Spanish verbMAPS

Phil McGowan

verbMAPS publishing

Published by verbMAPS publishing.

Copyright © 2014 Verbmaps Ltd.

A catalogue record for this book is available from the British Library.

ISBN 978-0-9929072-1-1

Contents

How to use this book

The specially designed verbMAPS layout displays Spanish verbs in a completely unique way. Before starting to use this book, familiarise yourself with the verbMAPS design by consulting the next page on "How to read a verbMAP". Once you are familiar with this design, you will find the book as a whole very easy to use because the method of presentation is exactly the same for every verb.

The Introduction explains how to use and how to form each of the tenses displayed by the verbMAPS as well as various other aspects of Spanish verbs. Students who are already familiar with the basics of Spanish verb grammar may wish to skip the Introduction and dive straight into the verbMAPS in Sections 1 to 3. Students who have a better understanding in some areas than in others may find the Glossary a useful tool; the terms used as labels on the actual verbMAPS have been highlighted in bold font (with page references to places where more information can be found).

The principal aim of this book is to provide the most efficient system for approaching the subject of Spanish verbs. With this in mind, the verbMAPS have been split into three sections: Section 1 is for -ar verbs, Section 2 looks at -er verbs, and Section 3 contains -ir verbs. Within each section, patterns that are followed by a large number of verbs have been placed near the front, while unique patterns are towards the back. To help you find your way around, each section begins with a summary page containing a contents table for that section.

In addition to being a powerful learning tool, verbMAPS can also be used for reference. The index at the back contains an alphabetical list of over 3,000 Spanish verbs, all of which have been cross-referenced to a model verbMAP.

How to read a verbMAP

➡ Start in the centre of the verbMAP (with the infinitive) and work outwards to the coloured boxes on the left-hand side.

➡ Boxes with a thin, grey outline contain instructions regarding the verb stems in each tense.

➡ The coloured boxes contain the actual verb forms for each of the tenses. The verb stem is always in black, whereas the verb endings appear in the same colour as the box (e.g. green for the imperfect tense).

➡ The small, grey arrows indicate where a verb form in one tense is being used as the basis for generating forms in one of the other tenses.

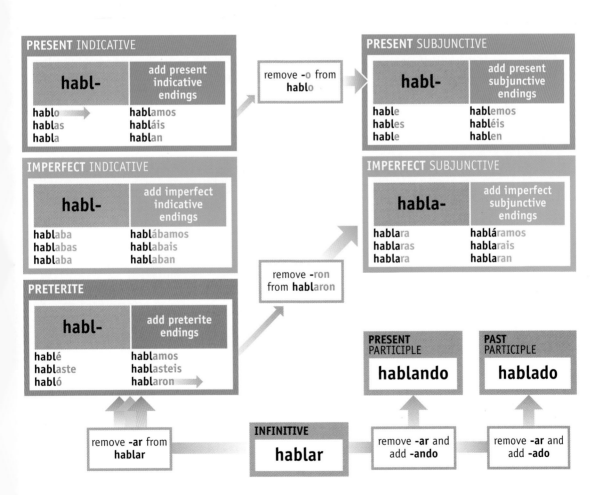

An introduction to Spanish verbs

A verb is a word that expresses action or a state of being. The basic form of a verb is its infinitive, which you can think of as the name of the verb. In English, the infinitive is the word "to" followed by a verb (to have, to be, to walk, etc.). The Spanish infinitive is always a single word with one of the following endings: -ar, -er or -ir. Here are a few examples of Spanish infinitives: *hablar* (to speak), *comer* (to eat) and *vivir* (to live). The infinitive is considered the basic form of a verb because it does not refer to any particular tense and is used as the basis for forming many of the tenses.

Spanish verbs change their form depending on the subject and the tense in which they are used. The subject is the person or thing about which the verb is saying something. For example, in the English sentence "he speaks Spanish", the pronoun "he" is the subject. In both English and Spanish, subjects are divided into three grammatical persons, each of which has a singular and a plural form.

The persons of the verb and their corresponding subject pronouns in English are as follows:

	Singular	Plural
First person	I	we
Second person	you	you
Third person	he/she	they

Here are the persons of the verb and their corresponding subject pronouns in Spanish:

	Singular	Plural
First person (I...we)	yo	nosotros/nosotras
Second person (you singular...you plural)	tú	vosotros/vosotras
Third person (he/she...they)	él/ella	ellos/ellas
Third person (you singular...you plural)	usted	ustedes

Comparing the two tables above, you will notice the following differences between English and Spanish:

➡ English has only one form for "you", whereas Spanish has four different forms. The second person (i.e. the form for *tú* or *vosotros/vosotras*) is the informal way to say "you" in Spanish. The *tú* form of the verb is used to address one person with whom you have an informal relationship (e.g. a friend, family member or classmate).

Tú eres mi mejor amigo.   *You are my best friend.*

➡ The *vosotros* form of the verb is used to address two or more people with whom you have an informal relationship. The spelling of *vosotros* changes to *vosotras* when referring to a group consisting solely of females.

Vosotros sois mis mejores amigos.   *You are my best friends.*
Vosotras venís a mi fiesta esta noche.   *You are coming to my party tonight.*

➡ The third person of the verb can be used as a more formal way of saying "you" in Spanish. *Usted* is the formal way to say "you" when you are speaking to one person. You should use the *usted* form to address an older person, a stranger or someone you don't know very well. *Ustedes* (the plural of *usted*) is used to address two or more people with whom you have a formal relationship.

Usted puede entrar ahora, señor.   *You may come in now, sir.*
Ustedes no pueden fumar aquí.   *You may not smoke here.*

Just as the spelling of *vosotros* changes to *vosotras*, other Spanish subject pronouns change form to make distinctions in gender:

➡ The Spanish equivalent of "we" can either be spelled as *nosotros* or as *nosotras* depending on the gender of the subjects. *Nosotros* is used to refer to groups of males or to mixed groups of males and females; the form *nosotras* can only be used for a group consisting solely of females.

Nosotros vamos a la playa.   *We are going to the beach.*
Nosotras somos hermanas.   *We are sisters.*

➡ The Spanish equivalent of "they" also has a masculine and feminine form. The masculine form *ellos* is used to refer to more than one male (or more than one masculine noun). The feminine form *ellas* is used for groups consisting solely of females (or feminine nouns).

Ellos van a visitar a sus amigos.   *They are going to visit their friends.*
Ellas son hermanas.   *They are sisters.*

An important difference between Spanish and English is that subject pronouns are not used very often in Spanish. English often requires subject pronouns to show who the subject of the verb is; in Spanish, the verb ending within the actual verb form nearly always makes it obvious who the subject is. Thus, Spanish verbs are used without subject pronouns most of the time. Spanish speakers tend to only add subject pronouns to a sentence for emphasis or greater clarity.

Introduction | An introduction to Spanish verbs

As we have seen, Spanish verbs can be used in three different grammatical persons, each of which has a singular and a plural form. The correct form required for each of these persons is determined by the verb tense in which the verb is being used. Spanish has several different verb tenses that give the listener (or reader) information about when an action or situation takes place. The verbMAPS in this book display thirteen Spanish verb tenses, each of which will be examined in detail in the remainder of this Introduction.

The simple tenses

➡ The simple tenses are tenses that consist of only one word. The verbMAPS display the seven simple (single-word) tenses shown below. The next few pages will teach you how to use and how to form each of these tenses.

THE PRESENT INDICATIVE TENSE

How to use the present indicative tense

1. The present indicative tense is used to refer to an action or a state of being that is taking place at the time of speaking (or writing).

    Limpia la cocina.   *He is cleaning the kitchen.*
    ¿Qué **haces**?   *What are you doing?*
    Estoy listo.   *I am ready.*

2. The present indicative tense is used to refer to an action that is habitual.

    Voy al colegio todos los días.   *I go to school every day.*
    Juega al fútbol los sábados.   *He plays football on Saturdays.*

3. The present indicative tense is used to express absolute and general truths.

    La Tierra **gira** alrededor del Sol.   *The Earth revolves around the Sun.*
    Noam Chomsky **es** un lingüista y   *Noam Chomsky is an American linguist*
    filósofo estadounidense.   *and philosopher.*

4. The present indicative tense is used to refer to an action that will take place in the near future, particularly when another part of the sentence makes it clear that the future is being referred to.

    Gabriela **llega** a las diez y media.   *Gabriela is arriving at half past ten.*
    Vamos a Barcelona en enero.   *We are going to Barcelona in January.*

5. The present tense is used to refer to an action that started in the past but continues into the present.

    Hace cinco meses que **trabaja** en   *He has been working at the bank for*
    el banco.   *five months.*
    Estudio español desde hace tres   *I have been studying Spanish for three*
    años.   *years.*

6. The present indicative tense is sometimes used for dramatic effect when a writer is referring to a past event and wishes to make it seem more immediate. This is called the historical present and you can think of it as a technique used to bring past events to life within a narrative.

THE PRESENT INDICATIVE TENSE

La Revolución Industrial **comienza** en 1760.

The Industrial Revolution begins in 1760.

Alexander Graham Bell **inventa** el teléfono en 1876.

Alexander Graham Bell invents the telephone in 1876.

 Useful tips

If you wish to emphasise the fact that something is happening right now, you can use the present continuous tense. The present continuous is a Spanish tense that is formed by adding the present participle to the present indicative tense of the verb *estar*. Here are a few examples:

Estás hablando demasiado rápido.   *You are speaking too fast.*
Está nevando.   *It's snowing.*

The present continuous is often referred to as the present progressive.

THE PRESENT INDICATIVE TENSE

How to form the present indicative tense

The stem of the present indicative tense is formed by removing the ending of the infinitive (i.e. by removing -ar, -er or -ir):

Infinitive	Stem
hablar ⟶	habl-
comer ⟶	com-
vivir ⟶	viv-

A set of endings is added to the present indicative stem depending on the subject (i.e. depending on who is doing the action). The three types of verb (-ar verbs, -er verbs and -ir verbs) each have a different set of endings added to their present indicative stems. The verbMAPS show the present indicative tense in the following way with the present indicative stem shown in **black** and the present indicative endings shown in light blue. Notice how the blue endings are different for each of the three models below.

hablar, a regular -ar verb:

PRESENT INDICATIVE

habl-	add present indicative endings
hablo	hablamos
hablas	habláis
habla	hablan

comer, a regular -er verb:

PRESENT INDICATIVE

com-	add present indicative endings
como	comemos
comes	coméis
come	comen

vivir, a regular -ir verb:

PRESENT INDICATIVE

viv-	add present indicative endings
vivo	vivimos
vives	vivís
vive	viven

Many verbs are irregular in the present indicative tense, which means they do not follow one of the three models shown above. Some of these irregular verbs are unique patterns in their own right, but many of them belong to families of verbs that can be learnt together. For this reason, every verbMAP (apart from those which are labelled as unique patterns) has a list of verbs that follow the same pattern as the main verb displayed by the verbMAP.

THE IMPERFECT INDICATIVE TENSE

How to use the imperfect indicative tense

1. The imperfect indicative tense is used to describe an action that happened regularly or habitually in the past.

    Tocaba el piano después de la escuela.　　*I used to play the piano after school.*

    Empezaba a trabajar a las ocho de la mañana.　　*She used to begin work at eight o'clock in the morning.*

2. The imperfect indicative tense is used to describe states or conditions that existed in the past (i.e. to describe what something or someone was like in the past). This includes things like describing the weather in the past and telling what time it was in the past.

    Era mediodía y estaba lloviendo.　　*It was midday and it was raining.*

    Cuando **tenía** cinco años, **tenía** el pelo rubio.　　*When he was five, he had blond hair.*

3. The imperfect indicative tense sometimes provides a background against which particular completed events are acted out. The imperfect indicative can do this in several ways:

    ➡ It can provide general background information.

    Era tarde cuando llegamos.　　*It was late when we arrived.*

    ➡ It can describe an action that was going on when another action occurred.

    Comía cuando llamaste.　　*I was eating when you called.*

4. The imperfect indicative tense is sometimes used in reported speech to report what someone said. When used in this way, the imperfect indicative tense will often follow verbs such as *decir* (to say) and *escribir* (to write) in a past tense.

    Me dijo que **iba** a la piscina.　　*He told me he was going to the swimming pool.*

    Me preguntó dónde **vivía**.　　*She asked me where I lived.*

THE IMPERFECT INDICATIVE TENSE

 Useful tips

The imperfect indicative tense is used to refer to continuous actions and states of being in the past or to habitual past actions. However, if you wish simply to refer to an action that was in progress in the past but is now completed, for this you will require the past continuous tense (which is also known as the past progressive). The past continuous tense is formed by adding the present participle to the imperfect indicative tense of the verb *estar*. Here are a few examples:

Estaba leyendo. *I was reading.*
Estaba haciendo los deberes. *He was doing his homework.*

THE IMPERFECT INDICATIVE TENSE

How to form the imperfect indicative tense

The stem of the imperfect indicative tense is formed by removing the ending of the infinitive (i.e. by removing -ar, -er or -ir):

Infinitive		Stem
hablar	⟹	habl-
comer	⟹	com-
vivir	⟹	viv-

A set of endings is added to the imperfect indicative stem depending on the subject (i.e. depending on who is doing the action). Verbs that end in -ar take the set of endings that is shown in green by the *hablar* model below. The *comer* and *vivir* models show the set of endings that is used for both -er and -ir verbs.

hablar, a regular -ar verb:

IMPERFECT INDICATIVE

habl-	add imperfect indicative endings
hablaba	hablábamos
hablabas	hablabais
hablaba	hablaban

comer, a regular -er verb:

IMPERFECT INDICATIVE

com-	add imperfect indicative endings
comía	comíamos
comías	comíais
comía	comían

vivir, a regular -ir verb:

IMPERFECT INDICATIVE

viv-	add imperfect indicative endings
vivía	vivíamos
vivías	vivíais
vivía	vivían

There are only three verbs that are irregular in the imperfect indicative tense: *ir* (to go), *ser* (to be) and *ver* (to see). These verbs are irregular because you cannot form their imperfect indicative stems by removing the ending of the infinitive:

Infinitive		Stem
ir	⟹	ib-
ser	⟹	er-
ver	⟹	ve-

THE PRETERITE TENSE

How to use the preterite tense

In Spanish, the preterite tense is the most common past tense. As a useful rule of thumb, use the preterite to refer to a past action if you know precisely when the action occurred or how many times it occurred.

1. The preterite tense is used to refer to actions that were completed at a specific point in the past. As such, the preterite tense is associated with words such as *ayer* (yesterday) and *anoche* (last night).

Mis primos **llegaron** ayer.	*My cousins arrived yesterday.*
Salí anoche.	*I went out last night.*

2. The completed past actions referred to by the preterite tense can be part of a series of events.

Fue al cine, **vio** una película y **compró** un libro.	*She went to the cinema, saw a film and bought a book.*

3. The preterite tense is used to refer to past actions that were performed a specific number of times.

David me **llamó** tres veces anoche.	*David called me three times last night.*
Leí el artículo dos veces.	*I read the article twice.*

4. The preterite tense is used to refer to events in the past that lasted for a specific period of time.

Trabajé de nueve a cinco.	*I worked from nine to five.*
Jugaron al tenis durante media hora.	*They played tennis for half an hour.*

5. The preterite tense is also used to indicate the beginning or the end of a past event.

Empezó a llover.	*It started to rain.*
Terminaron de construir la urbanización.	*They finished building the housing estate.*

THE PRETERITE TENSE

How to form the preterite tense

The stem of the preterite tense is formed by removing the ending of the infinitive (i.e. by removing -ar, -er or -ir):

Infinitive	Stem
hablar	⟹ habl-
comer	⟹ com-
vivir	⟹ viv-

A set of endings is added to the preterite stem depending on the subject (i.e. depending on who is doing the action). Verbs that end in -ar take the set of endings that is shown in **orange** by the *hablar* model below. The *comer* and *vivir* models show the set of endings that is used for both -er and -ir verbs.

hablar, a regular -ar verb:

PRETERITE	
habl-	add preterite endings
hablé	hablamos
hablaste	hablasteis
habló	hablaron

comer, a regular -er verb:

PRETERITE	
com-	add preterite endings
comí	comimos
comiste	comisteis
comió	comieron

vivir, a regular -ir verb:

PRETERITE	
viv-	add preterite endings
viví	vivimos
viviste	vivisteis
vivió	vivieron

There are many verbs that are irregular in the preterite tense. On the verbMAPS, the instruction box beneath the preterite tense box will point out if a verb has an irregular preterite stem or if the stem changes in the preterite tense.

THE FUTURE TENSE

How to use the future tense

The Spanish future tense is used in a similar way to the English future tense.

1. The future tense is used to refer to an action or a state of being that will take place in the future.

    Iré a Francia el año que viene.   *I will go to France next year.*
    Te **veré** delante del cine.   *I will meet you in front of the cinema.*

2. The future tense can be used for conjecture about the present.

    Tendrás hambre.   *You must be hungry.*
    ¿Qué hora **será**?   *I wonder what time it is.*

3. The future tense is used in si-clauses (if-clauses) to indicate what will happen if a certain condition is met.

    Si me ayudas, te **daré** diez euros.   *If you help me, I will give you ten euros.*
    Si no llueve, **andaré** al   *If it doesn't rain, I will walk to the*
        supermercado.   *supermarket.*

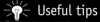 Useful tips

For actions that will occur in the near future, the present tense is more commonly used than the future tense:
    Llegamos mañana.   *We will arrive tomorrow.*

THE FUTURE TENSE

How to form the future tense

For all regular verbs, the infinitive is used as the stem in the future tense.

Infinitive   **Future Stem**
hablar   ⟹ hablar-
comer   ⟹ comer-
vivir   ⟹ vivir-

A special set of endings is added to the future stem depending on the subject (i.e. depending on who is doing the action). This set of future tense endings is the same for all verbs. The verbMAPS display the future tense in the following way with the future tense stem shown in **black** and the future tense endings shown in **dark blue**.

hablar, a regular -ar verb:

FUTURE

hablar-	add future endings
hablaré	hablaremos
hablarás	hablaréis
hablará	hablarán

comer, a regular -er verb:

FUTURE

comer-	add future endings
comeré	comeremos
comerás	comeréis
comerá	comerán

vivir, a regular -ir verb:

FUTURE

vivir-	add future endings
viviré	viviremos
vivirás	viviréis
vivirá	vivirán

Some verbs are irregular in the future tense; while they still have the future tense endings, the following verbs have irregular stems in the future tense.

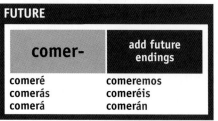

Infinitive   **Stem**
decir   ⟹ dir-
haber   ⟹ habr-
hacer   ⟹ har-
poder   ⟹ podr-
querer   ⟹ querr-

🔅 Useful tips

➡ Even for irregular verbs, the future stem always ends in **-r**.

THE CONDITIONAL TENSE

How to use the conditional tense

The conditional tense is used to refer to events that are somewhat hypothetical in nature.

1. The conditional tense is used to refer to an action or state of being that would occur if something else were possible.

Si tuviera tiempo, **aprendería** otro idioma.	*If I had the time, I would learn another language.*
Si fuera rico, **viajaría** por todo el mundo.	*If I were rich, I would travel all over the world.*

2. The conditional tense can be used to express desires and make polite requests.

Querría decir algo.	*I would like to say something.*
Querría un kilo de tomates.	*I would like a kilo of tomatoes.*

3. The conditional tense is used in reported speech to report statements that were in the future tense when they were spoken in direct speech.

Dijo que **volvería**.	*He said he would come back.*
Dijo que **averiguaría** la verdad.	*She said that she would find out the truth.*

4. The conditional tense can be used for conjecture about the past. In this way, the conditional tense is often used by speakers to express the probability of a past action.

Ayer **andaríamos** dieciséis millas.	*We must have walked sixteen miles yesterday.*
Probablemente **estaría** en la escuela.	*She must have been at school.*

THE CONDITIONAL TENSE

How to form the conditional tense

The conditional tense uses the same stem as the future tense. So, to form the conditional tense, add the conditional tense endings to the future stem. See page 17 to review how to form the future stem. The set of conditional tense endings is the same for all verbs.

The verbMAPS display the conditional tense in the following way: the stem is shown in **black** and the conditional tense endings are shown in **purple**.

hablar, a regular -ar verb:

CONDITIONAL	
hablar-	add conditional endings
hablaría	hablaríamos
hablarías	hablaríais
hablaría	hablarían

comer, a regular -er verb:

CONDITIONAL	
comer-	add conditional endings
comería	comeríamos
comerías	comeríais
comería	comerían

vivir, a regular -ir verb:

CONDITIONAL	
vivir-	add conditional endings
viviría	viviríamos
vivirías	viviríais
viviría	vivirían

Some verbs are irregular in the conditional tense; while they still have the conditional tense endings, the following verbs have irregular stems in the conditional tense.

Infinitive	Stem
decir	dir-
haber	habr-
hacer	har-
poder	podr-
querer	querr-

 Useful tips

➡ Verbs that are irregular in the future tense have the same irregular stem in the conditional.

The subjunctive mood

The subjunctive mood is mostly used in a dependent clause, which is a group of words that cannot stand alone as a sentence. Unlike the indicative mood, which is used to present objective facts, the subjunctive mood implies subjectivity. The subjunctive mood is used in a dependent clause when the subject of the main clause presents the event or situation described in the dependent clause with a certain kind of personal interpretation. The following is a summary of the four kinds of personal interpretation that trigger the use of the subjunctive mood.

1. Personal feelings or desires:

    In each of the examples below, the statement that indicates personal feelings or desires makes up the main clause that is said to trigger the use of the **bold**, subjunctive forms in the dependent clause.

Piensa que **tienes** razón.	*She thinks you're right.*
Me alegro de que **hayamos andado**.	*I am glad that we walked.*
Quiero que **pongas** la música.	*I want you to put the music on.*
Es importante que **cuentes** el dinero.	*It is important that you count the money.*

2. The belief that an event is unlikely:

    When the subject of the main clause expresses a belief that an event or situation is unlikely to occur or to have occurred, the subjunctive mood is required in the dependent clause.

No puedo creer que Rafael no **venga**.	*I can't believe that Rafael is not coming.*
Es sorprendente que el ordenador **ande** lento.	*It is surprising that the computer runs slow.*

3. Seeing an event as hypothetical or conditional on other events:

    This use of the subjunctive is triggered by conjunctions that express a condition and by conjunctions of time, such as *cuando* (meaning "when"). However, it is important to note that the subjunctive mood is only used after conjunctions of time if the dependent clause refers to an action that has not yet happened.

La llave no entra en la cerradura a no ser que la **fuerce**.	*The key does not fit in the lock unless I force it.*
Comeré cuando **lleguen**.	*I will eat when they arrive.*

4. Uncertainty over whether something exists:

When the object or person referred to in the main clause is not known to actually exist, the subjunctive is required in the dependent clause.

No conozco a nadie que **niegue** este hecho.	*I don't know anyone who denies this fact.*
¿Hay algo que **recomiendes**?	*Is there anything that you recommend?*

In Spanish, the subjunctive mood has four tenses: the present subjunctive tense, the imperfect subjunctive tense, the perfect subjunctive tense and the pluperfect subjunctive tense. As will be explained, the main difference between these tenses is the time of the action to which they refer (past, present or future). Any other characteristics that are particular to a given tense in the subjunctive mood are mentioned in the pages of this Introduction that have been specifically dedicated to that tense.

THE PRESENT SUBJUNCTIVE TENSE

How to use the present subjunctive tense

The present subjunctive is used when both of the following conditions are met:

➡ The verb or expression in the main clause that triggers the subjunctive is in the present indicative or the future tense.

➡ The action in the dependent clause can be seen as happening at the same time or after the action in the main clause.

Here are some example sentences that meet both of these conditions. Examples are given for each of the four categories that were introduced on page 20 as the kinds of personal interpretation on the part of the subject that trigger the use of the subjunctive mood.

1. Personal feelings or desires:

    Espero que **lleguéis** a tiempo.   *I hope that you will arrive on time.*
    Es importante que **averigüemos** el   *It is important that we find out the*
         alcance del problema.   *extent of the problem.*

2. The belief that an event is unlikely:

    Dudo que **quiera** salir.   *I doubt she wants to leave.*
    No creo que ella **vaya** a tener éxito.   *I do not think she will succeed.*

3. Seeing an event as hypothetical or conditional on other events:

    The present subjunctive is only used after conjunctions of time if the dependent clause refers to a future situation, that is to say something that has not yet happened.

    Comeré cuando **lleguen**.   *I will eat when they arrive.*
    ¿Quieres comer algo antes de que   *Do you want to have something to eat*
         empiece la obra?   *before the play starts?*

    When used to mean "if", the Spanish word *si* is never followed by a verb in the present subjunctive tense.

THE PRESENT SUBJUNCTIVE TENSE

4. Uncertainty over whether something exists:

No conozco a nadie que **hable** japonés.

I don't know anyone who speaks Japanese.

Cualquiera que **juegue** al fútbol sabe la importancia de trabajar en equipo.

Anyone who plays football knows the importance of working as a team.

THE PRESENT SUBJUNCTIVE TENSE

How to form the present subjunctive tense

The stem of the present subjunctive tense is formed by removing the -o ending from the first person singular form of the present indicative tense.

hablo	hable	habl-
como	come	com-
vivo	vive	viv-

On the verbMAPS, two small, grey arrows connect the first person singular form of the present indicative tense to an instruction box that tells you to remove the -o ending from that form. As shown below, a larger, blue arrow points to the stem that is derived by following the instruction given.

hablar, a regular -ar verb:

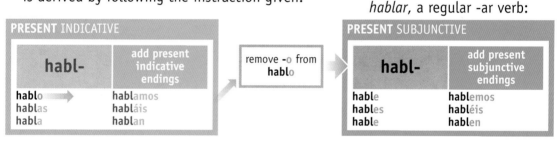

comer, a regular -er verb:

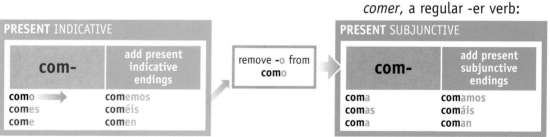

vivir, a regular -ir verb:

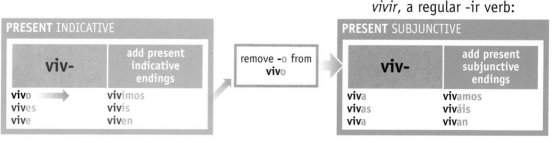

A set of endings has been added to the present subjunctive stem of each of the three models above. Verbs that end in -ar take the set of endings that is shown in blue by the *hablar* model. The *comer* and *vivir* models show the set of endings that is used for both -er and -ir verbs.

THE IMPERFECT SUBJUNCTIVE TENSE

How to use the imperfect subjunctive tense

The imperfect subjunctive is used when both of the following conditions are met:

➜ The verb or expression in the main clause that triggers the subjunctive is in the preterite tense, the imperfect indicative tense or the conditional tense.

➜ The action in the dependent clause can be seen as happening at the same time or after the action in the main clause.

Here are some example sentences that meet both of these conditions. Examples are given for each of the four categories that were introduced on page 20 as the kinds of personal interpretation on the part of the subject that trigger the use of the subjunctive mood.

1. Personal feelings or desires:

    Esperaba que los niños **pusieran** la   *I was hoping that the children would set*
        mesa.   *the table.*
    Me pidió que no **empezara** sin él.   *He asked me not to start without him.*

2. The belief that an event is unlikely:

    Dudaban que **pudiera** cuidarme.   *They doubted that I could take care of*
                                                    myself.
    No puedo creer que **lloviera** ayer.   *I can't believe that it rained yesterday.*

3. Seeing an event as hypothetical or conditional on other events:

    Estudié en caso de que **hubiera** un   *I studied in case there was an exam.*
        examen.
    Hice la cena para que no **tuviéramos**   *I made dinner so that we would not be*
        hambre.   *hungry.*

4. Uncertainty over whether something exists:

    Buscaba un estudiante que **hablara**   *I was looking for a student who spoke*
        español.   *Spanish.*

THE IMPERFECT SUBJUNCTIVE TENSE

There are a few other special uses of the imperfect subjunctive:

5. Unlike the present subjunctive, the imperfect subjunctive tense is used in the si-clauses (if-clauses) of conditional sentences. The imperfect subjunctive is used in this way to express unreal conditions in the present or unlikely conditions in the future. These si-clauses are known as contrary-to-fact clauses.

Si **comieras** más verduras, estarías más sano.	*If you ate more vegetables, you would be healthier.*
Si no la **conociera**, pensaría que está mintiendo.	*If I did not know her, I would think she was lying.*

    The imperfect subjunctive is also used after the expression *como si* (meaning "as if").

Sintió como si **fuera** a vomitar.	*She felt as though she was going to be sick.*

6. The imperfect subjunctive tense of *querer* (to want) is used in main clauses to make polite requests and to soften suggestions.

Quisiera un kilo de tomates.	*I would like a kilo of tomatoes.*

THE IMPERFECT SUBJUNCTIVE TENSE

How to form the imperfect subjunctive tense

The stem of the imperfect subjunctive tense is formed by removing the -ron ending from the third person plural form of the preterite tense.

hablaron ➤ habla~~ron~~ ➤ habla-
comieron ➤ comie~~ron~~ ➤ comie-
vivieron ➤ vivie~~ron~~ ➤ vivie-

In the first person plural of the imperfect subjunctive, an acute accent is added to the last letter of the stem. For example, the imperfect subjunctive stem **habla-** becomes **hablá-** in the first person plural.

A special set of endings is added to the imperfect subjunctive stem depending on the subject (i.e. depending on who is doing the action). This set of imperfect subjunctive endings is the same for all verbs. The verbMAPS display the imperfect subjunctive tense in the following way with the verb stem shown in **black** and the imperfect subjunctive endings shown in green.

hablar, a regular -ar verb:

IMPERFECT SUBJUNCTIVE	
habla-	add imperfect subjunctive endings
hablara	**hablá**ramos
hablaras	**habla**rais
hablara	**habla**ran

comer, a regular -er verb:

IMPERFECT SUBJUNCTIVE	
comie-	add imperfect subjunctive endings
comiera	**comié**ramos
comieras	**comie**rais
comiera	**comie**ran

vivir, a regular -ir verb:

IMPERFECT SUBJUNCTIVE	
vivie-	add imperfect subjunctive endings
viviera	**vivié**ramos
vivieras	**vivie**rais
viviera	**vivie**ran

The compound tenses

➡ Compound tenses are always made up of two parts: the appropriate form of the auxiliary verb *haber* and the past participle. The verbMAPS display the six compound tenses shown below. The next few pages will teach you how to use and how to form each of these compound tenses.

Past participle

The past participle of a verb will be used to form each of that verb's compound tenses. The regular pattern for obtaining the past participle is to take the infinitive of the verb and change the ending.

For infinitives ending in **-ar**, remove the **-ar** and add **-ado**.
habl**ar** ➡ habl**ado**
cant**ar** ➡ cant**ado**

For infinitives ending in **-er**, remove the **-er** and add **-ido**.
com**er** ➡ com**ido**
beb**er** ➡ beb**ido**

For infinitives ending in **-ir**, remove the **-ir** and add **-ido**.
viv**ir** ➡ viv**ido**
part**ir** ➡ part**ido**

Regular past participles of -er verbs and -ir verbs have the same ending. If the stem of an -er or -ir verb ends in a vowel, an acute accent is added over the "i" of the past participle ending -ido.
caer ➡ caído
leer ➡ leído
oír ➡ oído
reír ➡ reído

Many verbs have irregular past participles that do not follow any of the above patterns. Most irregular past participles end in -to.
escribir ➡ escrito
morir ➡ muerto
ver ➡ visto
volver ➡ vuelto

Two very common verbs have irregular past participles ending in -cho.
decir ➡ dicho
hacer ➡ hecho

The auxiliary verb haber

An auxiliary verb is a verb that precedes the past participle in the compound tenses. When forming the compound tenses, all Spanish verbs take *haber* as their auxiliary verb. As such, compound tenses in Spanish always consist of two parts: the appropriate form of the auxiliary verb *haber* plus the past participle. The chart below specifies in which tense *haber* must be used (i.e. the appropriate form) for each of the compound tenses.

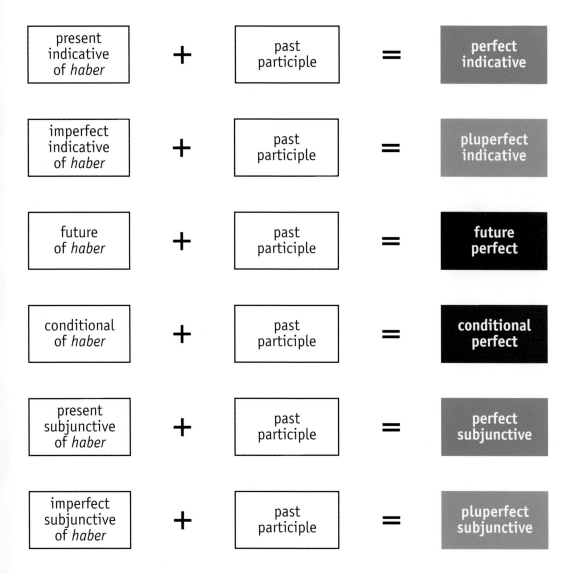

present indicative of *haber*	+	past participle	=	perfect indicative
imperfect indicative of *haber*	+	past participle	=	pluperfect indicative
future of *haber*	+	past participle	=	future perfect
conditional of *haber*	+	past participle	=	conditional perfect
present subjunctive of *haber*	+	past participle	=	perfect subjunctive
imperfect subjunctive of *haber*	+	past participle	=	pluperfect subjunctive

The next few pages demonstrate how to form each of these compound tenses by looking at three model verbs: *hablar* (a regular -ar verb), *comer* (a regular -er verb) and *vivir* (a regular -ir verb).

THE PERFECT INDICATIVE TENSE

How to use the perfect indicative tense

1. The perfect indicative tense is used to refer to something that happened at an unspecified time in the past.

He escrito el informe.	*I have written the report.*
El presidente **ha muerto** de un infarto.	*The president has died of a heart attack.*

2. The perfect indicative tense is also commonly used for past actions that either continue into the present or continue to affect the present in some way.

Hemos venido a verte.	*We have come to see you.*
He pedido a mi amigo que me ayude.	*I have asked my friend to help me.*

THE PERFECT INDICATIVE TENSE

How to form the perfect indicative tense

The perfect indicative tense is made up of two parts: the present indicative tense of *haber* (the auxiliary verb) plus the past participle. The verbMAPS show the perfect indicative tense in the following way with the auxiliary verb shown in light blue and the past participle shown in **black**.

hablar, a regular -ar verb:

PERFECT INDICATIVE

present indicative of haber	add past participle
he **hablado**	hemos **hablado**
has **hablado**	habéis **hablado**
ha **hablado**	han **hablado**

comer, a regular -er verb:

PERFECT INDICATIVE

present indicative of haber	add past participle
he **comido**	hemos **comido**
has **comido**	habéis **comido**
ha **comido**	han **comido**

vivir, a regular -ir verb:

PERFECT INDICATIVE

present indicative of haber	add past participle
he **vivido**	hemos **vivido**
has **vivido**	habéis **vivido**
ha **vivido**	han **vivido**

THE PLUPERFECT INDICATIVE TENSE

How to use the pluperfect indicative tense

1. The pluperfect indicative tense is used to refer to an action or event that had taken place before another action or event. An action or event that is in the pluperfect indicative tense is therefore specified as happening further back in the past than some other past action or event.

Para cuando llegamos al cine, la película ya **había empezado**.	*By the time we arrived at the cinema, the film had already started.*
Fernando **había vivido** feliz hasta que se casó.	*Fernando had lived happily until he got married.*

Note that the action before which the pluperfect indicative action took place (i.e. the more recent action) is sometimes implied rather than stated outright.

Ya **había visto** la película.	*She had already seen the film.*
Había visitado el museo antes.	*I had visited the museum before.*

THE PLUPERFECT INDICATIVE TENSE

How to form the pluperfect indicative tense

The pluperfect indicative tense is made up of two parts: the imperfect indicative tense of *haber* (the auxiliary verb) plus the past participle. The verbMAPS show the pluperfect indicative tense in the following way with the auxiliary verb shown in green and the past participle shown in **black**.

hablar, a regular -ar verb:

PLUPERFECT INDICATIVE

imperfect indicative of haber	add past participle
había **hablado**	habíamos **hablado**
habías **hablado**	habíais **hablado**
había **hablado**	habían **hablado**

comer, a regular -er verb:

PLUPERFECT INDICATIVE

imperfect indicative of haber	add past participle
había **comido**	habíamos **comido**
habías **comido**	habíais **comido**
había **comido**	habían **comido**

vivir, a regular -ir verb:

PLUPERFECT INDICATIVE

imperfect indicative of haber	add past participle
había **vivido**	habíamos **vivido**
habías **vivido**	habíais **vivido**
había **vivido**	habían **vivido**

THE FUTURE PERFECT TENSE

How to use the future perfect tense

1. The future perfect is used to describe an action that will have happened by a certain point in the future.

    | A las seis, **habrán conducido** cuatro horas sin parar. | *By six o'clock, they will have driven for four hours straight.* |
    | **Habrán vuelto** de Italia para el doce de febrero. | *They will have returned from Italy by the twelfth of February.* |

    There is a subtle difference between the future and the future perfect: the future tense is used to refer to an action that the speaker will do in the future, whereas the future perfect tense describes an action that the speaker will have completed by a specific point in the future.

2. The future perfect tense can be used to label a future action as one that is going to be completed before another future action takes place.

    | Para cuando vuelvan, **habré salido**. | *I will have left by the time they get back.* |
    | **Habré cocinado** la paella antes de que lleguen los invitados. | *I will have cooked the paella before the guests arrive.* |

3. The future perfect tense can also be used to speculate or make an assumption about what might have happened in the past.

    | **Habrá oído** lo que pasó. | *She must have heard what happened.* |
    | Paula **habrá andado** al trabajo. | *Paula must have walked to work.* |

Useful tips

➡ Watch out! The **future** perfect tense can be used to make guesses about what might have happened in the **past**.

THE FUTURE PERFECT TENSE

How to form the future perfect tense

The future perfect tense is made up of two parts: the future tense of *haber* (the auxiliary verb) plus the past participle. The verbMAPS show the future perfect tense in the following way with the auxiliary verb shown in **dark blue** and the past participle shown in **black**.

hablar, a regular -ar verb:

FUTURE PERFECT	
future of haber	add past participle
habré hablado	habremos hablado
habrás hablado	habréis hablado
habrá hablado	habrán hablado

comer, a regular -er verb:

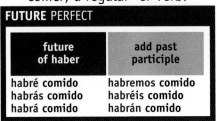

FUTURE PERFECT	
future of haber	add past participle
habré comido	habremos comido
habrás comido	habréis comido
habrá comido	habrán comido

vivir, a regular -ir verb:

FUTURE PERFECT	
future of haber	add past participle
habré vivido	habremos vivido
habrás vivido	habréis vivido
habrá vivido	habrán vivido

THE CONDITIONAL PERFECT TENSE

How to use the conditional perfect tense

1. The conditional perfect is used to refer to an action or event that would have taken place if past circumstances had been different.

Si hubiera hecho buen tiempo, **habríamos ido** a la playa.

If the weather had been good, we would have gone to the beach.

Si Olivia hubiera estudiado más, **habría aprobado** el examen.

If Olivia had studied harder, she would have passed the exam.

2. The conditional perfect can also be used for conjecture about the past, but it is less commonly used for this function than the future perfect.

Habría sido las dos cuando llegué a su casa.

It must have been two o'clock when I got to his house.

THE CONDITIONAL PERFECT TENSE

How to form the conditional perfect tense

The conditional perfect tense is made up of two parts: the conditional tense of *haber* (the auxiliary verb) plus the past participle. The verbMAPS show the conditional perfect tense in the following way with the auxiliary verb shown in **purple** and the past participle shown in **black**.

hablar, a regular -ar verb:

CONDITIONAL PERFECT	
conditional of haber	**add past participle**
habría **hablado**	habríamos **hablado**
habrías **hablado**	habríais **hablado**
habría **hablado**	habrían **hablado**

comer, a regular -er verb:

CONDITIONAL PERFECT	
conditional of haber	**add past participle**
habría **comido**	habríamos **comido**
habrías **comido**	habríais **comido**
habría **comido**	habrían **comido**

vivir, a regular -ir verb:

CONDITIONAL PERFECT	
conditional of haber	**add past participle**
habría **vivido**	habríamos **vivido**
habrías **vivido**	habríais **vivido**
habría **vivido**	habrían **vivido**

THE PERFECT SUBJUNCTIVE TENSE

How to use the perfect subjunctive tense

The perfect subjunctive is used when both of the following conditions are met:

➡ The verb or expression in the main clause that triggers the subjunctive is in the present indicative or the future tense.

➡ The action in the dependent clause can be seen as happening before the action in the main clause.

Here are some example sentences that meet both of these conditions. Examples are given for each of the four categories that were introduced on page 20 as the kinds of personal interpretation on the part of the subject that trigger the use of the subjunctive mood.

1. Personal feelings or desires:

Estoy tan contenta de que **hayas venido** a verme.	*I'm so glad you came to see me.*
Es bueno que **haya aprobado** el examen.	*It's good that he passed the test.*

2. The belief that an event is unlikely:

Dudo que **haya colgado** todos los cuadros.	*I doubt that he has hung up all of the pictures.*
No creo que **hayan salido**.	*I don't think they went out.*

3. Seeing an event as hypothetical or conditional on other events:

    The perfect subjunctive is only used after conjunctions of time if the dependent clause refers to a future situation, that is to say something that has not yet happened.

Una vez que **haya reunido** suficiente dinero, compraré un coche.	*Once I have raised enough money, I will buy a car.*
La clase empezará cuando **hayan llegado**.	*The lesson will begin when they have arrived.*

THE PERFECT SUBJUNCTIVE TENSE

When used to mean "if", the Spanish word *si* is never followed by a verb in the perfect subjunctive tense.

4. Uncertainty over whether something exists:

Busco un estudiante que se **haya graduado** recientemente.	*I am looking for a student who has recently graduated.*
¿Hay alguien que no **haya leído** "Don Quijote"?	*Is there anyone who has not read "Don Quijote"?*

THE PERFECT SUBJUNCTIVE TENSE

How to form the perfect subjunctive tense

The perfect subjunctive tense is made up of two parts: the present subjunctive tense of *haber* (the auxiliary verb) plus the past participle. The verbMAPS show the perfect subjunctive tense in the following way with the auxiliary verb shown in light blue and the past participle shown in **black**.

hablar, a regular -ar verb:

PERFECT SUBJUNCTIVE

present subjunctive of haber	add past participle
haya **hablado**	hayamos **hablado**
hayas **hablado**	hayáis **hablado**
haya **hablado**	hayan **hablado**

comer, a regular -er verb:

PERFECT SUBJUNCTIVE

present subjunctive of haber	add past participle
haya **comido**	hayamos **comido**
hayas **comido**	hayáis **comido**
haya **comido**	hayan **comido**

vivir, a regular -ir verb:

PERFECT SUBJUNCTIVE

present subjunctive of haber	add past participle
haya **vivido**	hayamos **vivido**
hayas **vivido**	hayáis **vivido**
haya **vivido**	hayan **vivido**

THE PLUPERFECT SUBJUNCTIVE TENSE

How to use the pluperfect subjunctive tense

The pluperfect subjunctive is used when both of the following conditions are met:

➡ The verb or expression in the main clause that triggers the subjunctive is in the preterite tense, the imperfect indicative tense or the conditional tense.

➡ The action in the dependent clause can be seen as happening before the action in the main clause.

Here are some example sentences that meet both of these conditions. Examples are given for each of the four categories that were introduced on page 20 as the kinds of personal interpretation on the part of the subject that trigger the use of the subjunctive mood.

1. Personal feelings or desires:

    Ojalá lo **hubieran traído**.   *I wish that they had brought it.*
    A mi abuelo le gustó que **hubieran**   *My grandfather liked that they had built*
      construido una biblioteca cerca   *a library near his house.*
      de su casa.

2. The belief that an event is unlikely:

    No parecía que **hubiéramos andado**   *It didn't seem that we had walked ten*
      diez millas.   *miles.*
    Parecía raro que la compañía **hubiera**   *It seemed odd that the company would*
      enviado un coche al aeropuerto.   *send a car to the airport.*

3. Seeing an event as hypothetical or conditional on other events:

    Le envié una carta en caso de que   *I sent him a letter in case he had not*
      no **hubiera recibido** el correo   *received the email.*
      electrónico.

4. Uncertainty over whether something exists:

    ¿Había alguien que no **hubiera**   *Was there anyone who had not heard of*
      oído hablar de Salvador Dalí?   *Salvador Dalí?*

THE PLUPERFECT SUBJUNCTIVE TENSE

The pluperfect subjunctive tense also has the additional usage of appearing in the si-clauses (if-clauses) of conditional sentences:

5. The pluperfect subjunctive is used in si-clauses to imagine that past circumstances had been different to what they actually were. As such, you can think of these si-clauses as contrary-to-past-fact clauses.

Si lo **hubiera sabido**, habría vuelto.   *If I had known, I would have come back.*
Si **hubiera gritado** más fuerte, le   *If he had shouted louder, I would have*
  habría oído.   *heard him.*

The pluperfect subjunctive is used in a similar way to the above examples after the expression *como si* (meaning "as if").

Actuabais como si nada **hubiera**   *You were acting as if nothing had*
  pasado.   *happened.*

THE PLUPERFECT SUBJUNCTIVE TENSE

How to form the pluperfect subjunctive tense

The pluperfect subjunctive tense is made up of two parts: the imperfect subjunctive tense of *haber* (the auxiliary verb) plus the past participle. The verbMAPS show the pluperfect subjunctive tense in the following way with the auxiliary verb shown in green and the past participle shown in **black**.

hablar, a regular -ar verb:

PLUPERFECT SUBJUNCTIVE

imperfect subjunctive of haber	add past participle
hubiera **hablado**	hubiéramos **hablado**
hubieras **hablado**	hubierais **hablado**
hubiera **hablado**	hubieran **hablado**

comer, a regular -er verb:

PLUPERFECT SUBJUNCTIVE

imperfect subjunctive of haber	add past participle
hubiera **comido**	hubiéramos **comido**
hubieras **comido**	hubierais **comido**
hubiera **comido**	hubieran **comido**

vivir, a regular -ir verb:

PLUPERFECT SUBJUNCTIVE

imperfect subjunctive of haber	add past participle
hubiera **vivido**	hubiéramos **vivido**
hubieras **vivido**	hubierais **vivido**
hubiera **vivido**	hubieran **vivido**

Present participle

The regular pattern for obtaining the present participle is to take the infinitive of the verb and change the ending.

For infinitives ending in **-ar**, remove the **-ar** and add **-ando**.
hablar ➡ habl**ando**
cantar ➡ cant**ando**

For infinitives ending in **-er**, remove the **-er** and add **-iendo**.
comer ➡ com**iendo**
beber ➡ beb**iendo**

For infinitives ending in **-ir**, remove the **-ir** and add **-iendo**.
vivir ➡ viv**iendo**
partir ➡ part**iendo**

Regular present participles of -er verbs and -ir verbs have the same ending. If the stem of an -er or -ir verb ends in a vowel, the ending of the present participle is changed to -yendo.
caer ➡ cayendo
leer ➡ leyendo
oír ➡ oyendo

Stem-changing -ir verbs have the same vowel in the stem of the present participle as in the third person of the preterite. This is demonstrated by the comparison below of the third person singular forms and the present participles of *dormir*, *elegir* and *pedir*.

	3rd pers. sing. of preterite	Present participle
dormir	durmió	durmiendo
elegir	eligió	eligiendo
pedir	pidió	pidiendo

Similarly, -ir verbs with irregular preterite stems have the same vowel in the stem of the present participle as the vowel used in the irregular preterite stem:

	3rd pers. sing. of preterite	Present participle
decir	dijo	diciendo
venir	vino	viniendo

The Spanish present participle is used to form the continuous (or progressive) tenses, such as the present continuous and the imperfect continuous.

The present continuous tense is used to describe an action that is happening right now. It is formed by adding the present participle to the present tense of the verb *estar*.

Estoy escribiendo una carta.	*I am writing a letter.*
Están dando un documental.	*They are showing a documentary.*

The imperfect continuous tense is used to describe a continuous action that was happening in the past. It is formed by adding the present participle to the imperfect tense of the verb *estar*.

La nieve **estaba cayendo** cuando llegamos.	*The snow was falling when we arrived.*
Estaba colgando de un gancho.	*It was hanging on a hook.*

Reflexive verbs

A reflexive verb is a verb that is used with a reflexive pronoun that refers back to the verb's subject. The infinitive form of a reflexive verb has -se attached to the end of it. For example, the reflexive form of *lavar* (to wash) is *lavarse* in the infinitive.

In each of the tenses, a reflexive pronoun needs to be placed before the conjugated forms of reflexive verbs. The reflexive pronoun required is determined by the subject of the verb. Here is a table showing the reflexive pronoun for each subject:

	Singular	Plural
First person	me	nos
Second person	te	os
Third person	se	se

The following examples demonstrate how these reflexive pronouns are placed before the conjugated forms of reflexive verbs:

lavarse in the present indicative:

PRESENT INDICATIVE

lav-	add present indicative endings
me lavo	nos lavamos
te lavas	os laváis
se lava	se lavan

meterse in the preterite:

PRETERITE

met-	add preterite endings
me metí	nos metimos
te metiste	os metisteis
se metió	se metieron

decidirse in the pluperfect indicative:

PLUPERFECT INDICATIVE

imperfect indicative of haber	add past participle
me había decidido	nos habíamos decidido
te habías decidido	os habíais decidido
se había decidido	se habían decidido

➡ A reflexive verb is used to express an action that the subject performs on itself.

Me estoy vistiendo.   *I am getting dressed.*
Anoche **se acostó** tarde.   *He went to bed late last night.*

➡ The normal way of describing actions in which subjects do things to their own bodies is to use a reflexive verb. When referring to parts of the body, Spanish uses a definite article (either *el, la, los* or *las*) where English uses a possessive determiner (e.g. his, my, their).

Se afeitó la barba esta mañana.	*He shaved off his beard this morning.*
Los niños **se lavan** las manos.	*The children are washing their hands.*

➡ Reflexive verbs can also be used to describe a situation where several subjects are doing things to each other.

Los dos profesores **se odian**.	*The two teachers hate each other.*
No **se conocen** bien.	*They don't know each other very well.*

Glossary of terms

This Glossary gives definitions of all of the grammatical terms used in this book. The terms in **bold** are used as labels on the verbMAPS.

Auxiliary verb	A verb that precedes the past participle in the compound tenses. When forming the compound tenses, all Spanish verbs take *haber* as their auxiliary verb. See page 31 for more information.
Clause	A group of words that contains a verb.
Compound tense	A tense that is made up of two parts: the auxiliary verb *haber* and a past participle.
Conditional	A simple tense used to refer to events that are somewhat hypothetical in nature. Instructions on how to use and how to form the conditional tense can be found on page 18.
Conditional perfect	A compound tense used to refer to an action or event that would have taken place if past circumstances had been different. Instructions on how to use and how to form the conditional perfect can be found on page 38.
Conjugation	The process by which a verb changes form depending on such things as the subject and the tense in which it is being used.
Conjunction	A type of word that is used to connect words or groups of words.
Continuous tenses	The tenses that are formed by adding the present participle to the conjugated forms of the verb *estar*. The continuous tenses are used to describe what is happening right now or what was happening in the past. See page 47 for more information.
Dependent clause	A group of words that cannot stand alone as a sentence because its meaning is dependent on a main clause. See Clause and Main clause.
Direct speech	The reproduction of speech in its original form. In writing, direct speech is usually enclosed in quotation marks.
Ending	A sequence of letters added to the stem of a verb.
Feminine	One of the two genders in Spanish. See Gender.

Future	A simple tense used to refer to something that will happen in the future. Instructions on how to use and how to form the future tense can be found on page 16.
Future stem	The stem to which endings are added in order to form the future and conditional tenses.
Future perfect	A compound tense used to refer to an action that will have happened by a certain point in the future. Instructions on how to use and how to form the future perfect tense can be found on page 36.
Gender	The division of nouns into two classes: masculine and feminine. This distinction often shows up in other parts of speech, such as pronouns, some of which take either a masculine or feminine form depending on the gender of the noun to which they refer.
Imperfect indicative	A simple tense used to refer to continuous actions and states of being in the past or to habitual past actions. Instructions on how to use and how to form the imperfect indicative tense can be found on page 11.
Imperfect subjunctive	A simple tense of the subjunctive. Instructions on how to use and how to form the imperfect subjunctive tense can be found on page 25. See Subjunctive.
Infinitive	The basic, unconjugated form of a verb. Spanish infinitives either end in -ar, -er or -ir.
Indicative	A grammatical mood that is used to present objective facts.
Irregular verb	A verb that does not follow any of the three model verb patterns that are considered to be regular. See Regular verb.
Main clause	A clause that expresses a complete idea and can stand alone as a sentence. See Clause.
Masculine	One of the two genders in Spanish. See Gender.
Noun	A word that names a person, an object or an abstract quality.
Number	The distinction between parts of speech that are singular and those which are plural.

Past participle	The form of a verb used with *haber* to form the compound tenses. Page 30 shows you how to form the past participle.
Perfect indicative	A compound tense used to refer to something that happened at an unspecified time in the past. Instructions on how to use and how to form the perfect indicative tense can be found on page 32.
Perfect subjunctive	A compound tense of the subjunctive. Instructions on how to use and how to form the perfect subjunctive tense can be found on page 40. See Subjunctive.
Person	The three categories into which verb forms can be classified indicating relationship to the speaker. The first person refers to the person or people speaking; the second person refers to the person or people being spoken to; the third person refers to the person or people being spoken about.
Pluperfect indicative	A compound tense used to specify a past action or event as having taken place before another past action or event. Instructions on how to use and how to form the pluperfect indicative tense can be found on page 34.
Pluperfect subjunctive	A compound tense of the subjunctive. Instructions on how to use and how to form the pluperfect subjunctive tense can be found on page 43. See Subjunctive.
Plural	A word or form denoting more than one.
Present indicative	A simple tense used to refer to something happening now or something that happens habitually. Instructions on how to use and how to form the present indicative tense can be found on page 8.
Present participle	The form of a verb used with *estar* to form the continuous tenses. Page 46 shows you how to form the present participle.
Present subjunctive	A simple tense of the subjunctive. Instructions on how to use and how to form the present subjunctive tense can be found on page 22. See Subjunctive.
Pronoun	A word that can take the place of a noun in order to stand for or represent that noun in a sentence. See Noun.

Preterite	A simple tense tense used to refer to a past action or a series of past actions that were completed at a specific point, lasted for a specific period of time or occurred a specific number of times. Instructions on how to use and how to form the preterite tense can be found on page 14.
Reflexive verb	A verb that is used with a reflexive pronoun that refers back to the verb's subject. See page 48 for more information.
Reflexive pronoun	A pronoun that is placed before the conjugated forms of reflexive verbs. See page 48 for more information.
Regular verb	A verb that follows one of the three model verb patterns that are considered to be regular. The three model verb patterns are "regular -ar verbs" (see *hablar*, page 56), "regular -er verbs" (see *comer*, page 96) and "regular -ir verbs" (see *vivir*, page 146).
Reported speech	A report of what someone has said that does not reproduce their exact words. Reported speech is sometimes referred to as indirect speech.
Sentence	A sequence of words that can stand on its own to convey a statement, question, exclamation or command.
Si-clause	A clause introduced by the word *si* that states a condition or possibility. See Clause.
Simple tense	A tense that consists of a single conjugated verb.
Singular	A word or form referring to just one person or thing.
Stem	The part of the verb to which endings are added.
Subject	The subject of a verb is the person or thing about which the verb is saying something. Spanish subjects are divided into three grammatical persons, each of which has a singular and a plural form.
Subject pronoun	A pronoun used to represent the subject of a verb. See pages 4 and 5 for a list of the Spanish subject pronouns as well as information on how these subject pronouns are used in the language.

Subjunctive

A grammatical mood that implies subjectivity. The circumstances that trigger the use of the subjunctive mood are discussed on page 20.

Tense

A form of the verb that indicates the time at which an event takes place.

Verb

A word that expresses action or a state of being.

-ar verbs

➜ -ar verbs are verbs that end in -ar in the infinitive

⚷–O Key points

➡ this verb follows the regular pattern for **-ar** verbs

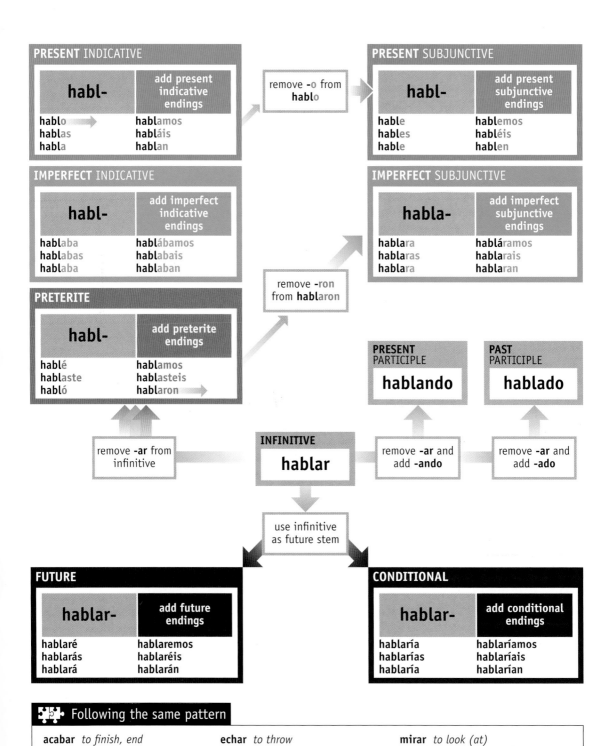

PRESENT INDICATIVE

habl-	add present indicative endings
hablo	hablamos
hablas	habláis
habla	hablan

remove **-o** from habl**o**

PRESENT SUBJUNCTIVE

habl-	add present subjunctive endings
hable	hablemos
hables	habléis
hable	hablen

IMPERFECT INDICATIVE

habl-	add imperfect indicative endings
hablaba	hablábamos
hablabas	hablabais
hablaba	hablaban

IMPERFECT SUBJUNCTIVE

habla-	add imperfect subjunctive endings
hablara	habláramos
hablaras	hablarais
hablara	hablaran

remove **-ron** from **habla**ron

PRETERITE

habl-	add preterite endings
hablé	hablamos
hablaste	hablasteis
habló	hablaron

PRESENT PARTICIPLE

hablando

PAST PARTICIPLE

hablado

remove **-ar** from infinitive

INFINITIVE

hablar

remove **-ar** and add **-ando**

remove **-ar** and add **-ado**

use infinitive as future stem

FUTURE

hablar-	add future endings
hablaré	hablaremos
hablarás	hablaréis
hablará	hablarán

CONDITIONAL

hablar-	add conditional endings
hablaría	hablaríamos
hablarías	hablaríais
hablaría	hablarían

⧩ Following the same pattern

acabar to finish, end	**echar** to throw	**mirar** to look (at)
cantar to sing	**entrar** to enter	**pasar** to pass (by); to happen
comprar to buy	**llamar** to call, name	**tratar** to try; to deal with

---

haber (in the correct simple tense) **+ past participle**

PERFECT INDICATIVE

present indicative of haber	add past participle
he **hablado**	hemos **hablado**
has **hablado**	habéis **hablado**
ha **hablado**	han **hablado**

PERFECT SUBJUNCTIVE

present subjunctive of haber	add past participle
haya **hablado**	hayamos **hablado**
hayas **hablado**	hayáis **hablado**
haya **hablado**	hayan **hablado**

PLUPERFECT INDICATIVE

imperfect indicative of haber	add past participle
había **hablado**	habíamos **hablado**
habías **hablado**	habíais **hablado**
había **hablado**	habían **hablado**

PAST PARTICIPLE
hablado

PLUPERFECT SUBJUNCTIVE

imperfect subjunctive of haber	add past participle
hubiera **hablado**	hubiéramos **hablado**
hubieras **hablado**	hubierais **hablado**
hubiera **hablado**	hubieran **hablado**

FUTURE PERFECT

future of haber	add past participle
habré **hablado**	habremos **hablado**
habrás **hablado**	habréis **hablado**
habrá **hablado**	habrán **hablado**

CONDITIONAL PERFECT

conditional of haber	add past participle
habría **hablado**	habríamos **hablado**
habrías **hablado**	habríais **hablado**
habría **hablado**	habrían **hablado**

Usage examples

Hablo francés con soltura. *I speak fluent French.*
No hablo alemán. *I don't speak German.*
¿Hablas español? *Do you speak Spanish?*
Aquí se habla inglés. *English is spoken here.*
¿Podría hablar más despacio, por favor? *Could you speak more slowly, please?*
hablar de *to talk about*
Hablan muy bien de ella. *People speak very highly of her.*
Hablamos sobre eso. *We talked about that.*
¿Es fácil hablar con los profesores? *Are the teachers easy to talk to?*
Hablaré con él. *I'll speak to him.*
No conozco a nadie que hable japonés. *I don't know anyone who speaks Japanese.*

He hablado con mi abogado. *I have spoken to my lawyer.*
Los ministros han hablado de la crisis económica mundial. *The ministers discussed the global economic crisis.*
Para cuando llegues, habré hablado con el profesor. *By the time you arrive, I will have spoken to the professor.*
En un país europeo, habrían hablado más inglés. *In a European country, they would have spoken more English.*
el español hablado *spoken Spanish*
países de habla portuguesa *Portuguese-speaking countries*
hablador *talkative, chatty*

-car verbs | the simple tenses

58 **-car verbs** | the simple tenses   **buscar** to look for

🔑 Key points

➡ spelling rule: **c** becomes **qu** before **e**

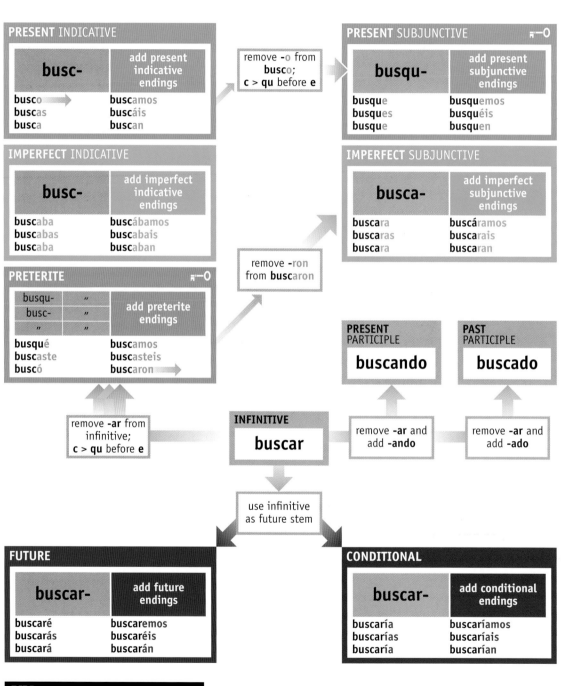

🧩 Following the same pattern

aplicar to apply	**explicar** to explain	**provocar** to cause; to provoke
atacar to attack	**indicar** to point out, indicate	**sacar** to take out; to get
comunicar to communicate	**practicar** to practise; to perform	**tocar** to touch; to play

---

haber (in the correct simple tense) + past participle

PERFECT INDICATIVE

present indicative of haber	add past participle
he **buscado**	hemos **buscado**
has **buscado**	habéis **buscado**
ha **buscado**	han **buscado**

PERFECT SUBJUNCTIVE

present subjunctive of haber	add past participle
haya **buscado**	hayamos **buscado**
hayas **buscado**	hayáis **buscado**
haya **buscado**	hayan **buscado**

PLUPERFECT INDICATIVE

imperfect indicative of haber	add past participle
había **buscado**	habíamos **buscado**
habías **buscado**	habíais **buscado**
había **buscado**	habían **buscado**

PAST PARTICIPLE
buscado

PLUPERFECT SUBJUNCTIVE

imperfect subjunctive of haber	add past participle
hubiera **buscado**	hubiéramos **buscado**
hubieras **buscado**	hubierais **buscado**
hubiera **buscado**	hubieran **buscado**

FUTURE PERFECT

future of haber	add past participle
habré **buscado**	habremos **buscado**
habrás **buscado**	habréis **buscado**
habrá **buscado**	habrán **buscado**

CONDITIONAL PERFECT

conditional of haber	add past participle
habría **buscado**	habríamos **buscado**
habrías **buscado**	habríais **buscado**
habría **buscado**	habrían **buscado**

Usage examples

buscar algo *to look for something*
Estoy buscando mi pasaporte. *I'm looking for my passport.*
¿Qué buscas? *What are you looking for?*
Buscamos un piso en el centro de Barcelona. *We are looking for a flat in the centre of Barcelona.*
Estaba buscando a Eduardo. *She was looking for Eduardo.*
Buscó por todas partes. *He looked everywhere.*
Fui a buscarlo al aeropuerto. *I went to pick him up from the airport.*
¿Has buscado bien? *Have you looked properly?*
Más de cien mil sirios han buscado refugio en los países vecinos. *More than one hundred thousand Syrians have sought refuge in neighbouring countries.*

Hubiera buscado el monedero, pero no tuve tiempo. *I would have looked for the purse, but I didn't have time.*
Busca y encontrarás. *Seek and you shall find.*
El sospechoso está siendo buscado por la policía. *The suspect is wanted by the police.*
"Se busca cocinero" *"Cook wanted"*
buscar excusas *to make excuses*
buscar una palabra en el diccionario *to look up a word in the dictionary*
buscar una aguja en un pajar *to look for a needle in a haystack*
la búsqueda *search*
en busca de *in search of*
un buscador *search engine*

🔑 Key points

➡ spelling rule: **z** becomes **c** before **e**

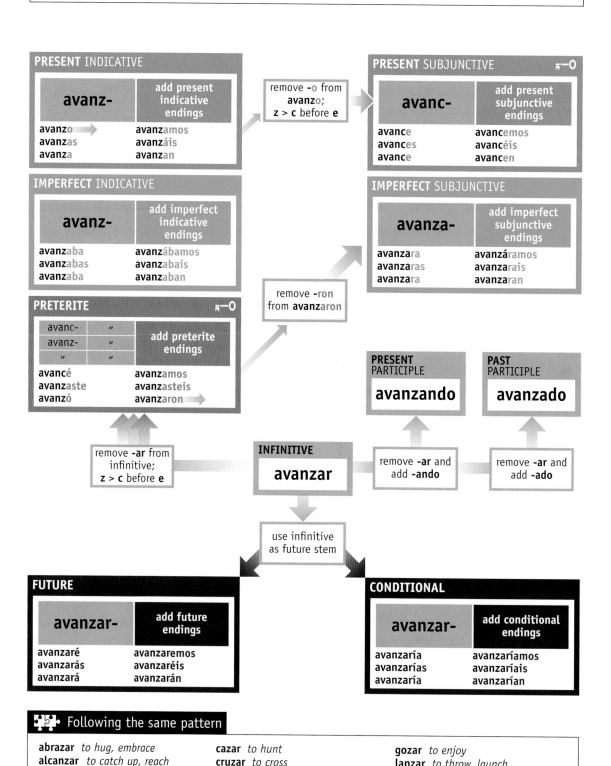

PRESENT INDICATIVE

avanz-	add present indicative endings
avanzo	avanzamos
avanzas	avanzáis
avanza	avanzan

remove -o from avanzo; z > c before e

PRESENT SUBJUNCTIVE 🔑

avanc-	add present subjunctive endings
avance	avancemos
avances	avancéis
avance	avancen

IMPERFECT INDICATIVE

avanz-	add imperfect indicative endings
avanzaba	avanzábamos
avanzabas	avanzabais
avanzaba	avanzaban

IMPERFECT SUBJUNCTIVE

avanza-	add imperfect subjunctive endings
avanzara	avanzáramos
avanzaras	avanzarais
avanzara	avanzaran

remove -ron from **avanz**aron

PRETERITE 🔑

avanc-	"	add preterite endings
avanz-	"	
"	"	
avancé	avanzamos
avanzaste	avanzasteis
avanzó	avanzaron

PRESENT PARTICIPLE

avanzando

PAST PARTICIPLE

avanzado

remove -ar from infinitive; z > c before e

INFINITIVE

avanzar

remove -ar and add -ando

remove -ar and add -ado

use infinitive as future stem

FUTURE

avanzar-	add future endings
avanzaré	avanzaremos
avanzarás	avanzaréis
avanzará	avanzarán

CONDITIONAL

avanzar-	add conditional endings
avanzaría	avanzaríamos
avanzarías	avanzaríais
avanzaría	avanzarían

🧩 Following the same pattern

abrazar *to hug, embrace*
alcanzar *to catch up, reach*
alzar *to raise*

cazar *to hunt*
cruzar *to cross*
garantizar *to guarantee*

gozar *to enjoy*
lanzar *to throw, launch*
utilizar *to use*

haber (in the correct simple tense) + past participle

PERFECT INDICATIVE

present indicative of haber	add past participle
he avanzado	hemos avanzado
has avanzado	habéis avanzado
ha avanzado	han avanzado

PERFECT SUBJUNCTIVE

present subjunctive of haber	add past participle
haya avanzado	hayamos avanzado
hayas avanzado	hayáis avanzado
haya avanzado	hayan avanzado

PLUPERFECT INDICATIVE

imperfect indicative of haber	add past participle
había avanzado	habíamos avanzado
habías avanzado	habíais avanzado
había avanzado	habían avanzado

PAST PARTICIPLE

avanzado

PLUPERFECT SUBJUNCTIVE

imperfect subjunctive of haber	add past participle
hubiera avanzado	hubiéramos avanzado
hubieras avanzado	hubierais avanzado
hubiera avanzado	hubieran avanzado

FUTURE PERFECT

future of haber	add past participle
habré avanzado	habremos avanzado
habrás avanzado	habréis avanzado
habrá avanzado	habrán avanzado

CONDITIONAL PERFECT

conditional of haber	add past participle
habría avanzado	habríamos avanzado
habrías avanzado	habríais avanzado
habría avanzado	habrían avanzado

Usage examples

Avanzaron lentamente. *They moved forward slowly.*

Los corredores avanzan hacia la línea de salida. *The runners moved towards the start line.*

Nos aburrimos según avanzaba la tarde. *We got bored as the evening wore on.*

El pelotón avanzó a una velocidad media de 50 km/h en las dos primeras horas. *The peloton advanced at an average speed of 50 km/h in the first two hours.*

Avancé un peón dos casillas. *I moved a pawn two squares forward.*

Avancé mucho en matemáticas el trimestre pasado. *I made a lot of progress in mathematics last term.*

No estoy avanzando nada con mis deberes. *I am not making any progress with my homework.*

Es probable que el campo de la medicina avance en el futuro. *It is likely that the field of medicine will make progress in the future.*

La genética ha avanzado enormemente en los últimos años. *Genetics has advanced greatly in recent years.*

El ejército habría avanzado hacia Stalingrado. *The army would have advanced on Stalingrad.*

un avance *an advance*

Las negociaciones concluyeron sin avances significativos. *The negotiations concluded without significant progress being made.*

avanzado, avanzada *advanced*

la tecnología de avanzada *advanced technology*

de edad avanzada *advanced in years*

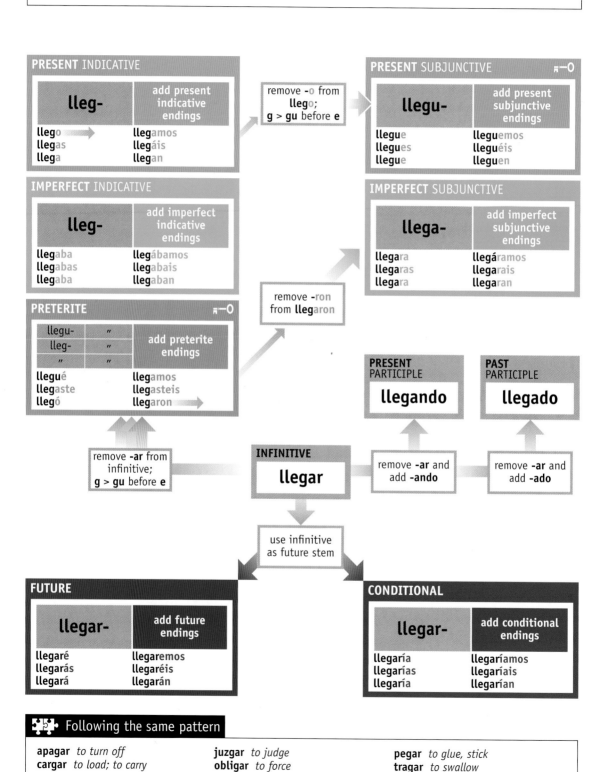

Key points

→ spelling rule: **g** becomes **gu** before **e**

PRESENT INDICATIVE

lleg-	add present indicative endings
llego	llegamos
llegas	llegáis
llega	llegan

remove **-o** from **lleg**o; **g > gu** before **e**

PRESENT SUBJUNCTIVE

llegu-	add present subjunctive endings
llegue	lleguemos
llegues	lleguéis
llegue	lleguen

IMPERFECT INDICATIVE

lleg-	add imperfect indicative endings
llegaba	llegábamos
llegabas	llegabais
llegaba	llegaban

IMPERFECT SUBJUNCTIVE

llega-	add imperfect subjunctive endings
llegara	llegáramos
llegaras	llegarais
llegara	llegaran

remove **-ron** from **lleg**aron

PRETERITE

llegu-	"	add preterite endings
lleg-	"	
"	"	
llegué	llegamos
llegaste	llegasteis
llegó	llegaron

remove **-ar** from infinitive; **g > gu** before **e**

INFINITIVE

llegar

use infinitive as future stem

PRESENT PARTICIPLE

llegando

remove **-ar** and add **-ando**

PAST PARTICIPLE

llegado

remove **-ar** and add **-ado**

FUTURE

llegar-	add future endings
llegaré	llegaremos
llegarás	llegaréis
llegará	llegarán

CONDITIONAL

llegar-	add conditional endings
llegaría	llegaríamos
llegarías	llegaríais
llegaría	llegarían

Following the same pattern

apagar *to turn off*	**juzgar** *to judge*	**pegar** *to glue, stick*
cargar *to load; to carry*	**obligar** *to force*	**tragar** *to swallow*
entregar *to deliver*	**pagar** *to pay*	**vengar** *to avenge*

haber (in the correct simple tense) + past participle

PERFECT INDICATIVE

present indicative of haber	add past participle
he **llegado**	hemos **llegado**
has **llegado**	habéis **llegado**
ha **llegado**	han **llegado**

PERFECT SUBJUNCTIVE

present subjunctive of haber	add past participle
haya **llegado**	hayamos **llegado**
hayas **llegado**	hayáis **llegado**
haya **llegado**	hayan **llegado**

PLUPERFECT INDICATIVE

imperfect indicative of haber	add past participle
había **llegado**	habíamos **llegado**
habías **llegado**	habíais **llegado**
había **llegado**	habían **llegado**

PAST PARTICIPLE

llegado

PLUPERFECT SUBJUNCTIVE

imperfect subjunctive of haber	add past participle
hubiera **llegado**	hubiéramos **llegado**
hubieras **llegado**	hubierais **llegado**
hubiera **llegado**	hubieran **llegado**

FUTURE PERFECT

future of haber	add past participle
habré **llegado**	habremos **llegado**
habrás **llegado**	habréis **llegado**
habrá **llegado**	habrán **llegado**

CONDITIONAL PERFECT

conditional of haber	add past participle
habría **llegado**	habríamos **llegado**
habrías **llegado**	habríais **llegado**
habría **llegado**	habrían **llegado**

Usage examples

Puede que Juan llegue un poco tarde. *Juan may arrive a bit late.*

¿Cuándo llegaste? *When did you arrive?*

Cuando llegué a su casa estaba lloviendo. *When I got to his house, it was raining.*

Samantha llegó hace un mes. *Samantha arrived a month ago.*

Llegaré al restaurante a la una y media de la tarde. *I will arrive at the restaurant at half past one in the afternoon.*

Espero que lleguéis a tiempo. *I hope that you will arrive on time.*

Habría llegado a tiempo pero mi coche tuvo una avería. *I would have arrived on time, but my car broke down.*

Ha llegado la primavera. *Spring has arrived.*

Más adelante, llegarás a una rotonda. *Farther on, you will come to a roundabout.*

El agua me llegaba a los tobillos. *The water came up to my ankles.*

No me llega el dinero. *I don't have enough money.*

No llego al estante. *I can't reach the shelf.*

Los gastos totales llegaron a mil euros. *The total expenditure came to a thousand euros.*

llegar a un acuerdo *to reach an agreement*

Quiero llegar a un acuerdo con ella antes de partir. *I want to reach an agreement with her before I leave.*

llegar a ser *to become*

Más tarde llegaría a ser gerente. *He would later become the manager.*

Key points

→ spelling rule: **gu** becomes **gü** before **e**

PRESENT INDICATIVE

averigu-	add present indicative endings
averiguo	averiguamos
averiguas	averiguáis
averigua	averiguan

remove **-o** *from* **averiguo**; **gu > gü** *before* **e**

PRESENT SUBJUNCTIVE

averigü-	add present subjunctive endings
averigüe	averigüemos
averigües	averigüéis
averigüe	averigüen

IMPERFECT INDICATIVE

averigu-	add imperfect indicative endings
averiguaba	averiguábamos
averiguabas	averiguabais
averiguaba	averiguaban

IMPERFECT SUBJUNCTIVE

averigua-	add imperfect subjunctive endings
averiguara	averiguáramos
averiguaras	averiguarais
averiguara	averiguaran

remove **-ron** *from* **averiguaron**

PRETERITE

averigü-	"	add preterite endings
averigu-	"	
"	"	
averigüé	averiguamos
averiguaste	averiguasteis
averiguó	averiguaron

PRESENT PARTICIPLE

averiguando

PAST PARTICIPLE

averiguado

remove **-ar** *from infinitive;* **gu > gü** *before* **e**

INFINITIVE

averiguar

remove **-ar** *and add* **-ando**

remove **-ar** *and add* **-ado**

use infinitive as future stem

FUTURE

averiguar-	add future endings
averiguaré	averiguaremos
averiguarás	averiguaréis
averiguará	averiguarán

CONDITIONAL

averiguar-	add conditional endings
averiguaría	averiguaríamos
averiguarías	averiguaríais
averiguaría	averiguarían

Following the same pattern

aguar *to dilute*
apaciguar *to pacify*
menguar *to diminish, decrease*

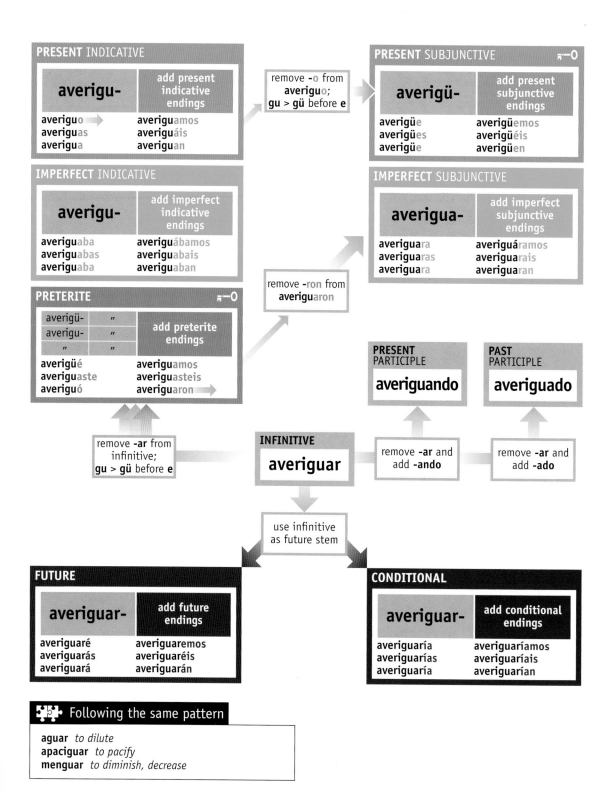

---

haber (in the correct simple tense) + past participle

PERFECT INDICATIVE

present indicative of haber	add past participle
he averiguado	hemos averiguado
has averiguado	habéis averiguado
ha averiguado	han averiguado

PERFECT SUBJUNCTIVE

present subjunctive of haber	add past participle
haya averiguado	hayamos averiguado
hayas averiguado	hayáis averiguado
haya averiguado	hayan averiguado

PLUPERFECT INDICATIVE

imperfect indicative of haber	add past participle
había averiguado	habíamos averiguado
habías averiguado	habíais averiguado
había averiguado	habían averiguado

PAST PARTICIPLE

averiguado

PLUPERFECT SUBJUNCTIVE

imperfect subjunctive of haber	add past participle
hubiera averiguado	hubiéramos averiguado
hubieras averiguado	hubierais averiguado
hubiera averiguado	hubieran averiguado

FUTURE PERFECT

future of haber	add past participle
habré averiguado	habremos averiguado
habrás averiguado	habréis averiguado
habrá averiguado	habrán averiguado

CONDITIONAL PERFECT

conditional of haber	add past participle
habría averiguado	habríamos averiguado
habrías averiguado	habríais averiguado
habría averiguado	habrían averiguado

Usage examples

¿Cómo has averiguando eso? *How did you find that out?*

No pudimos averiguar nada. *We couldn't find out anything.*

Averiguaremos la solución pronto. *We will soon find out the answer.*

Dijo que averiguaría la verdad. *She said that she would find out the truth.*

¿Cuándo lo averiguaste? *When did you find out?*

¿Has averiguado si van a venir? *Have you found out if they are coming?*

Llamó por teléfono para averiguar la hora del vuelo. *He called to find out the time of the flight.*

Me pregunto si han averiguado quién fue el ladrón. *I wonder if they have discovered who the thief was.*

Es importante que averigüemos el alcance del problema. *It is important that we find out the extent of the problem.*

Ha ido a averiguar su paradero. *She has gone to find out his whereabouts.*

Le prometo que se lo diré cuando hayamos averiguado la causa del problema. *I promise I will tell you when we have established the cause of the problem.*

No han averiguado la identidad de la persona que ha asesinado a su amigo. *The identity of the person who killed his friend has not been established.*

Trato de averiguar la información de contacto del Ministerio de Educación. *I am trying to find out the contact details for the Department of Education.*

la averiguación *verification; investigation, inquiry*

⚷ Key points

→ **e** of stem changes to **ie** for stressed syllables in present indicative

→ **ie** of stem reverts to **e** for unstressed syllables in present subjunctive

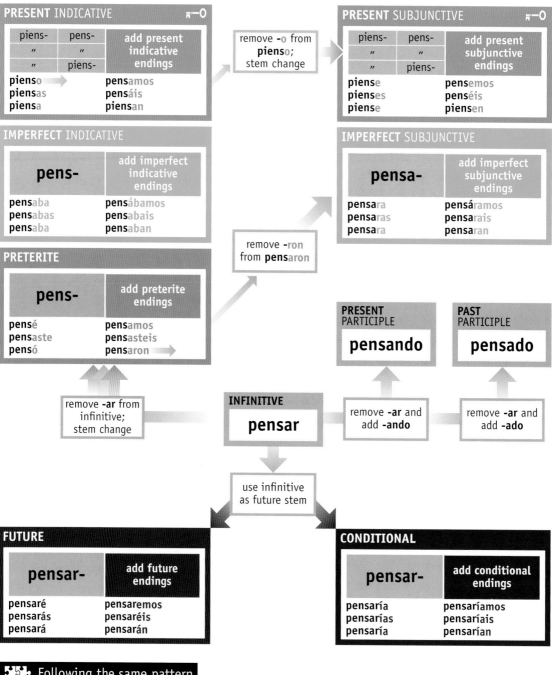

PRESENT INDICATIVE ⚷

piens-	pens-	add present indicative endings
"	"	
"	piens-	

pienso	pensamos
piensas	penséis
piensa	piensan

remove -o from **piens**o; *stem change*

PRESENT SUBJUNCTIVE ⚷

piens-	pens-	add present subjunctive endings
"	"	
"	piens-	

piense	pensemos
pienses	penséis
piense	piensen

IMPERFECT INDICATIVE

| **pens-** | add imperfect indicative endings |

pensaba	pensábamos
pensabas	pensabais
pensaba	pensaban

IMPERFECT SUBJUNCTIVE

| **pensa-** | add imperfect subjunctive endings |

pensara	pensáramos
pensaras	pensarais
pensara	pensaran

remove -ron from **pens**aron

PRETERITE

| **pens-** | add preterite endings |

pensé	pensamos
pensaste	pensasteis
pensó	pensaron

PRESENT PARTICIPLE

pensando

PAST PARTICIPLE

pensado

remove -ar from infinitive; stem change

INFINITIVE

pensar

remove -ar and add -ando

remove -ar and add -ado

use infinitive as future stem

FUTURE

| **pensar-** | add future endings |

pensaré	pensaremos
pensarás	pensaréis
pensará	pensarán

CONDITIONAL

| **pensar-** | add conditional endings |

pensaría	pensaríamos
pensarías	pensaríais
pensaría	pensarían

▚ Following the same pattern

calentar *to heat (up)*
cerrar *to close, shut*
confesar *to confess; to admit*

despertarse *to wake (up)*
enterrar *to bury*
gobernar *to govern*

manifestar *to declare; to show*
recomendar *to recommend*
sentarse *to sit down*

---

haber (in the correct simple tense) + **past participle**

PERFECT INDICATIVE

present indicative of haber	add past participle
he **pensado**	hemos **pensado**
has **pensado**	habéis **pensado**
ha **pensado**	han **pensado**

PERFECT SUBJUNCTIVE

present subjunctive of haber	add past participle
haya **pensado**	hayamos **pensado**
hayas **pensado**	hayáis **pensado**
haya **pensado**	hayan **pensado**

PLUPERFECT INDICATIVE

imperfect indicative of haber	add past participle
había **pensado**	habíamos **pensado**
habías **pensado**	habíais **pensado**
había **pensado**	habían **pensado**

PAST PARTICIPLE
pensado

PLUPERFECT SUBJUNCTIVE

imperfect subjunctive of haber	add past participle
hubiera **pensado**	hubieramos **pensado**
hubieras **pensado**	hubierais **pensado**
hubiera **pensado**	hubieran **pensado**

FUTURE PERFECT

future of haber	add past participle
habré **pensado**	habremos **pensado**
habrás **pensado**	habréis **pensado**
habrá **pensado**	habrán **pensado**

CONDITIONAL PERFECT

conditional of haber	add past participle
habría **pensado**	habríamos **pensado**
habrías **pensado**	habríais **pensado**
habría **pensado**	habrían **pensado**

◥▼ Usage examples

Lo hizo sin pensar. *He did it without thinking.*
Lo pensaré. *I'll think about it.*
Deja que piense en ello. *Let me think about it.*
Me has dado mucho en que pensar. *You have given me a lot to think about.*
No me importa lo que piensen. *I don't care what they think.*
¿Qué piensan los niños? *What do the children think?*
¿Qué piensas de mi idea? *What do you think of my idea?*
Piensa que tienes razón. *She thinks you're right.*
Pienso que debes venir. *I think you should come.*
Pensé que ella lo sabía. *I thought she knew.*
¿En qué estás pensando? *What are you thinking about?*

Pienso en ti. *I'm thinking about you.*
Estaban pensando en mudarse al campo. *They were thinking of moving to the country.*
Pienso quedarme unos días. *I intend to stay a few days.*
Pensamos irnos esta noche. *We intend to leave tonight.*
¿Qué piensas hacer mañana? *What do you plan to do tomorrow?*
¿Cuándo piensas volver? *When do you intend to return?*
Lo pensó mejor. *He thought better of it.*
¡Ni pensarlo! *No way!*
el pensamiento *thought*
pensativo, pensativa *pensive, thoughtful*

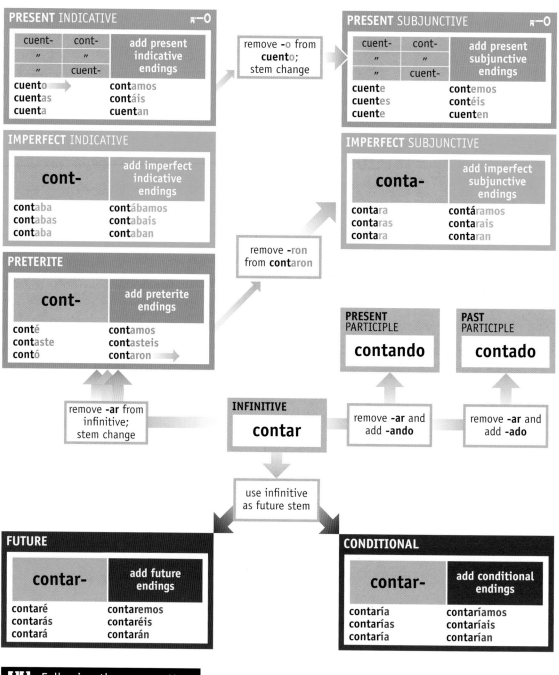

🔑 Key points

➡️ **o** of stem changes to **ue** for stressed syllables in present indicative

➡️ **ue** of stem reverts to **o** for unstressed syllables in present subjunctive

PRESENT INDICATIVE

cuent-	cont-	add present indicative endings
"	"	
"	cuent-	

cuento	contamos
cuentas	contáis
cuenta	cuentan

remove **-o** from **cuento**; stem change

PRESENT SUBJUNCTIVE

cuent-	cont-	add present subjunctive endings
"	"	
"	cuent-	

cuente	contemos
cuentes	contéis
cuente	cuenten

IMPERFECT INDICATIVE

| **cont-** | add imperfect indicative endings |

contaba	contábamos
contabas	contabais
contaba	contaban

IMPERFECT SUBJUNCTIVE

| **conta-** | add imperfect subjunctive endings |

contara	contáramos
contaras	contarais
contara	contaran

PRETERITE

| **cont-** | add preterite endings |

conté	contamos
contaste	contasteis
contó	contaron

remove **-ron** from **contaron**

PRESENT PARTICIPLE

contando

PAST PARTICIPLE

contado

remove **-ar** from infinitive; stem change

INFINITIVE

contar

remove **-ar** and add **-ando**

remove **-ar** and add **-ado**

use infinitive as future stem

FUTURE

| **contar-** | add future endings |

contaré	contaremos
contarás	contaréis
contará	contarán

CONDITIONAL

| **contar-** | add conditional endings |

contaría	contaríamos
contarías	contaríais
contaría	contarían

🧩 Following the same pattern

comprobar to check
demostrar to prove; to demonstrate

encontrar to find
mostrar to show
probar to prove; to try; to test

recordar to remember; to remind
sonar to ring; to sound
volar to fly

---

haber (in the correct simple tense) + past participle

PERFECT INDICATIVE

present indicative of haber	add past participle
he **contado**	hemos **contado**
has **contado**	habéis **contado**
ha **contado**	han **contado**

PERFECT SUBJUNCTIVE

present subjunctive of haber	add past participle
haya **contado**	hayamos **contado**
hayas **contado**	hayáis **contado**
haya **contado**	hayan **contado**

PLUPERFECT INDICATIVE

imperfect indicative of haber	add past participle
había **contado**	habíamos **contado**
habías **contado**	habíais **contado**
había **contado**	habían **contado**

PAST PARTICIPLE

contado

PLUPERFECT SUBJUNCTIVE

imperfect subjunctive of haber	add past participle
hubiera **contado**	hubiéramos **contado**
hubieras **contado**	hubierais **contado**
hubiera **contado**	hubieran **contado**

FUTURE PERFECT

future of haber	add past participle
habré **contado**	habremos **contado**
habrás **contado**	habréis **contado**
habrá **contado**	habrán **contado**

CONDITIONAL PERFECT

conditional of haber	add past participle
habría **contado**	habríamos **contado**
habrías **contado**	habríais **contado**
habría **contado**	habrían **contado**

◥◢ Usage examples

¿No sabes contar? *Can't you count?*
Mi hermana menor sólo sabe contar hasta diez. *My younger sister can only count to ten.*
Conté hasta veinte. *I counted up to twenty.*
Es importante que cuentes el dinero. *It is important that you count the money.*
¿Ha contado los pasajeros? *Has he counted the passengers?*
Estaba contando los días. *I was counting the days.*
Puedes contar conmigo. *You can count on me.*
Cuento contigo. *I'm counting on you.*
Mañana te cuento. *I'll tell you tomorrow.*
Te voy a contar un cuento. *I am going to tell you a story.*
Te contaré un secreto. *I will tell you a secret.*

No se lo contaría a nadie. *She wouldn't tell anyone.*
Mi abuelo contaba chistes. *My grandad used to tell jokes.*
Eso no cuenta. *That doesn't count.*
¿Qué te cuentas? *How's it going?*
una cuenta *calculation, sum; count; bill*
una cuenta bancaria *bank account*
un(a) contable *accountant*
un cuento *story, tale*
un cuento corto *short story*
un cuento infantil *children's story*
un cuento de hadas *fairy tale*
un(a) cuentista *storyteller*
un contador *meter*
un contador de gas *gas meter*

⌦─O Key points

→ **i** of stem changes to **í** for stressed syllables in present indicative

→ **í** of stem reverts to **i** for unstressed syllables in present subjunctive

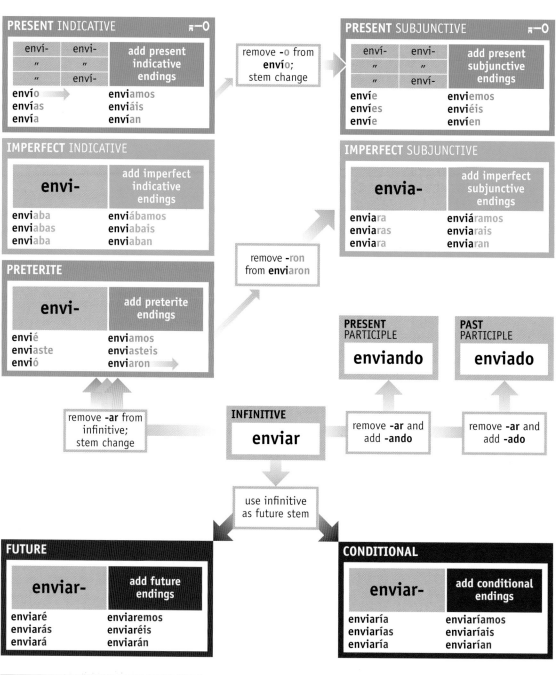

PRESENT INDICATIVE ⌦─O

enví-	enví-	add present indicative endings
"	"	
"	enví-	

envío	enviamos
envías	enviáis
envía	envían

PRESENT SUBJUNCTIVE ⌦─O

remove **-o** from **envío**; stem change

enví-	enví-	add present subjunctive endings
"	"	
"	enví-	

envíe	enviemos
envíes	enviéis
envíe	envíen

IMPERFECT INDICATIVE

envi-	add imperfect indicative endings

enviaba	enviábamos
enviabas	enviabais
enviaba	enviaban

IMPERFECT SUBJUNCTIVE

envia-	add imperfect subjunctive endings

enviara	enviáramos
enviaras	enviarais
enviara	enviaran

PRETERITE

envi-	add preterite endings

envié	enviamos
enviaste	enviasteis
envió	enviaron

remove **-ron** from **enviaron**

PRESENT PARTICIPLE

enviando

PAST PARTICIPLE

enviado

remove **-ar** from infinitive; stem change

INFINITIVE

enviar

remove **-ar** and add **-ando**

remove **-ar** and add **-ado**

use infinitive as future stem

FUTURE

enviar-	add future endings

enviaré	enviaremos
enviarás	enviaréis
enviará	enviarán

CONDITIONAL

enviar-	add conditional endings

enviaría	enviaríamos
enviarías	enviaríais
enviaría	enviarían

⧉ Following the same pattern

ampliar *to expand; to extend*
confiar *to trust; to entrust*
criar *to breed, rear; to bring up*

desafiar *to challenge, dare; to defy*
desviar *to divert; to deviate*

fotografiar *to photograph*
guiar *to guide*
variar *to vary*

haber (in the correct simple tense) + past participle

PERFECT INDICATIVE

present indicative of haber	add past participle
he **enviado**	hemos **enviado**
has **enviado**	habéis **enviado**
ha **enviado**	han **enviado**

PERFECT SUBJUNCTIVE

present subjunctive of haber	add past participle
haya **enviado**	hayamos **enviado**
hayas **enviado**	hayáis **enviado**
haya **enviado**	hayan **enviado**

PLUPERFECT INDICATIVE

imperfect indicative of haber	add past participle
había **enviado**	habíamos **enviado**
habías **enviado**	habíais **enviado**
había **enviado**	habían **enviado**

PAST PARTICIPLE

enviado

PLUPERFECT SUBJUNCTIVE

imperfect subjunctive of haber	add past participle
hubiera **enviado**	hubiéramos **enviado**
hubieras **enviado**	hubierais **enviado**
hubiera **enviado**	hubieran **enviado**

FUTURE PERFECT

future of haber	add past participle
habré **enviado**	habremos **enviado**
habrás **enviado**	habréis **enviado**
habrá **enviado**	habrán **enviado**

CONDITIONAL PERFECT

conditional of haber	add past participle
habría **enviado**	habríamos **enviado**
habrías **enviado**	habríais **enviado**
habría **enviado**	habrían **enviado**

Usage examples

enviar un mensaje de texto *to send a text message*
enviar por correo electrónico *to send by email*
Él me pidió que enviara la carta por correo. *He asked me to send the letter by post.*
¿Le enviaste un mensaje de texto a Miguel? *Did you send a text message to Miguel?*
Habrá enviado el correo electrónico para entonces. *She will have sent the email by then.*
Necesitamos que envíe un acuse de recibo. *We need you to send an acknowledgement of receipt.*
Te habría enviado la carta, pero no pude encontrar un sello. *I would have sent the letter, but I could not find a stamp.*
Enviaremos más información a su debido tiempo. *We will send further information in due course.*

Enviaron el paquete por avión. *They sent the package by plane.*
¿Cuándo envías las invitaciones? *When are you sending out the invitations?*
Les estoy enviando una postal. *I am sending them a postcard.*
Albert envía recuerdos. *Albert sends his regards.*
Pedro dijo que lo enviaría por mensajero. *Pedro said that he would send it by courier.*
Parecía raro que la compañía hubiera enviado un coche al aeropuerto. *It seemed odd that the company would send a car to the airport.*
un enviado *envoy*
enviado especial, enviada especial *special correspondent*

Key points

➡ **u** of stem changes to **ú** for stressed syllables in present indicative

➡ **ú** of stem reverts to **u** for unstressed syllables in present subjunctive

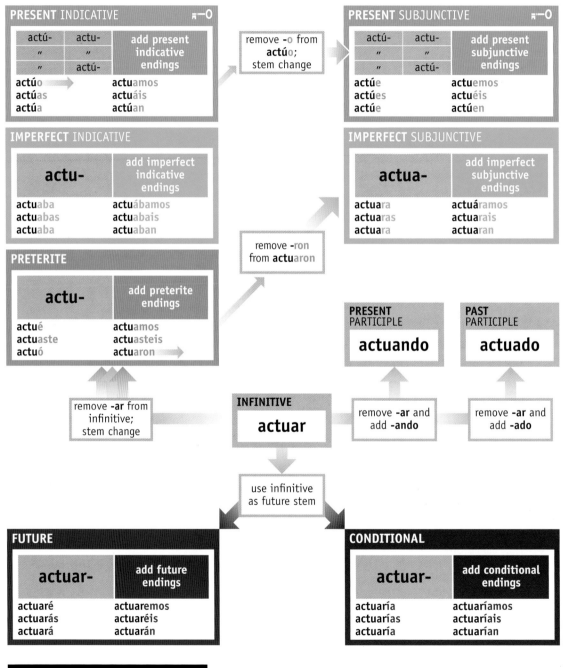

PRESENT INDICATIVE

actú-	actu-	add present indicative endings
"	"	
"	actú-	

actúo	actuamos
actúas	actuáis
actúa	actúan

remove **-o** from **actúo**; stem change

PRESENT SUBJUNCTIVE

actú-	actu-	add present subjunctive endings
"	"	
"	actú-	

actúe	actuemos
actúes	actuéis
actúe	actúen

IMPERFECT INDICATIVE

actu-	add imperfect indicative endings

actuaba	actuábamos
actuabas	actuabais
actuaba	actuaban

IMPERFECT SUBJUNCTIVE

actua-	add imperfect subjunctive endings

actuara	actuáramos
actuaras	actuarais
actuara	actuaran

remove **-ron** from **actuaron**

PRETERITE

actu-	add preterite endings

actué	actuamos
actuaste	actuasteis
actuó	actuaron

PRESENT PARTICIPLE

actuando

PAST PARTICIPLE

actuado

remove **-ar** from infinitive; stem change

INFINITIVE

actuar

remove **-ar** and add **-ando**

remove **-ar** and add **-ado**

use infinitive as future stem

FUTURE

actuar-	add future endings

actuaré	actuaremos
actuarás	actuaréis
actuará	actuarán

CONDITIONAL

actuar-	add conditional endings

actuaría	actuaríamos
actuarías	actuaríais
actuaría	actuarían

Following the same pattern

continuar *to continue*
efectuar *to carry out*
evaluar *to evaluate*

insinuar *to insinuate*
perpetuar *to perpetuate*
situar *to place, put; to locate*

---

haber (in the correct simple tense) **+ past participle**

PERFECT INDICATIVE

present indicative of haber	add past participle
he **actuado**	hemos **actuado**
has **actuado**	habéis **actuado**
ha **actuado**	han **actuado**

PERFECT SUBJUNCTIVE

present subjunctive of haber	add past participle
haya **actuado**	hayamos **actuado**
hayas **actuado**	hayáis **actuado**
haya **actuado**	hayan **actuado**

PLUPERFECT INDICATIVE

imperfect indicative of haber	add past participle
había **actuado**	habíamos **actuado**
habías **actuado**	habíais **actuado**
había **actuado**	habían **actuado**

PAST PARTICIPLE

actuado

PLUPERFECT SUBJUNCTIVE

imperfect subjunctive of haber	add past participle
hubiera **actuado**	hubiéramos **actuado**
hubieras **actuado**	hubierais **actuado**
hubiera **actuado**	hubieran **actuado**

FUTURE PERFECT

future of haber	add past participle
habré **actuado**	habremos **actuado**
habrás **actuado**	habréis **actuado**
habrá **actuado**	habrán **actuado**

CONDITIONAL PERFECT

conditional of haber	add past participle
habría **actuado**	habríamos **actuado**
habrías **actuado**	habríais **actuado**
habría **actuado**	habrían **actuado**

Usage examples

Actuaremos con decisión. *We will act decisively.*
Sabes que me molesta que actúes de esa manera. *You know I don't like to act that way.*
Actuamos de buena fe. *We acted in good faith.*
Actué precipitadamente. *I acted rashly.*
Actuaban de una forma rara. *They were acting strangely.*
Hemos actuado con honradez. *We have acted with integrity.*
Nunca actuaría de una forma tan irresponsable. *I would never act so irresponsibly.*
No acordamos con su forma de actuar. *We don't agree with his way of doing things.*
¡Déjate de actuar como un niño! *Stop acting like a baby!*

Actuabais como si nada hubiera pasado. *You were acting as if nothing had happened.*
Actuaba como si hubiera ganado las elecciones. *He was acting as if he had won the election.*
Está actuando en una película. *She is acting in a film.*
Javier Bardem actuó en esa película. *Javier Bardem acted in that film.*
El grupo actuará en Londres. *The band will perform in London.*
Este es el abogado que actúa en nombre del acusado. *This is the lawyer acting on behalf of the defendant.*
el acto *act*
en el acto *there and then*
un actor, una actriz *actor*
actuación *performance*

⚷–O Key points

→ **e** of stem changes to **ie** for stressed syllables in present indicative

→ spelling rule: **z** becomes **c** before **e**

→ **ie** of stem reverts to **e** for unstressed syllables in present subjunctive

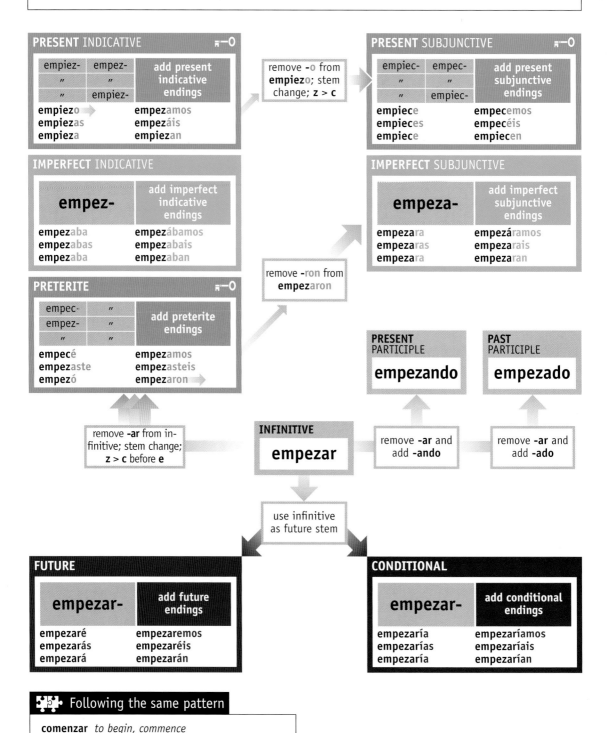

PRESENT INDICATIVE   ⚷–O

empiez-	empez-	add present indicative endings
"	"	
"	empiez-	

empiezo → empezamos
empiezas   empezáis
empieza   empiezan

remove **-o** from **empiezo**; stem change; **z > c**

PRESENT SUBJUNCTIVE   ⚷–O

empiec-	empec-	add present subjunctive endings
"	"	
"	empiec-	

empiece   empecemos
empieces   empecéis
empiece   empiecen

IMPERFECT INDICATIVE

| empez- | add imperfect indicative endings |

empezaba   empezábamos
empezabas   empezabais
empezaba   empezaban

IMPERFECT SUBJUNCTIVE

| empeza- | add imperfect subjunctive endings |

empezara   empezáramos
empezaras   empezarais
empezara   empezaran

PRETERITE   ⚷–O

empec-	"	add preterite endings
empez-	"	
"	"	

empecé   empezamos
empezaste empezasteis
empezó   empezaron →

remove **-ron** from **empezaron**

PRESENT PARTICIPLE

empezando

PAST PARTICIPLE

empezado

remove **-ar** from infinitive; stem change; **z > c** before **e**

INFINITIVE

empezar

remove **-ar** and add **-ando**

remove **-ar** and add **-ado**

use infinitive as future stem

FUTURE

| empezar- | add future endings |

empezaré   empezaremos
empezarás   empezaréis
empezará   empezarán

CONDITIONAL

| empezar- | add conditional endings |

empezaría   empezaríamos
empezarías   empezaríais
empezaría   empezarían

⟊ Following the same pattern

comenzar *to begin, commence*
recomenzar *to recommence*
tropezar *to stumble, trip*

---

haber (in the correct simple tense) + past participle

PERFECT INDICATIVE

present indicative of haber	add past participle
he empezado	hemos empezado
has empezado	habéis empezado
ha empezado	han empezado

PERFECT SUBJUNCTIVE

present subjunctive of haber	add past participle
haya empezado	hayamos empezado
hayas empezado	hayáis empezado
haya empezado	hayan empezado

PLUPERFECT INDICATIVE

imperfect indicative of haber	add past participle
había empezado	habíamos empezado
habías empezado	habíais empezado
había empezado	habían empezado

PAST PARTICIPLE

empezado

PLUPERFECT SUBJUNCTIVE

imperfect subjunctive of haber	add past participle
hubiera empezado	hubiéramos empezado
hubieras empezado	hubierais empezado
hubiera empezado	hubieran empezado

FUTURE PERFECT

future of haber	add past participle
habré empezado	habremos empezado
habrás empezado	habréis empezado
habrá empezado	habrán empezado

CONDITIONAL PERFECT

conditional of haber	add past participle
habría empezado	habríamos empezado
habrías empezado	habríais empezado
habría empezado	habrían empezado

◥◤ Usage examples

¿A qué hora empieza la película? *What time does the film start?*

El partido de fútbol empieza a las seis. *The football match starts at six o'clock.*

El nuevo trimestre empezará pronto. *The new term will start soon.*

¿Quieres comer algo antes de que empiece la obra? *Do you want to have something to eat before the play starts?*

No sé por dónde empezar. *I don't know where to begin.*

Si no llegas a las cuatro, empezamos sin ti. *If you don't arrive at four o'clock, we'll start without you.*

Si yo fuera tú, empezaría desde cero. *If I were you, I would start from scratch.*

Me pidió que no empezara sin él. *He asked me not to start without him.*

La conjunción "y" se convierte en "e" cuando la palabra que le sigue empieza por "i". *The conjunction "y" changes to "e" when the word that follows begins with "i".*

Empezó a llover. *It started to rain.*

Está empezando a nevar. *It's starting to snow.*

Empezaba a preocuparme. *I was starting to worry.*

La película ya había empezado para cuando llegamos al cine. *The film had already started by the time we arrived at the cinema.*

¿Ha empezado ya el partido? *Has the match started yet?*

Para cuando llegue Juan, ya habréis empezado. *By the time Juan arrives, you will have already started.*

⚡–O Key points

➡ **e** of stem changes to **ie** for stressed syllables in present indicative

➡ spelling rule: **g** becomes **gu** before **e**

➡ **ie** of stem reverts to **e** for unstressed syllables in present subjunctive

PRESENT INDICATIVE ⚡–O

nieg-	neg-	add present indicative endings
"	"	
"	nieg-	

niego	negamos
niegas	negáis
niega	niegan

→ remove **-o** from **niego**; stem change; **g > gu**

PRESENT SUBJUNCTIVE ⚡–O

niegu-	negu-	add present subjunctive endings
"	"	
"	niegu-	

niegue	neguemos
niegues	neguéis
niegue	nieguen

IMPERFECT INDICATIVE

neg-	add imperfect indicative endings

negaba	negábamos
negabas	negabais
negaba	negaban

IMPERFECT SUBJUNCTIVE

nega-	add imperfect subjunctive endings

negara	negáramos
negaras	negarais
negara	negaran

remove **-ron** from **negaron**

PRETERITE ⚡–O

negu-	"	add preterite endings
neg-	"	
"	"	

negué	negamos
negaste	negasteis
negó	negaron

PRESENT PARTICIPLE

negando

PAST PARTICIPLE

negado

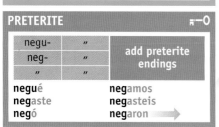 remove **-ar** from infinitive; stem change; **g > gu** before **e**

INFINITIVE

negar

 remove **-ar** and add **-ando**

 remove **-ar** and add **-ado**

use infinitive as future stem

FUTURE

negar-	add future endings

negaré	negaremos
negarás	negaréis
negará	negarán

CONDITIONAL

negar-	add conditional endings

negaría	negaríamos
negarías	negaríais
negaría	negarían

🧩 Following the same pattern

denegar *to deny, refuse*
fregar *to wash (the dishes), scrub*
plegar *to fold, bend*

regar *to water, irrigate*
renegar *to deny strongly*
segar *to reap, cut*

---

haber (in the correct simple tense) **+ past participle**

PERFECT INDICATIVE

present indicative of haber	add past participle
he **negado**	hemos **negado**
has **negado**	habéis **negado**
ha **negado**	han **negado**

PERFECT SUBJUNCTIVE

present subjunctive of haber	add past participle
haya **negado**	hayamos **negado**
hayas **negado**	hayáis **negado**
haya **negado**	hayan **negado**

PLUPERFECT INDICATIVE

imperfect indicative of haber	add past participle
había **negado**	habíamos **negado**
habías **negado**	habíais **negado**
había **negado**	habían **negado**

PAST PARTICIPLE

negado

PLUPERFECT SUBJUNCTIVE

imperfect subjunctive of haber	add past participle
hubiera **negado**	hubieramos **negado**
hubieras **negado**	hubierais **negado**
hubiera **negado**	hubieran **negado**

FUTURE PERFECT

future of haber	add past participle
habré **negado**	habremos **negado**
habrás **negado**	habréis **negado**
habrá **negado**	habrán **negado**

CONDITIONAL PERFECT

conditional of haber	add past participle
habría **negado**	habríamos **negado**
habrías **negado**	habríais **negado**
habría **negado**	habrían **negado**

Usage examples

No lo puedes negar. *You can't deny it.*
Lo niegan todo. *They deny everything.*
Lo habría negado de todos modos. *He would have denied it anyway.*
El presidente negaba las acusaciones. *The president was denying the accusations.*
Negaría la acusación. *I would deny the charge.*
Ni confirmó ni negó los rumores. *He neither confirmed nor denied the rumours.*
¿Por qué negáis la existencia de Dios? *Why do you deny the existence of God?*
No conozco a nadie que niegue este hecho. *I don't know anyone who denies this fact.*
No niego que es un buen profesor. *I don't deny that he is a good teacher.*

No me negarás que la película es popular. *You can't deny that the film is popular.*
Niega haber robado el dinero. *He denies having stolen the money.*
A los estudiantes se les negó la autorización para salir. *The students were refused permission to leave.*
Le habían negado el tratamiento. *He had been refused treatment.*
negarse *to refuse*
Mi nieta se negó a acostarse. *My granddaughter refused to go to bed.*
Mi resfriado se niega a desaparecer. *My cold refuses to go away.*
la negación *denial, negation*
innegable *undeniable*

⚷—O Key points

➡ **o** of stem changes to **ue** for stressed syllables in present indicative

➡ spelling rule: **z** becomes **c** before **e**

➡ **ue** of stem reverts to **o** for unstressed syllables in present subjunctive

PRESENT INDICATIVE ⚷—O

fuerz-	forz-	add present indicative endings
"	"	
"	fuerz-	

fuerzo	forzamos
fuerzas	forzáis
fuerza	fuerzan

remove -o from **fuerzo**; stem change; **z > c**

PRESENT SUBJUNCTIVE ⚷—O

fuerc-	forc-	add present subjunctive endings
"	"	
"	fuerc-	

fuerce	forcemos
fuerces	forcéis
fuerce	fuercen

IMPERFECT INDICATIVE

forz-	add imperfect indicative endings

forzaba	forzábamos
forzabas	forzabais
forzaba	forzaban

remove -ron from **forzaron**

IMPERFECT SUBJUNCTIVE

forza-	add imperfect subjunctive endings

forzara	forzáramos
forzaras	forzarais
forzara	forzaran

PRETERITE ⚷—O

forc-	"	add preterite endings
forz-	"	
"	"	

forcé	forzamos
forzaste	forzasteis
forzó	forzaron

PRESENT PARTICIPLE

forzando

PAST PARTICIPLE

forzado

remove -ar from infinitive; stem change; **z > c** *before* **e**

INFINITIVE

forzar

remove -ar and add -ando

remove -ar and add -ado

use infinitive as future stem

FUTURE

forzar-	add future endings

forzaré	forzaremos
forzarás	forzaréis
forzará	forzarán

CONDITIONAL

forzar-	add conditional endings

forzaría	forzaríamos
forzarías	forzaríais
forzaría	forzarían

🧩 Following the same pattern

almorzar *to have lunch*
esforzar *to strain*
reforzar *to reinforce, strengthen*

haber (in the correct simple tense) **+ past participle**

PERFECT INDICATIVE

present indicative of haber	add past participle
he **forzado**	hemos **forzado**
has **forzado**	habéis **forzado**
ha **forzado**	han **forzado**

PERFECT SUBJUNCTIVE

present subjunctive of haber	add past participle
haya **forzado**	hayamos **forzado**
hayas **forzado**	hayáis **forzado**
haya **forzado**	hayan **forzado**

PLUPERFECT INDICATIVE

imperfect indicative of haber	add past participle
había **forzado**	habíamos **forzado**
habías **forzado**	habíais **forzado**
había **forzado**	habían **forzado**

PAST PARTICIPLE

forzado

PLUPERFECT SUBJUNCTIVE

imperfect subjunctive of haber	add past participle
hubiera **forzado**	hubiéramos **forzado**
hubieras **forzado**	hubierais **forzado**
hubiera **forzado**	hubieran **forzado**

FUTURE PERFECT

future of haber	add past participle
habré **forzado**	habremos **forzado**
habrás **forzado**	habréis **forzado**
habrá **forzado**	habrán **forzado**

CONDITIONAL PERFECT

conditional of haber	add past participle
habría **forzado**	habríamos **forzado**
habrías **forzado**	habríais **forzado**
habría **forzado**	habrían **forzado**

Usage examples

Sus padres la forzaron a casarse. *Her parents forced her to get married.*

Los matones le forzaron a abrir la caja fuerte y se llevaron un buen botín. *The thugs forced him to open the safe and took off with a good haul.*

Me forzará a firmar el acuerdo. *He will force me to sign the contract.*

El ladrón forzó la puerta. *The burglar forced the door.*

Forzaría la puerta. *I would force the door.*

La llave no entra en la cerradura a no ser que la fuerce. *The key does not fit in the lock unless I force it.*

Tuve que forzarme a comer. *I had to force myself to eat.*

No puedes forzarme hacer eso. *You can't force me to do that.*

Usó una herramienta especial para forzar cerraduras. *He used a special tool for picking locks.*

Reconoció que había forzado la entrada. *He admitted that he had broken in.*

¿Por qué estás forzando la vista? *Why are you straining your eyes?*

Tuve que forzar la vista para verlo. *I had to strain my eyes to see it.*

forzado, forzada *forced*
la fuerza *strength, force, power*
la fuerza bruta *brute force*
la fuerza de trabajo *workforce*
las fuerzas armadas *armed forces*
las fuerzas de seguridad *security forces*
forzadamente *forcibly, by force*

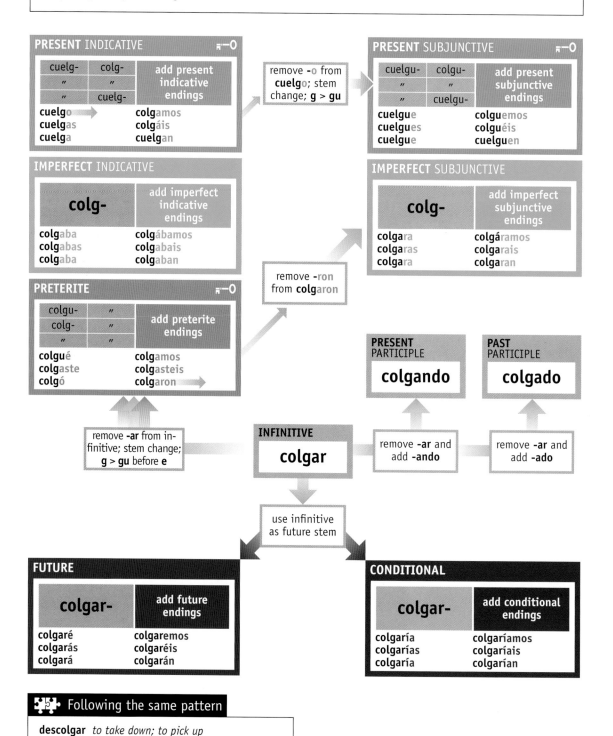

🔑 Key points

➡ **o** of stem changes to **ue** for stressed syllables in present indicative

➡ spelling rule: **g** becomes **gu** before **e**

➡ **ue** of stem reverts to **o** for unstressed syllables in present subjunctive

PRESENT INDICATIVE 🔑

cuelg-	colg-	add present indicative endings
"	"	
"	cuelg-	

cuelgo	colgamos
cuelgas	colgáis
cuelga	cuelgan

remove **-o** from **cuelgo**; stem change; **g > gu**

PRESENT SUBJUNCTIVE 🔑

cuelgu-	colgu-	add present subjunctive endings
"	"	
"	cuelgu-	

cuelgue	colguemos
cuelgues	colguéis
cuelgue	cuelguen

IMPERFECT INDICATIVE

colg-	add imperfect indicative endings

colgaba	colgábamos
colgabas	colgabais
colgaba	colgaban

IMPERFECT SUBJUNCTIVE

colg-	add imperfect subjunctive endings

colgara	colgáramos
colgaras	colgarais
colgara	colgaran

remove **-ron** from **colgaron**

PRETERITE 🔑

colgu-	"	add preterite endings
colg-	"	
"	"	

colgué	colgamos
colgaste	colgasteis
colgó	colgaron

PRESENT PARTICIPLE

colgando

PAST PARTICIPLE

colgado

remove **-ar** from infinitive; stem change; **g > gu** before **e**

INFINITIVE

colgar

remove **-ar** and add **-ando**

remove **-ar** and add **-ado**

use infinitive as future stem

FUTURE

colgar-	add future endings

colgaré	colgaremos
colgarás	colgaréis
colgará	colgarán

CONDITIONAL

colgar-	add conditional endings

colgaría	colgaríamos
colgarías	colgaríais
colgaría	colgarían

🧩 Following the same pattern

descolgar to take down; to pick up (telephone)

rogar to beg; to plead; to pray

haber (in the correct simple tense) + **past participle**

PERFECT INDICATIVE

present indicative of haber	add past participle
he **colgado**	hemos **colgado**
has **colgado**	habéis **colgado**
ha **colgado**	han **colgado**

PERFECT SUBJUNCTIVE

present subjunctive of haber	add past participle
haya **colgado**	hayamos **colgado**
hayas **colgado**	hayáis **colgado**
haya **colgado**	hayan **colgado**

PLUPERFECT INDICATIVE

imperfect indicative of haber	add past participle
había **colgado**	habíamos **colgado**
habías **colgado**	habíais **colgado**
había **colgado**	habían **colgado**

PAST PARTICIPLE

colgado

PLUPERFECT SUBJUNCTIVE

imperfect subjunctive of haber	add past participle
hubiera **colgado**	hubiéramos **colgado**
hubieras **colgado**	hubierais **colgado**
hubiera **colgado**	hubieran **colgado**

FUTURE PERFECT

future of haber	add past participle
habré **colgado**	habremos **colgado**
habrás **colgado**	habréis **colgado**
habrá **colgado**	habrán **colgado**

CONDITIONAL PERFECT

conditional of haber	add past participle
habría **colgado**	habríamos **colgado**
habrías **colgado**	habríais **colgado**
habría **colgado**	habrían **colgado**

◥◣ Usage examples

Te he colgado el abrigo. *I've hung your coat up.*

Colgaremos los cuadros en la sala de estar. *We will hang up the pictures in the living room.*

¿Colgaste el cuadro? *Have you hung up the picture?*

Dudo que haya colgado todos los cuadros. *I doubt that he has hung up all of the pictures.*

La araña de luces cuelga del techo. *The chandelier is suspended from the ceiling.*

Nunca cuelga su ropa. *He never hangs his clothes up.*

Estaba colgando de un gancho. *It was hanging on a hook.*

Los pescadores colgaron la red por la borda del barco. *The fishermen hung the net over the side of the boat.*

Colgaba de un hilo. *It was hanging by a thread.*

Te habría colgado la chaqueta pero no había espacio en el vestíbulo. *I would have hung up your jacket, but there was no room in the hall.*

Los cables colgaban del enchufe. *The wires were dangling from the socket.*

Las llaves colgaban de una cadena de hierro. *The keys were dangling from an iron chain.*

Colgué el teléfono. *I hung up.*

Habrá colgado el teléfono. *He must have hung up.*

Me ha colgado. *He's hung up on me.*

¿Por qué has colgado? *Why did you hang up?*

Mi ordenador se cuelga todo el tiempo. *My computer is crashing all the time.*

colgante *hanging*

un colgante *pendant*

🔑 Key points

➜ irregular stem in preterite: **estuv-**

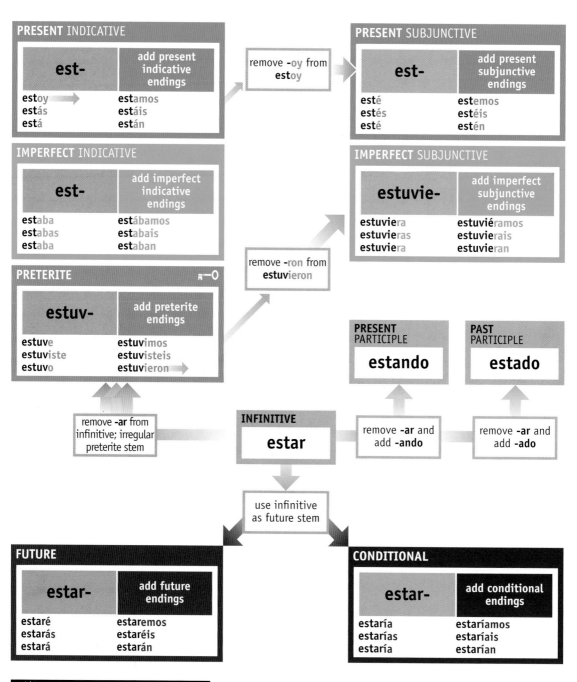

PRESENT INDICATIVE

est-	add present indicative endings
estoy	estamos
estás	estáis
está	están

remove **-oy** from estoy

PRESENT SUBJUNCTIVE

est-	add present subjunctive endings
esté	estemos
estés	estéis
esté	estén

IMPERFECT INDICATIVE

est-	add imperfect indicative endings
estaba	estábamos
estabas	estabais
estaba	estaban

IMPERFECT SUBJUNCTIVE

estuvie-	add imperfect subjunctive endings
estuviera	estuviéramos
estuvieras	estuvierais
estuviera	estuvieran

remove **-ron** from estuvieron

PRETERITE 🔑

estuv-	add preterite endings
estuve	estuvimos
estuviste	estuvisteis
estuvo	estuvieron

PRESENT PARTICIPLE

estando

PAST PARTICIPLE

estado

remove **-ar** from infinitive; irregular preterite stem

INFINITIVE

estar

remove **-ar** and add **-ando**

remove **-ar** and add **-ado**

use infinitive as future stem

FUTURE

estar-	add future endings
estaré	estaremos
estarás	estaréis
estará	estarán

CONDITIONAL

estar-	add conditional endings
estaría	estaríamos
estarías	estaríais
estaría	estarían

💡 Useful tips

Ser and **estar** both mean "to be", but they are used in different ways. **Estar** is used with adjectives indicating non-characteristic features, such as a person's mood or temporary physical state: **Está triste** (She's sad); **Estuvo cansado** (She was tired); **Estoy en la oficina** (I'm in the office). See page 128 to learn about **ser**.

haber (in the correct simple tense) + past participle

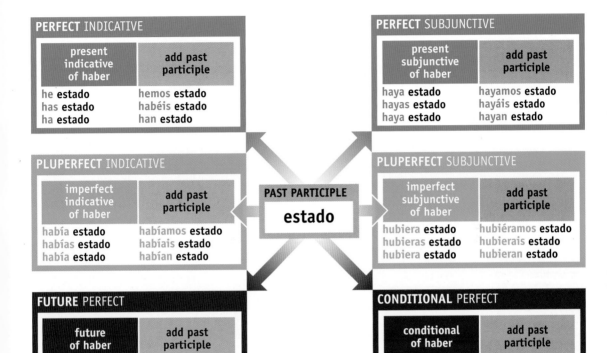

PERFECT INDICATIVE

present indicative of haber	add past participle
he **estado**	hemos **estado**
has **estado**	habéis **estado**
ha **estado**	han **estado**

PERFECT SUBJUNCTIVE

present subjunctive of haber	add past participle
haya **estado**	hayamos **estado**
hayas **estado**	hayáis **estado**
haya **estado**	hayan **estado**

PLUPERFECT INDICATIVE

imperfect indicative of haber	add past participle
había **estado**	habíamos **estado**
habías **estado**	habíais **estado**
había **estado**	habían **estado**

PAST PARTICIPLE

estado

PLUPERFECT SUBJUNCTIVE

imperfect subjunctive of haber	add past participle
hubiera **estado**	hubiéramos **estado**
hubieras **estado**	hubierais **estado**
hubiera **estado**	hubieran **estado**

FUTURE PERFECT

future of haber	add past participle
habré **estado**	habremos **estado**
habrás **estado**	habréis **estado**
habrá **estado**	habrán **estado**

CONDITIONAL PERFECT

conditional of haber	add past participle
habría **estado**	habríamos **estado**
habrías **estado**	habríais **estado**
habría **estado**	habrían **estado**

❧ Usage examples

¿Cómo estás? *How are you?*
¿Cómo está usted, señor? *How are you, sir?*
Estoy muy bien, gracias. *I am very well, thanks.*
Estamos muy cansados. *We are very tired.*
Estás enfermo. *You are ill.*
Este café está frío. *This coffee is cold.*
La Torre Eiffel está en Paris. *The Eiffel Tower is in Paris.*
Las sillas no están en el comedor. *The chairs are not in the dining room.*
¿Dónde está mi cartera? *Where is my wallet?*
¿Dónde estabas? *Where were you?*
Las llaves estaban en la mesa. *The keys were on the table.*
Las tiendas estarán cerradas. *The shops will be closed.*

Estaría en la escuela. *She must have been at school.*
Su nueva casa está bien construida. *Their new house is well built.*
¿A qué hora estaréis aquí? *What time will you be here?*
Hoy estaré en la oficina. *I will be in the office today.*
Si estuviéramos en Barcelona, estaríamos en la playa. *If we were in Barcelona, we would be on the beach.*
Está lloviendo. *It's raining.*
Estoy escribiendo una carta. *I am writing a letter.*
Hoy mi padre está trabajando en casa. *Today my father is working at home.*
¿Qué estás haciendo? *What are you doing?*
¿A qué día estamos? *What is the date today?*
Estamos a 17 de abril. *It's the 17th of April.*
un estado *state, condition*

⚏─O Key points

➜ add slightly modified endings to regular stem, particularly in preterite

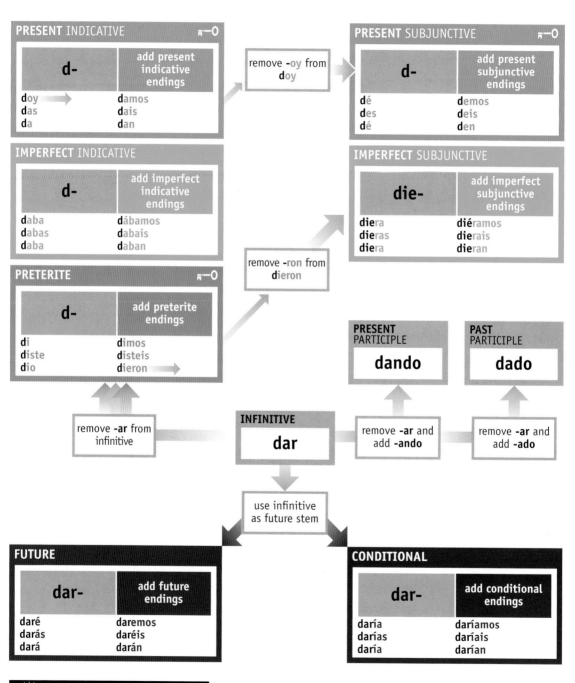

PRESENT INDICATIVE ⚏─O

d-	add present indicative endings
doy	damos
das	dais
da	dan

remove **-oy** from **d**oy

PRESENT SUBJUNCTIVE ⚏─O

d-	add present subjunctive endings
dé	demos
des	deis
dé	den

IMPERFECT INDICATIVE

d-	add imperfect indicative endings
daba	dábamos
dabas	dabais
daba	daban

IMPERFECT SUBJUNCTIVE

die-	add imperfect subjunctive endings
diera	diéramos
dieras	dierais
diera	dieran

remove **-ron** from **d**ieron

PRETERITE ⚏─O

d-	add preterite endings
di	dimos
diste	disteis
dio	dieron

remove **-ar** from infinitive

PRESENT PARTICIPLE

dando

PAST PARTICIPLE

dado

INFINITIVE

dar

remove **-ar** and add **-ando**

remove **-ar** and add **-ado**

use infinitive as future stem

FUTURE

dar-	add future endings
daré	daremos
darás	daréis
dará	darán

CONDITIONAL

dar-	add conditional endings
daría	daríamos
darías	daríais
daría	darían

☀ Useful tips

The verb **dar** is used in many common set phrases. For example, **dar la mano** means "to shake hands", **dar las gracias** means "to thank" and **dar la bienvenida** means "to welcome".

haber (in the correct simple tense) **+ past participle**

PERFECT INDICATIVE

present indicative of haber	add past participle
he **dado**	hemos **dado**
has **dado**	habéis **dado**
ha **dado**	han **dado**

PERFECT SUBJUNCTIVE

present subjunctive of haber	add past participle
haya **dado**	hayamos **dado**
hayas **dado**	hayáis **dado**
haya **dado**	hayan **dado**

PLUPERFECT INDICATIVE

imperfect indicative of haber	add past participle
había **dado**	habíamos **dado**
habías **dado**	habíais **dado**
había **dado**	habían **dado**

PAST PARTICIPLE

dado

PLUPERFECT SUBJUNCTIVE

imperfect subjunctive of haber	add past participle
hubiera **dado**	hubiéramos **dado**
hubieras **dado**	hubierais **dado**
hubiera **dado**	hubieran **dado**

FUTURE PERFECT

future of haber	add past participle
habré dado	habremos dado
habrás dado	habréis dado
habrá dado	habrán dado

CONDITIONAL PERFECT

conditional of haber	add past participle
habría dado	habríamos dado
habrías dado	habríais dado
habría dado	habrían dado

Usage examples

Les doy regalos a mis hermanos. *I give presents to my brothers.*

Dio todo lo que pudo. *She gave all that she could.*

El presidente dio una charla ayer. *The president gave a speech yesterday.*

Si me ayudas, te daré diez euros. *If you help me, I will give you ten euros.*

Si solicitaras el empleo, probablemente te lo darían. *If you were to apply for the job, they would probably give it to you.*

Les vendería las pinturas si me dieran más dinero por ellas. *I would sell them the paintings if they were to give me more money for them.*

Sus palabras me han dado ánimos. *Your words have given me encouragement.*

Te doy hasta el domingo. *I'll give you until Sunday.*

Le dimos las gracias. *We thanked him.*

Están dando un documental. *They are showing a documentary.*

Mi ventana da al jardín. *My window looks out on the garden.*

¿Has dado de comer al gato? *Have you fed the cat?*

dar un paseo *to go for a walk*

David daba un paseo por el parque con frecuencia. *David often used to go for a walk in the park.*

¡Me da rabia! *It makes me mad!*

Para ser sincero, me da lo mismo. *To be honest, it's all the same to me.*

Me da igual. *I don't mind.*

Ese árbol da frutos. *This tree bears fruit.*

🔑─O Key points

➡ irregular stem in preterite: **anduv-**

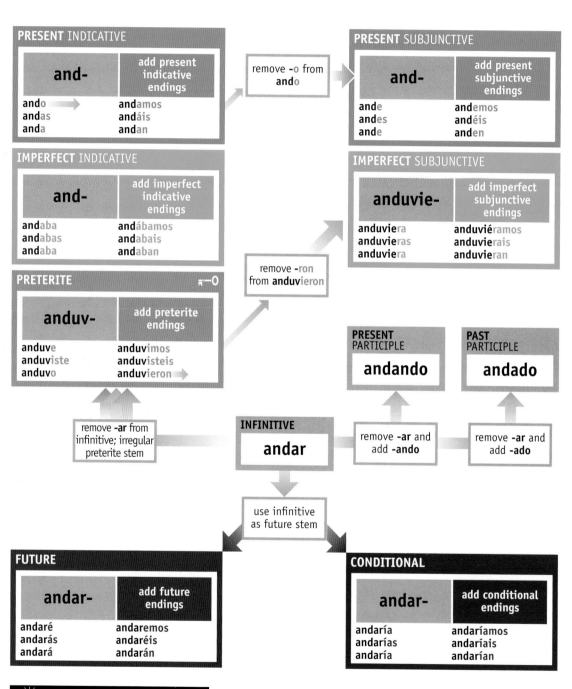

PRESENT INDICATIVE

and-	add present indicative endings
ando	andamos
andas	andáis
anda	andan

remove -o from **ando**

PRESENT SUBJUNCTIVE

and-	add present subjunctive endings
ande	andemos
andes	andéis
ande	anden

IMPERFECT INDICATIVE

and-	add imperfect indicative endings
andaba	andábamos
andabas	andabais
andaba	andaban

remove -ron from **anduvieron**

IMPERFECT SUBJUNCTIVE

anduvie-	add imperfect subjunctive endings
anduviera	anduviéramos
anduvieras	anduvierais
anduviera	anduvieran

PRETERITE 🔑─O

anduv-	add preterite endings
anduve	anduvimos
anduviste	anduvisteis
anduvo	anduvieron

PRESENT PARTICIPLE

andando

PAST PARTICIPLE

andado

remove **-ar** from infinitive; irregular preterite stem

INFINITIVE

andar

remove **-ar** and add **-ando**

remove **-ar** and add **-ado**

use infinitive as future stem

FUTURE

andar-	add future endings
andaré	andaremos
andarás	andaréis
andará	andarán

CONDITIONAL

andar-	add conditional endings
andaría	andaríamos
andarías	andaríais
andaría	andarían

☀ Useful tips

Spanish has two verbs meaning "to walk": **andar** (above) and **caminar** (a regular -ar verb). **Andar** is more common in Spain, whereas you are more likely to hear **caminar** used in Latin America.

haber (in the correct simple tense) + past participle

PERFECT INDICATIVE

present indicative of haber	add past participle
he **andado**	hemos **andado**
has **andado**	habéis **andado**
ha **andado**	han **andado**

PERFECT SUBJUNCTIVE

present subjunctive of haber	add past participle
haya **andado**	hayamos **andado**
hayas **andado**	hayáis **andado**
haya **andado**	hayan **andado**

PLUPERFECT INDICATIVE

imperfect indicative of haber	add past participle
había **andado**	habíamos **andado**
habías **andado**	habíais **andado**
había **andado**	habían **andado**

PAST PARTICIPLE

andado

PLUPERFECT SUBJUNCTIVE

imperfect subjunctive of haber	add past participle
hubiera **andado**	hubiéramos **andado**
hubieras **andado**	hubierais **andado**
hubiera **andado**	hubieran **andado**

FUTURE PERFECT

future of haber	add past participle
habré **andado**	habremos **andado**
habrás **andado**	habréis **andado**
habrá **andado**	habrán **andado**

CONDITIONAL PERFECT

conditional of haber	add past participle
habría **andado**	habríamos **andado**
habrías **andado**	habríais **andado**
habría **andado**	habrían **andado**

◥ Usage examples

Tuve que andar porque se me averió el coche. *I had to walk because my car broke down.*

Anda arrastrando los pies. *He shuffles his feet when he walks.*

No andáis muy deprisa. *You don't walk very fast.*

Calculo que ayer anduvimos dieciséis millas. *We must have walked sixteen miles yesterday.*

Estuvo andando todo el día. *She walked all day long.*

Anduvieron a la escuela. *They walked to school.*

Andábamos por el río. *We used to walk along the river.*

Había andado durante cinco horas. *I had been walking for five hours.*

Habríamos ido andando a la estación, pero estábamos demasiado cansados. *We would have walked to the station, but we were too tired.*

No parecía que hubiéramos andado diez millas. *It didn't seem that we had walked ten miles.*

Me advirtió que no anduviera sola por la noche. *He warned me not to walk alone at night.*

Es sorprendente que el ordenador ande lento. *It is surprising that the computer runs slow.*

Paula habrá andado al trabajo. *Paula must have walked to work.*

No había andado mucho cuando la divisó entre el gentío. *He had not gone far when he spotted her in the crowd.*

Si no llueve, iré andando al supermercado. *If it doesn't rain, I will walk to the supermarket.*

Me alegro de que hayamos andado. *I am glad that we walked.*

Key points

→ **u** of stem changes to **ue** for stressed syllables in present indicative
→ spelling rule: **g** becomes **gu** before **e**

→ **ue** of stem reverts to **u** for unstressed syllables in present subjunctive

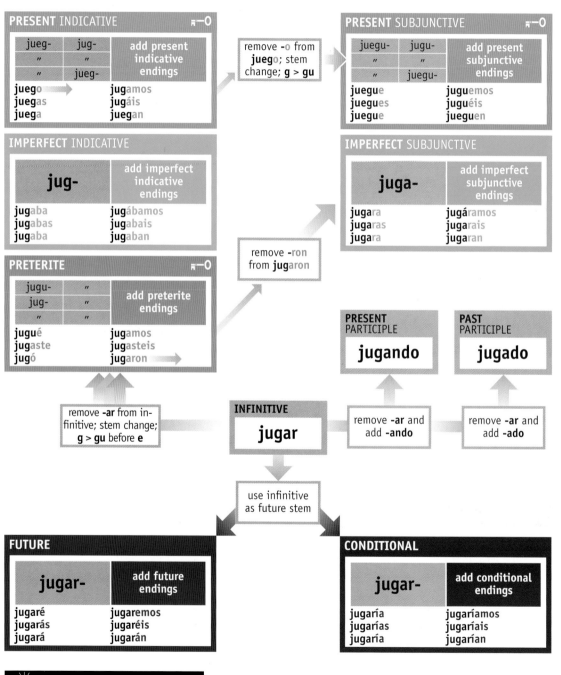

PRESENT INDICATIVE

jueg-	jug-	add present indicative endings
"	"	
"	jueg-	

juego → jugamos
juegas   jugáis
juega   juegan

remove **-o** from **juego**; stem change; **g > gu**

PRESENT SUBJUNCTIVE

juegu-	jugu-	add present subjunctive endings
"	"	
"	juegu-	

juegue   juguemos
juegues   juguéis
juegue   jueguen

IMPERFECT INDICATIVE

jug-	add imperfect indicative endings

jugaba   jugábamos
jugabas   jugabais
jugaba   jugaban

IMPERFECT SUBJUNCTIVE

juga-	add imperfect subjunctive endings

jugara   jugáramos
jugaras   jugarais
jugara   jugaran

remove **-ron** from **jugaron**

PRETERITE

jugu-	"	add preterite endings
jug-	"	
"	"	

jugué   jugamos
jugaste   jugasteis
jugó   jugaron

PRESENT PARTICIPLE

jugando

PAST PARTICIPLE

jugado

remove **-ar** from infinitive; stem change; **g > gu** before **e**

INFINITIVE

jugar

remove **-ar** and add **-ando**

remove **-ar** and add **-ado**

use infinitive as future stem

FUTURE

jugar-	add future endings

jugaré   jugaremos
jugarás   jugaréis
jugará   jugarán

CONDITIONAL

jugar-	add conditional endings

jugaría   jugaríamos
jugarías   jugaríais
jugaría   jugarían

Useful tips

Although **jugar** is used to talk about playing a sport or a game, the verb **tocar** (which literally means "to touch") is used to talk about playing a musical instrument.

---

haber (in the correct simple tense) + past participle

PERFECT INDICATIVE

present indicative of haber	add past participle
he **jugado**	hemos **jugado**
has **jugado**	habéis **jugado**
ha **jugado**	han **jugado**

PERFECT SUBJUNCTIVE

present subjunctive of haber	add past participle
haya **jugado**	hayamos **jugado**
hayas **jugado**	hayáis **jugado**
haya **jugado**	hayan **jugado**

PLUPERFECT INDICATIVE

imperfect indicative of haber	add past participle
había **jugado**	habíamos **jugado**
habías **jugado**	habíais **jugado**
había **jugado**	habían **jugado**

PAST PARTICIPLE

jugado

PLUPERFECT SUBJUNCTIVE

imperfect subjunctive of haber	add past participle
hubiera **jugado**	hubieramos **jugado**
hubieras **jugado**	hubierais **jugado**
hubiera **jugado**	hubieran **jugado**

FUTURE PERFECT

future of haber	add past participle
habré jugado	habremos jugado
habrás jugado	habréis jugado
habrá jugado	habrán jugado

CONDITIONAL PERFECT

conditional of haber	add past participle
habría jugado	habríamos jugado
habrías jugado	habríais jugado
habría jugado	habrían jugado

◥◣ Usage examples

Los niños están jugando en el jardín. *The children are playing in the garden.*

Mi nieto estuvo jugando todo el día. *My grandson played all day.*

Jugué contra él tres veces. *I played him three times.*

¿Jugáis al baloncesto? *Do you play basketball?*

No me gusta jugar al ajedrez. *I don't like playing chess.*

Jugábamos al fútbol todos los domingos. *I used to play football every Sunday.*

Habrían jugado al tenis pero se olvidaron de traer las raquetas. *They would have played tennis, but they forgot to bring the rackets.*

Nunca jugaría a la lotería. *I would never play the lottery.*

Ya había jugado dos partidos esa semana. *I had already played two matches that week.*

Si no haces los deberes, no jugaremos con los videojuegos. *If you do not do your homework, we will not play video games.*

Aprendo a jugar al golf. *I am learning to play golf.*

Cualquiera que juegue al fútbol sabe la importancia de trabajar en equipo. *Anyone who plays football knows the importance of working as a team.*

La repetición juega un papel importante en el aprendizaje de idiomas. *Repetition plays an important role in language learning.*

el juego *play; game; gambling*

un juguete *toy*

juguetón, juguetona *playful*

⚷━O Key points

➡ **err** of stem changes to **yerr** for stressed syllables in present indicative

➡ **yerr** of stem reverts to **err** for unstressed syllables in present subjunctive

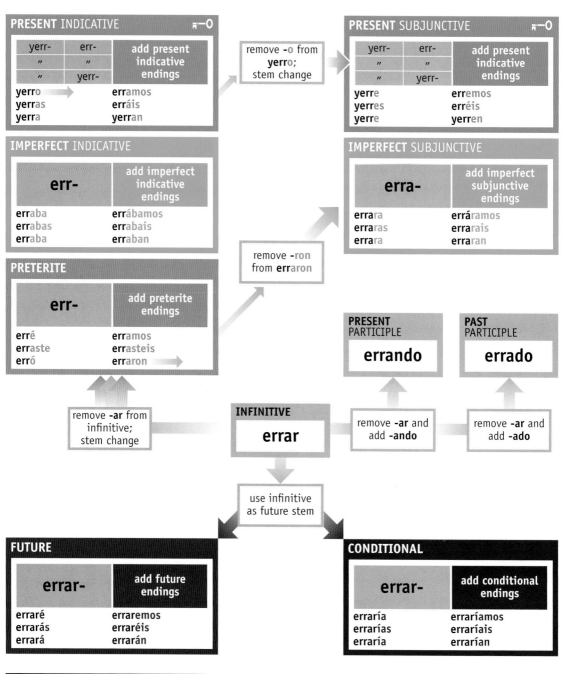

PRESENT INDICATIVE ⚷━O

yerr-	err-	add present indicative endings
"	"	
"	yerr-	

yerro	erramos
yerras	erráis
yerra	yerran

remove -o from yerro; stem change

PRESENT SUBJUNCTIVE ⚷━O

yerr-	err-	add present indicative endings
"	"	
"	yerr-	

yerre	erremos
yerres	erréis
yerre	yerren

IMPERFECT INDICATIVE

err-	add imperfect indicative endings

erraba	errábamos
errabas	errabais
erraba	erraban

IMPERFECT SUBJUNCTIVE

erra-	add imperfect subjunctive endings

errara	erráramos
erraras	errarais
errara	erraran

remove -ron from erraron

PRETERITE

err-	add preterite endings

erré	erramos
erraste	errasteis
erró	erraron

PRESENT PARTICIPLE

errando

PAST PARTICIPLE

errado

remove -ar from infinitive; stem change

INFINITIVE

errar

remove -ar and add -ando

remove -ar and add -ado

use infinitive as future stem

FUTURE

errar-	add future endings

erraré	erraremos
errarás	erraréis
errará	errarán

CONDITIONAL

errar-	add conditional endings

erraría	erraríamos
errarías	erraríais
erraría	errarían

💡 Useful tips

As well as reading through the example sentences, pay attention to the related words listed on the opposite page. Rather than just learning the verb **errar** on its own, also learning words such as **errante** (wandering) and **erróneo** (wrong) is a great way to improve your Spanish vocabulary.

haber (in the correct simple tense) **+ past participle**

PERFECT INDICATIVE

present indicative of haber	add past participle
he **errado**	hemos **errado**
has **errado**	habéis **errado**
ha **errado**	han **errado**

PERFECT SUBJUNCTIVE

present subjunctive of haber	add past participle
haya **errado**	hayamos **errado**
hayas **errado**	hayáis **errado**
haya **errado**	hayan **errado**

PLUPERFECT INDICATIVE

imperfect indicative of haber	add past participle
había **errado**	habíamos **errado**
habías **errado**	habíais **errado**
había **errado**	habían **errado**

PAST PARTICIPLE
errado

PLUPERFECT SUBJUNCTIVE

imperfect subjunctive of haber	add past participle
hubiera **errado**	hubiéramos **errado**
hubieras **errado**	hubierais **errado**
hubiera **errado**	hubieran **errado**

FUTURE PERFECT

future of haber	add past participle
habré **errado**	habremos **errado**
habrás **errado**	habréis **errado**
habrá **errado**	habrán **errado**

CONDITIONAL PERFECT

conditional of haber	add past participle
habría **errado**	habríamos **errado**
habrías **errado**	habríais **errado**
habría **errado**	habrían **errado**

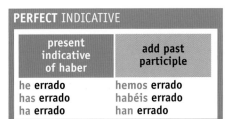

◥◤ Usage examples

Errar es humano, perdonar es divino. *To err is human, to forgive is divine.*

"Quien poco piensa, mucho yerra." - Leonardo da Vinci *"He who thinks little, errs much." - Leonardo da Vinci*

Erré el tiro. *I missed the shot.*

La bomba había errado el blanco. *The bomb had missed the target.*

Han errado en su decisión. *They have made the wrong decision.*

Es posible que haya errado en sus cálculos. *It is possible that he has made a mistake in his calculations.*

Dejé errar mi imaginación. *I let my imagination wander.*

"Erraba solitario como una nube." - William Wordsworth *"I wandered lonely as a cloud." - William Wordsworth*

un error *mistake, error*
un error de bulto *glaring error*
un grave error *serious mistake*
un error garrafal *bad error*
por error *by mistake*
un mensaje de error *error message*
un yerro *error, mistake*
una errata *misprint, erratum*
un error de imprenta *misprint*
errante *wandering, roving, roaming*
erróneo *wrong, erroneous*
erróneamente *wrongly, erroneously*

🔑 Key points

➡ **o** of stem changes to **üe** for stressed syllables in present indicative

➡ **üe** of stem reverts to **o** for unstressed syllables in present subjunctive

➡ spelling rule: **z** becomes **c** before **e**

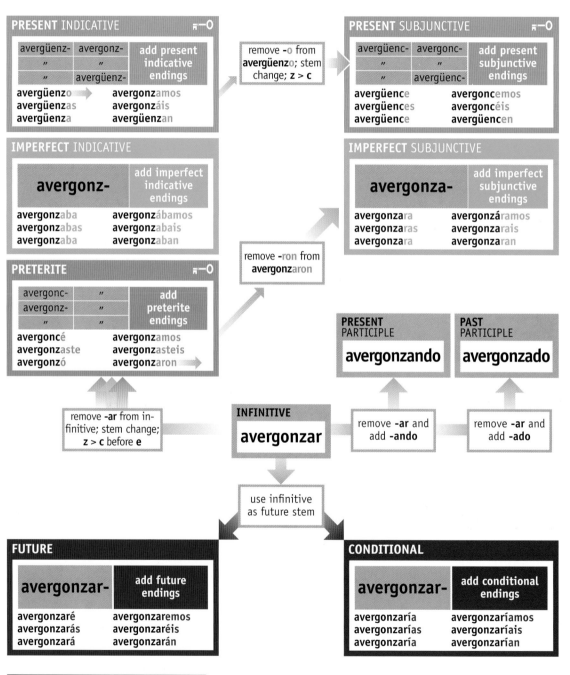

PRESENT INDICATIVE 🔑

avergüenz-	avergonz-	add present indicative endings
"	"	
"	avergüenz-	

avergüenzo → avergonzamos
avergüenzas · avergonzáis
avergüenza · avergüenzan

remove -o from **avergüenzo**; stem change; **z > c**

PRESENT SUBJUNCTIVE 🔑

avergüenc-	avergonc-	add present subjunctive endings
"	"	
"	avergüenc-	

avergüence · avergoncemos
avergüences · avergoncéis
avergüence · avergüencen

IMPERFECT INDICATIVE

avergonz-	add imperfect indicative endings

avergonzaba · avergonzábamos
avergonzabas · avergonzabais
avergonzaba · avergonzaban

IMPERFECT SUBJUNCTIVE

avergonza-	add imperfect subjunctive endings

avergonzara · avergonzáramos
avergonzaras · avergonzarais
avergonzara · avergonzaran

remove -ron from **avergonzaron**

PRETERITE 🔑

avergonc-	"	add preterite endings
avergonz-	"	
"	"	

avergoncé · avergonzamos
avergonzaste · avergonzasteis
avergonzó → avergonzaron

PRESENT PARTICIPLE
avergonzando

PAST PARTICIPLE
avergonzado

remove -ar from infinitive; stem change; **z > c** before **e**

INFINITIVE
avergonzar

remove -ar and add **-ando**

remove -ar and add **-ado**

use infinitive as future stem

FUTURE

avergonzar-	add future endings

avergonzaré · avergonzaremos
avergonzarás · avergonzaréis
avergonzará · avergonzarán

CONDITIONAL

avergonzar-	add conditional endings

avergonzaría · avergonzaríamos
avergonzarías · avergonzaríais
avergonzaría · avergonzarían

💡 Useful tips

The Spanish word for "shame" is the noun **la vergüenza**. Knowing the meaning of this noun will help you to remember that the verb **avergonzar** means "to shame". In addition, the spelling of **la vergüenza** will help you to remember the stem change (**o > üe**) undergone by **avegonzar**.

> **haber** (in the correct simple tense) **+ past participle**

PERFECT INDICATIVE

present indicative of haber	add past participle
he avergonzado	hemos avergonzado
has avergonzado	habéis avergonzado
ha avergonzado	han avergonzado

PERFECT SUBJUNCTIVE

present subjunctive of haber	add past participle
haya avergonzado	hayamos avergonzado
hayas avergonzado	hayáis avergonzado
haya avergonzado	hayan avergonzado

PLUPERFECT INDICATIVE

imperfect indicative of haber	add past participle
había avergonzado	habíamos avergonzado
habías avergonzado	habíais avergonzado
había avergonzado	habían avergonzado

PAST PARTICIPLE

avergonzado

PLUPERFECT SUBJUNCTIVE

imperfect subjunctive of haber	add past participle
hubiera avergonzado	hubiéramos avergonzado
hubieras avergonzado	hubierais avergonzado
hubiera avergonzado	hubieran avergonzado

FUTURE PERFECT

future of haber	add past participle
habré avergonzado	habremos avergonzado
habrás avergonzado	habréis avergonzado
habrá avergonzado	habrán avergonzado

CONDITIONAL PERFECT

conditional of haber	add past participle
habría avergonzado	habríamos avergonzado
habrías avergonzado	habríais avergonzado
habría avergonzado	habrían avergonzado

Usage examples

Se avergüenza de ello. *She's ashamed of it.*

Abogó por la política de "nombrar y avergonzar" a los países que no respeten la igualdad de género. *He advocated the policy of naming and shaming the countries that do not respect gender equality.*

La información pueda avergonzar al primer ministro. *The information may embarrass the prime minister.*

Mi hermano me suele avergonzar delante de mis amigos. *My brother usually embarrasses me in front of my friends.*

avergonzarse *to be ashamed; to be embarrassed*

Debería avergonzarse. *You ought to be ashamed of yourself.*

No debes avergonzarte de tus raíces. *You should not be ashamed of your roots.*

¿Cómo no te avergüenza hacerlo? *Aren't you ashamed to do so?*

Me avergonzaría decírselo. *I would be ashamed to tell him.*

Se avergonzaron por las cosas que habían hecho. *They felt shame for the things they had done.*

Si te pillaran con las manos en la masa, te avergonzarías. *You'll be embarrassed if they catch you red-handed.*

Se habría avergonzado si alguien la hubiera visto. *She would have been embarrassed had anyone seen her.*

avergonzado *ashamed*

la vergüenza *embarrassment; shame; disgrace*

desvergonzado, desvergonzada *shameless; impudent*

la desvergüenza *shamelessness; impudence*

-er verbs

➡ -er verbs are verbs that end in -er in the infinitive.

➡ this verb follows the regular pattern for **-er** verbs

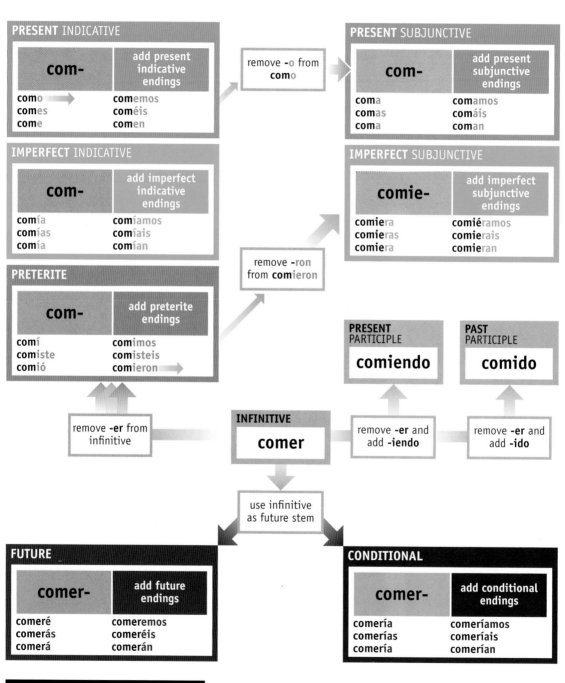

PRESENT INDICATIVE

com-	add present indicative endings
como	comemos
comes	coméis
come	comen

remove **-o** from **com**o

PRESENT SUBJUNCTIVE

com-	add present subjunctive endings
coma	comamos
comas	comáis
coma	coman

IMPERFECT INDICATIVE

com-	add imperfect indicative endings
comía	comíamos
comías	comíais
comía	comían

IMPERFECT SUBJUNCTIVE

comie-	add imperfect subjunctive endings
comiera	comiéramos
comieras	comierais
comiera	comieran

remove **-ron** from **com**ieron

PRETERITE

com-	add preterite endings
comí	comimos
comiste	comisteis
comió	comieron

PRESENT PARTICIPLE

comiendo

PAST PARTICIPLE

comido

remove **-er** from infinitive

INFINITIVE

comer

remove **-er** and add **-iendo**

remove **-er** and add **-ido**

use infinitive as future stem

FUTURE

comer-	add future endings
comeré	comeremos
comerás	comeréis
comerá	comerán

CONDITIONAL

comer-	add conditional endings
comería	comeríamos
comerías	comeríais
comería	comerían

🧩 Following the same pattern

aprender to learn	**comprender** to understand	**responder** to answer
barrer to sweep	**correr** to run	**temer** to fear, dread
beber to drink	**deber** to have to, must; to owe	**vender** to sell

haber (in the correct simple tense) + past participle

PERFECT INDICATIVE

present indicative of haber	add past participle
he **comido**	hemos **comido**
has **comido**	habéis **comido**
ha **comido**	han **comido**

PERFECT SUBJUNCTIVE

present subjunctive of haber	add past participle
haya **comido**	hayamos **comido**
hayas **comido**	hayáis **comido**
haya **comido**	hayan **comido**

PLUPERFECT INDICATIVE

imperfect indicative of haber	add past participle
había **comido**	habíamos **comido**
habías **comido**	habíais **comido**
había **comido**	habían **comido**

PAST PARTICIPLE
comido

PLUPERFECT SUBJUNCTIVE

imperfect subjunctive of haber	add past participle
hubiera **comido**	hubiéramos **comido**
hubieras **comido**	hubierais **comido**
hubiera **comido**	hubieran **comido**

FUTURE PERFECT

future of haber	add past participle
habré **comido**	habremos **comido**
habrás **comido**	habréis **comido**
habrá **comido**	habrán **comido**

CONDITIONAL PERFECT

conditional of haber	add past participle
habría **comido**	habríamos **comido**
habrías **comido**	habríais **comido**
habría **comido**	habrían **comido**

◥◤ Usage examples

¿Quieres comer algo? *Would you like something to eat?*
No come carne. *She doesn't eat meat.*
Mi familia y yo siempre comemos juntos por la noche.
  My family and I always eat together at night.
Comíamos cuando sonó el teléfono. *We were eating*
  when the phone rang.
Comí en la cafetería. *I ate in the cafeteria.*
Comeré cuando lleguen. *I will eat when they arrive.*
He comido demasiado...me siento mal. *I have eaten*
  too much...I don't feel well.
Si comieras más verduras, estarías más sano. *If you*
  ate more vegetables, you would be healthier.
No comería una hamburguesa porque soy vegetariano.
  I would not eat a hamburger because I am a
  vegetarian.

¿Qué has comido hoy? *What have you eaten today?*
Todavía no han comido. *They have not eaten yet.*
Había comido más temprano. *He had eaten earlier.*
Habría comido si tuviera hambre. *I would have eaten*
  if I had been hungry.
He estado comiendo mucho últimamente. *I have been*
  eating a lot recently.
El agua salada comió la piedra. *The salt water wore*
  away the stone.
Se le come la ira. *He's consumed with anger.*
comerse *to eat up*
Me comí una pizza entera. *I ate a whole pizza.*
la comida *food; meal*
un comedor *dining room*
comestible *edible*

Key points

➡ spelling rule: **c** becomes **zc** before **o**

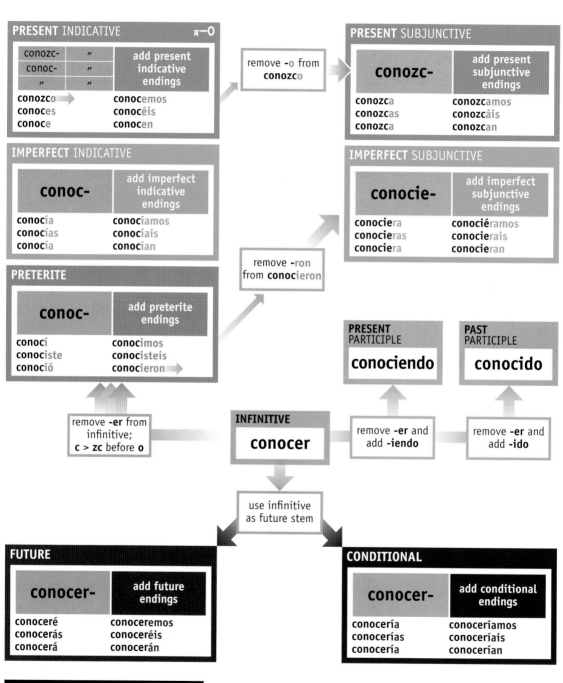

PRESENT INDICATIVE

conozc-	"	add present indicative endings
conoc-	"	
"	"	

conozco	conocemos
conoces	conocéis
conoce	conocen

remove -o from conozco

PRESENT SUBJUNCTIVE

| conozc- | add present subjunctive endings |

conozca	conozcamos
conozcas	conozcáis
conozca	conozcan

IMPERFECT INDICATIVE

| conoc- | add imperfect indicative endings |

conocía	conocíamos
conocías	conocíais
conocía	conocían

IMPERFECT SUBJUNCTIVE

| conocie- | add imperfect subjunctive endings |

conociera	conociéramos
conocieras	conocierais
conociera	conocieran

remove -ron from conocieron

PRETERITE

| conoc- | add preterite endings |

conocí	conocimos
conociste	conocisteis
conoció	conocieron

PRESENT PARTICIPLE

conociendo

PAST PARTICIPLE

conocido

remove -er from infinitive;
c > zc before **o**

INFINITIVE

conocer

remove -er and add -iendo

remove -er and add -ido

use infinitive as future stem

FUTURE

| conocer- | add future endings |

conoceré	conoceremos
conocerás	conoceréis
conocerá	conocerán

CONDITIONAL

| conocer- | add conditional endings |

conocería	conoceríamos
conocerías	conoceríais
conocería	conocerían

Following the same pattern

agradecer *to thank*	**merecer** *to deserve*	**ofrecer** *to offer*
complacer *to please*	**nacer** *to be born*	**pertenecer** *to belong to*
crecer *to grow*	**obedecer** *to obey*	**reconocer** *to recognise*

haber (in the correct simple tense) + past participle

PERFECT INDICATIVE

present indicative of haber	add past participle
he **conocido**	hemos **conocido**
has **conocido**	habéis **conocido**
ha **conocido**	han **conocido**

PERFECT SUBJUNCTIVE

present subjunctive of haber	add past participle
haya **conocido**	hayamos **conocido**
hayas **conocido**	hayáis **conocido**
haya **conocido**	hayan **conocido**

PLUPERFECT INDICATIVE

imperfect indicative of haber	add past participle
había **conocido**	habíamos **conocido**
habías **conocido**	habíais **conocido**
había **conocido**	habían **conocido**

PAST PARTICIPLE
conocido

PLUPERFECT SUBJUNCTIVE

imperfect subjunctive of haber	add past participle
hubiera **conocido**	hubiéramos **conocido**
hubieras **conocido**	hubierais **conocido**
hubiera **conocido**	hubieran **conocido**

FUTURE PERFECT

future of haber	add past participle
habré conocido	habremos conocido
habrás conocido	habréis conocido
habrá conocido	habrán conocido

CONDITIONAL PERFECT

conditional of haber	add past participle
habría conocido	habríamos conocido
habrías conocido	habríais conocido
habría conocido	habrían conocido

Usage examples

¿Conoces a Luca? *Have you met Luke?*
La conozco de vista. *I know her by sight.*
Las conozco de oídas. *I have heard of them.*
Ellos conocían a su familia. *They knew his family.*
Ayer conocí a tu primo. *I met your cousin yesterday.*
Nos conocimos en una fiesta. *We met at a party.*
La reconocerás. *You will recognise her.*
Quiero que conozcas a mis padres. *I want you to meet my parents.*
Si no la conociera, pensaría que está mintiendo. *If I did not know her, I would think she was lying.*
Estoy conociendo a los estudiantes. *I am getting to know my students.*
Conoce el camino a casa. *She knows the way home.*
Conozco Londres muy bien. *I know London very well.*

¿Conoces las obras de Dickens? *Do you know the works of Dickens?*
Todos mis amigos conocen mi pasión por los animales. *All my friends know of my passion for animals.*
Es importante que conozca sus derechos. *It is important that he knows his rights.*
conocerse *to know one another*
Se conocen de la universidad. *They know one another from university.*
conocido *famous, well-known; familiar*
desconocido, desconocida *unknown*
un conocido, una conocida *acquaintance*
un desconocido, una desconocida *stranger*
el conocimiento *knowledge*
el desconocimiento *ignorance*

🔑 Key points

➡ spelling rule: **c** becomes **z** before **o**

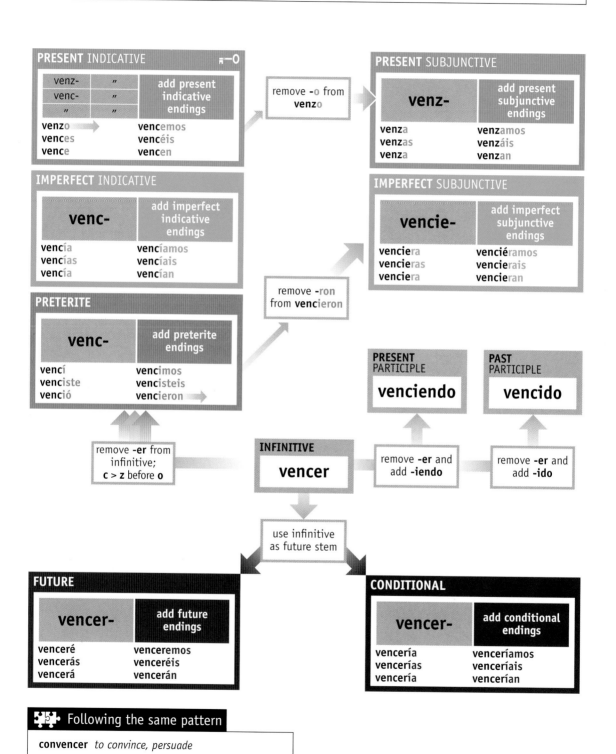

PRESENT INDICATIVE 🔑

venz-	"	add present indicative endings
venc-	"	
"	"	

venzo	vencemos
vences	vencéis
vence	vencen

remove -o from **venzo**

PRESENT SUBJUNCTIVE

venz-	add present subjunctive endings

venza	venzamos
venzas	venzáis
venza	venzan

IMPERFECT INDICATIVE

venc-	add imperfect indicative endings

vencía	vencíamos
vencías	vencíais
vencía	vencían

IMPERFECT SUBJUNCTIVE

vencie-	add imperfect subjunctive endings

venciera	venciéramos
vencieras	vencierais
venciera	vencieran

remove -ron from **vencieron**

PRETERITE

venc-	add preterite endings

vencí	vencimos
venciste	vencisteis
venció	vencieron

PRESENT PARTICIPLE

venciendo

PAST PARTICIPLE

vencido

remove -er from infinitive; **c > z** *before* **o**

INFINITIVE

vencer

remove -er and add -iendo

remove -er and add -ido

use infinitive as future stem

FUTURE

vencer-	add future endings

venceré	venceremos
vencerás	venceréis
vencerá	vencerán

CONDITIONAL

vencer-	add conditional endings

vencería	venceríamos
vencerías	venceríais
vencería	vencerían

🧩 Following the same pattern

convencer *to convince, persuade*

---

haber (in the correct simple tense) + past participle

PERFECT INDICATIVE

present indicative of haber	add past participle
he **vencido**	hemos **vencido**
has **vencido**	habéis **vencido**
ha **vencido**	han **vencido**

PERFECT SUBJUNCTIVE

present subjunctive of haber	add past participle
haya **vencido**	hayamos **vencido**
hayas **vencido**	hayáis **vencido**
haya **vencido**	hayan **vencido**

PLUPERFECT INDICATIVE

imperfect indicative of haber	add past participle
había **vencido**	habíamos **vencido**
habías **vencido**	habíais **vencido**
había **vencido**	habían **vencido**

PAST PARTICIPLE

vencido

PLUPERFECT SUBJUNCTIVE

imperfect subjunctive of haber	add past participle
hubiera **vencido**	hubiéramos **vencido**
hubieras **vencido**	hubierais **vencido**
hubiera **vencido**	hubieran **vencido**

FUTURE PERFECT

future of haber	add past participle
habré **vencido**	habremos **vencido**
habrás **vencido**	habréis **vencido**
habrá **vencido**	habrán **vencido**

CONDITIONAL PERFECT

conditional of haber	add past participle
habría **vencido**	habríamos **vencido**
habrías **vencido**	habríais **vencido**
habría **vencido**	habrían **vencido**

◥◣ Usage examples

Llegué, vi y vencí. *I came, I saw, I conquered.*

Siempre venzo a mis enemigos. *I always conquer my enemies.*

David venció a Goliat. *David conquered Goliath.*

Me venció el miedo. *I was overcome by fear.*

Venceremos. *We shall overcome.*

Vencieron a los otros equipos. *They defeated the other teams.*

Habríamos vencido. *We would have won.*

Mi pasaporte vence el tres de junio. *My passport expires on the third of June.*

Tu permiso de trabajo vence en abril. *Your work permit expires in April.*

Mi carnet de identidad vencerá en 2014. *My identity card will expire in 2014.*

Mi visado de turista ya ha vencido. *My tourist visa has already expired.*

El plazo vence el viernes. *The deadline is Friday.*

Nos mudaremos antes de que el contrato de arrendamiento venza. *We will move out before the lease expires.*

La pata de la mesa se venció por el peso. *The table leg gave way under the weight.*

vencerse *to give way, break; to expire*

vencedor, vencedora *victorious*

un vencedor, una vencedora *winner, victor*

vencido *defeated; expired; due, payable; sagging*

los vencidos *the losers, the defeated*

invencible *invincible*

la invencibilidad *invincibility*

🔑 Key points

→ spelling rule: **g** becomes **j** before **o**

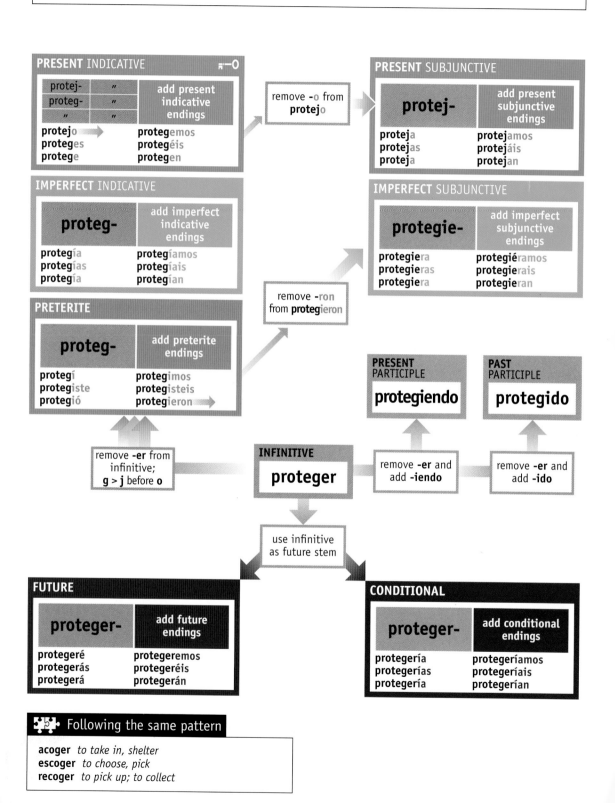

PRESENT INDICATIVE

protej-	"	add present indicative endings
proteg-	"	
"	"	

protejo	protegemos
proteges	protegéis
protege	protegen

remove **-o** from **protej**o

PRESENT SUBJUNCTIVE

protej-	add present subjunctive endings

proteja	protejamos
protejas	protejáis
proteja	protejan

IMPERFECT INDICATIVE

proteg-	add imperfect indicative endings

protegía	protegíamos
protegías	protegíais
protegía	protegían

IMPERFECT SUBJUNCTIVE

protegie-	add imperfect subjunctive endings

protegiera	protegiéramos
protegieras	protegierais
protegiera	protegieran

remove **-ron** from **proteg**ieron

PRETERITE

proteg-	add preterite endings

protegí	protegimos
protegiste	protegisteis
protegió	protegieron

PRESENT PARTICIPLE
protegiendo

PAST PARTICIPLE
protegido

remove **-er** from infinitive; **g > j** before **o**

INFINITIVE
proteger

remove **-er** and add **-iendo**

remove **-er** and add **-ido**

use infinitive as future stem

FUTURE

proteger-	add future endings

protegeré	protegeremos
protegerás	protegeréis
protegerá	protegerán

CONDITIONAL

proteger-	add conditional endings

protegería	protegeríamos
protegerías	protegeríais
protegería	protegerían

🧩 Following the same pattern

acoger *to take in, shelter*
escoger *to choose, pick*
recoger *to pick up; to collect*

haber (in the correct simple tense) **+ past participle**

PERFECT INDICATIVE

present indicative of haber	add past participle
he **protegido**	hemos **protegido**
has **protegido**	habéis **protegido**
ha **protegido**	han **protegido**

PERFECT SUBJUNCTIVE

present subjunctive of haber	add past participle
haya **protegido**	hayamos **protegido**
hayas **protegido**	hayáis **protegido**
haya **protegido**	hayan **protegido**

PLUPERFECT INDICATIVE

imperfect indicative of haber	add past participle
había **protegido**	habíamos **protegido**
habías **protegido**	habíais **protegido**
había **protegido**	habían **protegido**

PAST PARTICIPLE

protegido

PLUPERFECT SUBJUNCTIVE

imperfect subjunctive of haber	add past participle
hubiera **protegido**	hubiéramos **protegido**
hubieras **protegido**	hubierais **protegido**
hubiera **protegido**	hubieran **protegido**

FUTURE PERFECT

future of haber	add past participle
habré **protegido**	habremos **protegido**
habrás **protegido**	habréis **protegido**
habrá **protegido**	habrán **protegido**

CONDITIONAL PERFECT

conditional of haber	add past participle
habría **protegido**	habríamos **protegido**
habrías **protegido**	habríais **protegido**
habría **protegido**	habrían **protegido**

Usage examples

Protejo a mi familia. *I protect my family.*

El perro protege la casa. *The dog protects the house.*

Protegeremos la libertad de expresión a toda costa. *We will protect freedom of expression at any cost.*

La nueva ley protegerá los derechos de los trabajadores. *The new law will protect workers' rights.*

Creo que el proyecto habría protegido al consumidor. *I believe that the bill would have protected the consumer.*

El gobierno tiene que tomar medidas para proteger el medio ambiente. *The government must take measures to protect the environment.*

El chaleco antibalas le protegió. *The bulletproof vest protected him.*

Tuvimos que ponernos la crema del sol para proteger la piel. *We had to put on sun cream to protect our skin.*

Fueron protegidos por los guardaespaldas. *They were protected by the bodyguards.*

Este abrigo te protegerá del frío. *This coat will protect you from the cold.*

protegerse *to protect oneself*

Estaba tratando de protegerme del frío. *I was trying to protect myself from the cold.*

protegido, protegida *protected; subsidised*

una especie protegida *protected species*

la protección *protection*

protector, protectora *protective*

un/una protector *protector; patron*

🔑—O Key points

➡ **e** of stem changes to **ie** for stressed syllables in present indicative

➡ **ie** of stem reverts to **e** for unstressed syllables in present subjunctive

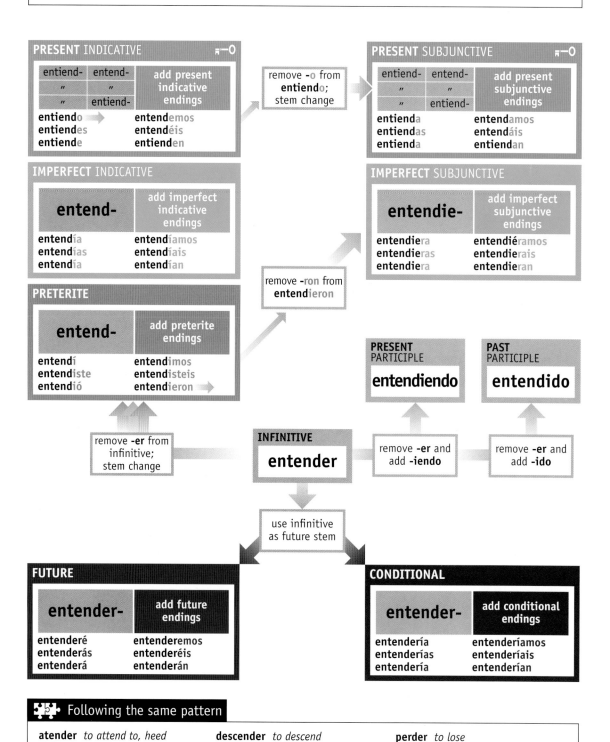

PRESENT INDICATIVE 🔑—O

entiend-	entend-	add present indicative endings
"	"	
"	entiend-	

entiendo	entendemos
entiendes	entendéis
entiende	entienden

PRESENT SUBJUNCTIVE 🔑—O

entiend-	entend-	add present subjunctive endings
"	"	
"	entiend-	

entienda	entendamos
entiendas	entendáis
entienda	entiendan

remove **-o** from **entiendo**; stem change

IMPERFECT INDICATIVE

entend-	add imperfect indicative endings

entendía	entendíamos
entendías	entendíais
entendía	entendían

IMPERFECT SUBJUNCTIVE

entendie-	add imperfect subjunctive endings

entendiera	entendiéramos
entendieras	entendierais
entendiera	entendieran

remove **-ron** from **entendieron**

PRETERITE

entend-	add preterite endings

entendí	entendimos
entendiste	entendisteis
entendió	entendieron

PRESENT PARTICIPLE
entendiendo

PAST PARTICIPLE
entendido

remove **-er** from infinitive; stem change

INFINITIVE
entender

remove **-er** and add **-iendo**

remove **-er** and add **-ido**

use infinitive as future stem

FUTURE

entender-	add future endings

entenderé	entenderemos
entenderás	entenderéis
entenderá	entenderán

CONDITIONAL

entender-	add conditional endings

entendería	entenderíamos
entenderías	entenderíais
entendería	entenderían

🧩 Following the same pattern

atender to attend to, heed	**descender** to descend	**perder** to lose
defender to defend	**encender** to turn on	**tender** to lay (out)
desatender to neglect	**extender** to spread out, extend	**verter** to pour

---

haber (in the correct simple tense) **+ past participle**

PERFECT INDICATIVE

present indicative of haber	add past participle
he **entendido**	hemos **entendido**
has **entendido**	habéis **entendido**
ha **entendido**	han **entendido**

PERFECT SUBJUNCTIVE

present subjunctive of haber	add past participle
haya **entendido**	hayamos **entendido**
hayas **entendido**	hayáis **entendido**
haya **entendido**	hayan **entendido**

PLUPERFECT INDICATIVE

imperfect indicative of haber	add past participle
había **entendido**	habíamos **entendido**
habías **entendido**	habíais **entendido**
había **entendido**	habían **entendido**

PAST PARTICIPLE
entendido

PLUPERFECT SUBJUNCTIVE

imperfect subjunctive of haber	add past participle
hubiera **entendido**	hubiéramos **entendido**
hubieras **entendido**	hubierais **entendido**
hubiera **entendido**	hubieran **entendido**

FUTURE PERFECT

future of haber	add past participle
habré **entendido**	habremos **entendido**
habrás **entendido**	habréis **entendido**
habrá **entendido**	habrán **entendido**

CONDITIONAL PERFECT

conditional of haber	add past participle
habría **entendido**	habríamos **entendido**
habrías **entendido**	habríais **entendido**
habría **entendido**	habrían **entendido**

Usage examples

No lo entiendo. *I don't understand.*

¿Entiendes? *Do you understand?*

Entiende italiano. *She understands Italian.*

¿Entendiste la pregunta? *Did you understand the question?*

¿Qué entiendes tú por "democracia"? *What do you understand by the word "democracy"?*

No entiendo nada de matemáticas. *I don't know a thing about mathematics.*

Entendían mucho de política. *They used to know a lot about politics.*

Con el tiempo lo entenderás. *One day you'll understand.*

No te preocupes, lo entenderá. *Don't worry, she'll understand.*

Se entiende en catalán. *He makes himself understood in Catalan.*

Tengo entendido que te jubilas. *I understand that you are retiring.*

Habéis entendido mal el problema. *You have misunderstood the problem.*

Si no he entendido mal, quieres aceptar la oferta. *Unless I've misunderstood, you want to accept the offer.*

entenderse con alguien *to get along with someone*

Nos entendemos bien con ella. *We get on very well with her.*

a mi entender *in my opinion*

el entendimiento *understanding; mind*

entiendo, entienda *understood; expert*

⌨–O Key points

➡ **o** of stem changes to **ue** for stressed syllables in present indicative

➡ **ue** of stem reverts to **o** for unstressed syllables in present subjunctive

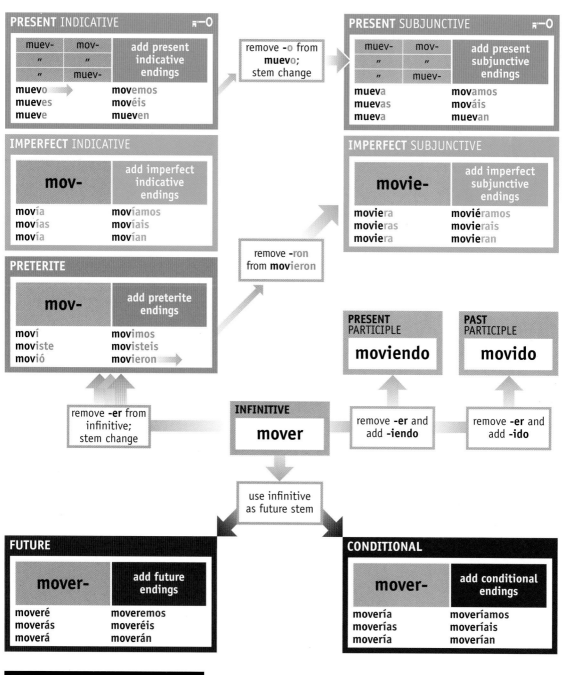

PRESENT INDICATIVE   ⌨–O

muev-	mov-	add present indicative endings
"	"	
"	muev-	

muevo	movemos
mueves	movéis
mueve	mueven

remove **-o** from **muevo**; stem change

PRESENT SUBJUNCTIVE   ⌨–O

muev-	mov-	add present subjunctive endings
"	"	
"	muev-	

mueva	movamos
muevas	mováis
mueva	muevan

IMPERFECT INDICATIVE

| mov- | add imperfect indicative endings |

movía	movíamos
movías	movíais
movía	movían

IMPERFECT SUBJUNCTIVE

| movie- | add imperfect subjunctive endings |

moviera	moviéramos
movieras	movierais
moviera	movieran

remove **-ron** from **movieron**

PRETERITE

| mov- | add preterite endings |

moví	movimos
moviste	movisteis
movió	movieron

PRESENT PARTICIPLE

moviendo

PAST PARTICIPLE

movido

remove **-er** from infinitive; stem change

INFINITIVE

mover

remove **-er** and add **-iendo**

remove **-er** and add **-ido**

use infinitive as future stem

FUTURE

| mover- | add future endings |

moveré	moveremos
moverás	moveréis
moverá	moverán

CONDITIONAL

| mover- | add conditional endings |

movería	moveríamos
moverías	moveríais
movería	moverían

Following the same pattern

conmover *to move (to pity), touch*   **morder** *to bite*
llover *to rain*   **promover** *to promote*
moler *to grind*   **remover** *to stir, turn over*

> ## haber (in the correct simple tense) + past participle

PERFECT INDICATIVE

present indicative of haber	add past participle
he **movido**	hemos **movido**
has **movido**	habéis **movido**
ha **movido**	han **movido**

PERFECT SUBJUNCTIVE

present subjunctive of haber	add past participle
haya **movido**	hayamos **movido**
hayas **movido**	hayáis **movido**
haya **movido**	hayan **movido**

PLUPERFECT INDICATIVE

imperfect indicative of haber	add past participle
había **movido**	habíamos **movido**
habías **movido**	habíais **movido**
había **movido**	habían **movido**

PAST PARTICIPLE

movido

PLUPERFECT SUBJUNCTIVE

imperfect subjunctive of haber	add past participle
hubiera **movido**	hubieramos **movido**
hubieras **movido**	hubierais **movido**
hubiera **movido**	hubieran **movido**

FUTURE PERFECT

future of haber	add past participle
habré **movido**	habremos **movido**
habrás **movido**	habréis **movido**
habrá **movido**	habrán **movido**

CONDITIONAL PERFECT

conditional of haber	add past participle
habría **movido**	habríamos **movido**
habrías **movido**	habríais **movido**
habría **movido**	habrían **movido**

◥◣ Usage examples

No puedo moverlo porque es demasiado pesado para que yo lo levante. *I can't move it because it's too heavy for me to lift.*

¿Has movido las sillas? *Have you moved the chairs?*

No puede mover el brazo derecho. *He can't move his right arm.*

Moveré cielo y tierra para estar contigo. *I will move heaven and earth to be with you.*

¿Por qué los perros mueven la cola? *Why do dogs wag their tails?*

El viento mueve los árboles. *The wind is shaking the trees.*

Es tu turno de mover. *It's your turn to move.*

No sé qué le movió a hacerlo. *I don't know what made him do it.*

Le mueve la codicia. *He's driven by greed.*

El aire mueve las aspas. *The wind drives the sails.*

Un motor eléctrico mueve el ascensor. *An electric motor powers the lift.*

moverse *to move*

La Tierra se mueve alrededor del Sol. *The Earth moves around the Sun.*

Cuando se hace enroque, el rey se mueve dos casillas hacia la torre. *When castling, the king moves two squares towards the rook.*

Se movían lentamente. *They moved slowly.*

el movimiento *movement, motion*

en movimiento *in motion, moving*

movible *movable*

la movilidad *mobility*

Key points

→ **o** of stem changes to **ue** for stressed syllables in present indicative

→ **ue** of stem reverts to **o** for unstressed syllables in present subjunctive

→ irregular past participle: **vuelto**

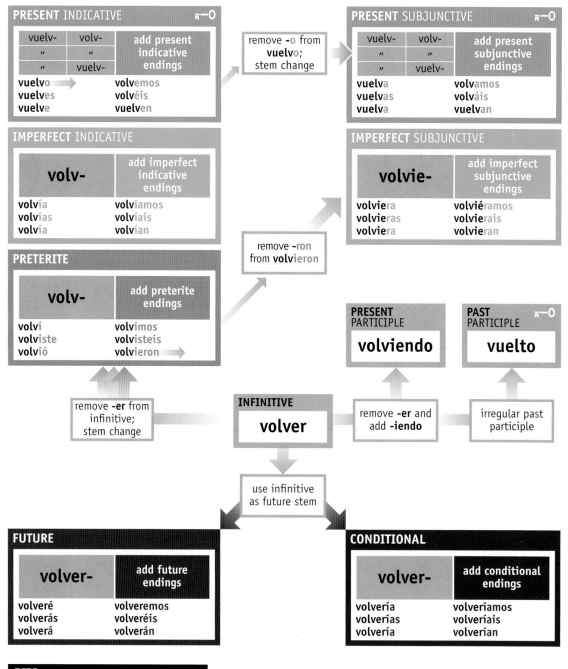

PRESENT INDICATIVE

vuelv-	volv-	add present indicative endings
"	"	
"	vuelv-	

vuelvo	volvemos
vuelves	volvéis
vuelve	volven

remove **-o** from **vuelvo**; stem change

PRESENT SUBJUNCTIVE

vuelv-	volv-	add present subjunctive endings
"	"	
"	vuelv-	

vuelva	volvamos
vuelvas	volváis
vuelva	vuelvan

IMPERFECT INDICATIVE

volv-	add imperfect indicative endings

volvía	volvíamos
volvías	volvíais
volvía	volvían

IMPERFECT SUBJUNCTIVE

volvie-	add imperfect subjunctive endings

volviera	volviéramos
volvieras	volvierais
volviera	volvieran

remove **-ron** from **volvieron**

PRETERITE

volv-	add preterite endings

volví	volvimos
volviste	volvisteis
volvió	volvieron

PRESENT PARTICIPLE
volviendo

PAST PARTICIPLE
vuelto

remove **-er** from infinitive; stem change

INFINITIVE
volver

remove **-er** and add **-iendo**

irregular past participle

use infinitive as future stem

FUTURE

volver-	add future endings

volveré	volveremos
volverás	volveréis
volverá	volverán

CONDITIONAL

volver-	add conditional endings

volvería	volveríamos
volverías	volveríais
volvería	volverían

Following the same pattern

absolver *to absolve; to acquit*
devolver *to give back, return; to throw up*
disolver *to dissolve; to break up*
envolver *to wrap (up)*
resolver *to solve, resolve; to settle*

---

haber (in the correct simple tense) + past participle

PERFECT INDICATIVE

present indicative of haber	add past participle
he **vuelto**	hemos **vuelto**
has **vuelto**	habéis **vuelto**
ha **vuelto**	han **vuelto**

PERFECT SUBJUNCTIVE

present subjunctive of haber	add past participle
haya **vuelto**	hayamos **vuelto**
hayas **vuelto**	hayáis **vuelto**
haya **vuelto**	hayan **vuelto**

PLUPERFECT INDICATIVE

imperfect indicative of haber	add past participle
había **vuelto**	habíamos **vuelto**
habías **vuelto**	habíais **vuelto**
había **vuelto**	habían **vuelto**

PAST PARTICIPLE

vuelto

PLUPERFECT SUBJUNCTIVE

imperfect subjunctive of haber	add past participle
hubiera **vuelto**	hubieramos **vuelto**
hubieras **vuelto**	hubierais **vuelto**
hubiera **vuelto**	hubieran **vuelto**

FUTURE PERFECT

future of haber	add past participle
habré **vuelto**	habremos **vuelto**
habrás **vuelto**	habréis **vuelto**
habrá **vuelto**	habrán **vuelto**

CONDITIONAL PERFECT

conditional of haber	add past participle
habría vuelto	habríamos vuelto
habrías vuelto	habríais vuelto
habría vuelto	habrían vuelto

◥▸ Usage examples

Mi hermano vuelve mañana. *My brother is coming back tomorrow.*

¿Cuándo vuelves? *When are you coming back?*

¿A qué hora vuelve a casa? *What time is he coming home?*

Volveremos el domingo. *We will be back next Sunday.*

Dijo que volvería. *He said he would come back.*

Para cuando vuelvan, habré salido. *I will have left by the time they get back.*

Volvía cansado del trabajo. *I used to come back tired from work.*

Habremos vuelto antes del jueves. *We will have returned before Tuesday.*

La vida vuelve a la normalidad tras el terremoto. *Life is getting back to normal after the earthquake.*

No hay vuelta de hoja. *There is no turning back.*

Es bueno que haya vuelto. *It is good that he came back.*

Volveré a intentarlo. *I'll try it again.*

¿Volveré a verte? *Will I see you again?*

Vuelvo a llamar más tarde. *I'll call back later.*

El boxeador volvió en sí. *The boxer regained consciousness.*

volverse *to turn (around); to become*

Se ha vuelto loco. *He's gone mad.*

Querían que sus hijos volvieran. *They wanted their children to come back.*

Ya ha vuelto. *He has already returned.*

Si lo hubiera sabido, habría vuelto. *If I had known, I would have come back.*

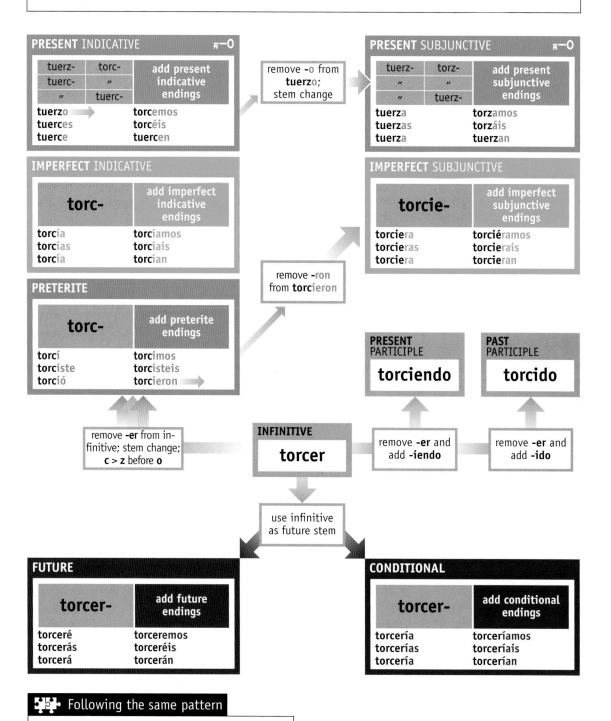

Key points

→ **o** of stem changes to **ue** for stressed syllables in present indicative
→ spelling rule: **c** becomes **z** before **o**

→ **ue** of stem reverts to **o** for unstressed syllables in present subjunctive

PRESENT INDICATIVE

tuerz-	torc-	add present indicative endings
tuerc-	"	
"	tuerc-	

tuerzo → torcemos
tuerces   torcéis
tuerce   tuercen

remove **-o** from **tuerzo**; stem change

PRESENT SUBJUNCTIVE

tuerz-	torz-	add present subjunctive endings
"	"	
"	tuerz-	

tuerza   torzamos
tuerzas   torzáis
tuerza   tuerzan

IMPERFECT INDICATIVE

torc-	add imperfect indicative endings

torcía   torcíamos
torcías   torcíais
torcía   torcían

IMPERFECT SUBJUNCTIVE

torcie-	add imperfect subjunctive endings

torciera   torciéramos
torcieras   torcierais
torciera   torcieran

remove **-ron** from **torcieron**

PRETERITE

torc-	add preterite endings

torcí   torcimos
torciste   torcisteis
torció   torcieron →

PRESENT PARTICIPLE

torciendo

PAST PARTICIPLE

torcido

remove **-er** from infinitive; stem change; **c > z** before **o**

INFINITIVE

torcer

remove **-er** and add **-iendo**

remove **-er** and add **-ido**

use infinitive as future stem

FUTURE

torcer-	add future endings

torceré   torceremos
torcerás   torceréis
torcerá   torcerán

CONDITIONAL

torcer-	add conditional endings

torcería   torceríamos
torcerías   torceríais
torcería   torcerían

Following the same pattern

retorcer to twist; to wring

---

haber (in the correct simple tense) **+ past participle**

PERFECT INDICATIVE

present indicative of haber	add past participle
he **torcido**	hemos **torcido**
has **torcido**	habéis **torcido**
ha **torcido**	han **torcido**

PERFECT SUBJUNCTIVE

present subjunctive of haber	add past participle
haya **torcido**	hayamos **torcido**
hayas **torcido**	hayáis **torcido**
haya **torcido**	hayan **torcido**

PLUPERFECT INDICATIVE

imperfect indicative of haber	add past participle
había **torcido**	habíamos **torcido**
habías **torcido**	habíais **torcido**
había **torcido**	habían **torcido**

PAST PARTICIPLE

torcido

PLUPERFECT SUBJUNCTIVE

imperfect subjunctive of haber	add past participle
hubiera **torcido**	hubiéramos **torcido**
hubieras **torcido**	hubierais **torcido**
hubiera **torcido**	hubieran **torcido**

FUTURE PERFECT

future of haber	add past participle
habré torcido	habremos torcido
habrás torcido	habréis torcido
habrá torcido	habrán torcido

CONDITIONAL PERFECT

conditional of haber	add past participle
habría torcido	habríamos torcido
habrías torcido	habríais torcido
habría torcido	habrían torcido

◢◤ Usage examples

!Me torció el brazo! *She twisted my arm!*

Torció la cabeza para mirar por la ventana. *He twisted his head to look out the window.*

Me tuerzo al andar. *I can't walk straight.*

Estás torciendo la barra. *You are bending the bar.*

Prohibido torcer a la izquierda. *No left turn.*

El coche torció a la derecha en el cruce. *The car turned right at the junction.*

Deberíamos haber torcido a la izquierda. *We should have turned left.*

El camino tuerce a la derecha. *The path bends round to the right.*

Torció el gesto. *She made a face.*

Tiene tendencia a torcer los ojos. *He has a tendency to squint.*

torcerse *to twist, sprain; to bend; to go wrong, go astray*

Se torció el tobillo durante el partido. *He twisted his ankle during the match.*

Si no tienes cuidado, te torcerás el tobillo. *If you are not careful, you will twist your ankle.*

torcido, torcida *crooked, twisted; bent*

torcidamente *in a twisted way, crookedly*

una torcedura *sprain, twist*

tortuoso, tortuosa *winding, tortuous; devious*

una vuelta de tuerca *twist (in a story)*

La historia tiene una vuelta de tuerca. *The story has a twist.*

una tuerca *nut (for a bolt)*

tuerto, tuerta *one-eyed; blind in one eye; twisted*

🔑 Key points

➡ add the ending **-yendo** for present participle   ➡ add the ending **-ído** for past participle

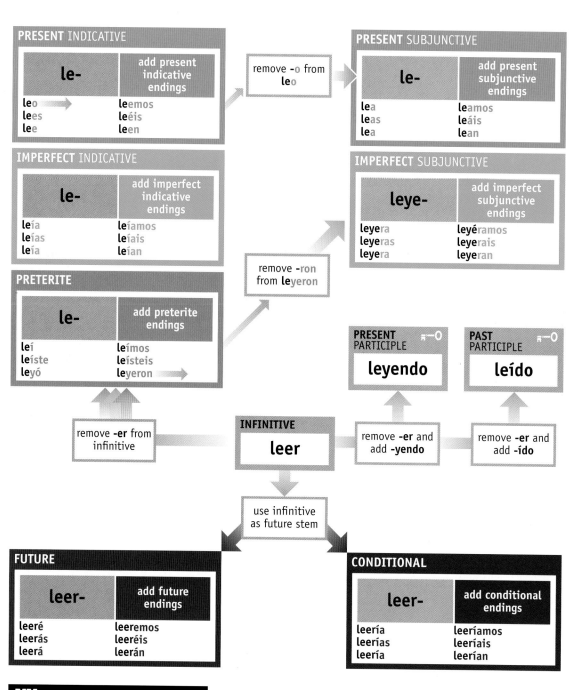

PRESENT INDICATIVE

le-	add present indicative endings
leo	leemos
lees	leéis
lee	leen

remove **-o** from **le**o

PRESENT SUBJUNCTIVE

le-	add present subjunctive endings
lea	leamos
leas	leáis
lea	lean

IMPERFECT INDICATIVE

le-	add imperfect indicative endings
leía	leíamos
leías	leíais
leía	leían

IMPERFECT SUBJUNCTIVE

leye-	add imperfect subjunctive endings
leyera	leyéramos
leyeras	leyerais
leyera	leyeran

remove **-ron** from **le**yeron

PRETERITE

le-	add preterite endings
leí	leímos
leíste	leísteis
leyó	leyeron

PRESENT PARTICIPLE 🔑

leyendo

PAST PARTICIPLE 🔑

leído

remove **-er** from infinitive

INFINITIVE

leer

remove **-er** and add **-yendo**

remove **-er** and add **-ído**

use infinitive as future stem

FUTURE

leer-	add future endings
leeré	leeremos
leerás	leeréis
leerá	leerán

CONDITIONAL

leer-	add conditional endings
leería	leeríamos
leerías	leeríais
leería	leerían

🧩 Following the same pattern

creer *to believe*   **proveer** *to provide, supply*
desposeer *to dispossess*   **releer** *to reread*
poseer *to possess*

haber (in the correct simple tense) + past participle

PERFECT INDICATIVE

present indicative of haber	add past participle
he **leído**	hemos **leído**
has **leído**	habéis **leído**
ha **leído**	han **leído**

PERFECT SUBJUNCTIVE

present subjunctive of haber	add past participle
haya **leído**	hayamos **leído**
hayas **leído**	hayáis **leído**
haya **leído**	hayan **leído**

PLUPERFECT INDICATIVE

imperfect indicative of haber	add past participle
había **leído**	habíamos **leído**
habías **leído**	habíais **leído**
había **leído**	habían **leído**

PAST PARTICIPLE
leído

PLUPERFECT SUBJUNCTIVE

imperfect subjunctive of haber	add past participle
hubiera **leído**	hubiéramos **leído**
hubieras **leído**	hubierais **leído**
hubiera **leído**	hubieran **leído**

FUTURE PERFECT

future of haber	add past participle
habré **leído**	habremos **leído**
habrás **leído**	habréis **leído**
habrá **leído**	habrán **leído**

CONDITIONAL PERFECT

conditional of haber	add past participle
habría **leído**	habríamos **leído**
habrías **leído**	habríais **leído**
habría **leído**	habrían **leído**

◥ Usage examples

Estoy leyendo. *I am reading.*
Leían cuando llegó. *They were reading when he arrived.*
Crees todo lo que lees. *You believe everything that you read.*
Quiero leer esa novela. *I want to read that novel.*
¿Qué libro leíste? *Which book did you read?*
He leído el periódico hoy. *I have read the newspaper today.*
El actor leyó el guión. *The actor read the script.*
Quiero que leas mi ensayo. *I want you to read my essay.*
Te leeré un cuento. *I will read you a story.*
Lo había leído detenidamente antes de responder. *He had read it carefully before responding.*

¿Lo habrías leído? *Would you have read it?*
Es una lástima que no hayas leído estos libros. *It is a shame that you have not read these books.*
Cuando vuelvas a casa, lo habré leído de tapa a tapa. *By the time you come home, I will have read it from cover to cover.*
¿Sabes leer en japonés? *Can you read Japanese?*
No sé leer música. *I can't read music.*
Si yo fuera tú, leería la letra pequeña. *I would read the small print if I were you.*
Preferiría que lo leyera después. *I would prefer that you read it later.*
No sabe leer. *He can't read.*
la lectura *reading*
lector, lectora *reader*

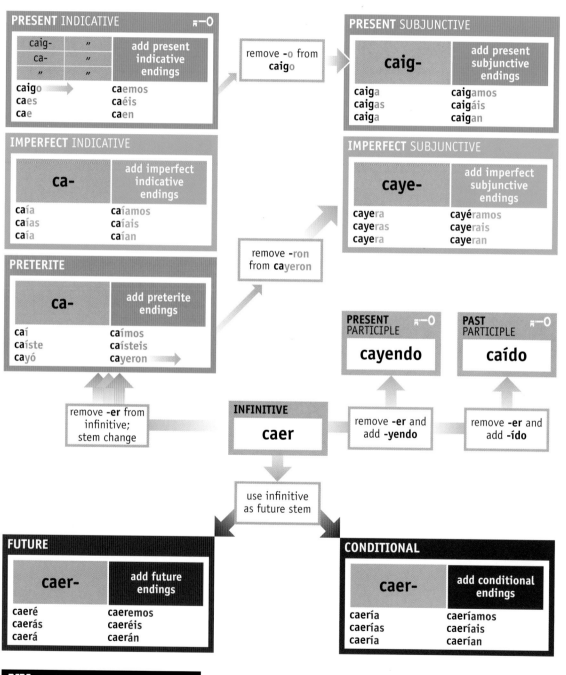

Key points

→ stem changes to **caig-** in 1st person singular of present indicative

→ add the ending **-yendo** for present participle
→ add the ending **-ído** for past participle

PRESENT INDICATIVE

caig-	"	add present indicative endings
ca-	"	
"	"	

caigo → caemos
caes   caéis
cae   caen

remove -o from **caig**o

PRESENT SUBJUNCTIVE

| **caig-** | add present subjunctive endings |

caiga   caigamos
caigas   caigáis
caiga   caigan

IMPERFECT INDICATIVE

| **ca-** | add imperfect indicative endings |

caía   caíamos
caías   caíais
caía   caían

IMPERFECT SUBJUNCTIVE

| **caye-** | add imperfect subjunctive endings |

cayera   cayéramos
cayeras   cayerais
cayera   cayeran

remove -ron from **ca**yeron

PRETERITE

| **ca-** | add preterite endings |

caí   caímos
caíste   caísteis
cayó   cayeron

PRESENT PARTICIPLE

cayendo

PAST PARTICIPLE

caído

remove -er from infinitive; stem change

INFINITIVE

caer

remove -er and add -yendo

remove -er and add -ído

use infinitive as future stem

FUTURE

| **caer-** | add future endings |

caeré   caeremos
caerás   caeréis
caerá   caerán

CONDITIONAL

| **caer-** | add conditional endings |

caería   caeríamos
caerías   caeríais
caería   caerían

Following the same pattern

decaer *to decline; to decay; to deteriorate*
recaer *to (have a) relapse*

haber (in the correct simple tense) + past participle

PERFECT INDICATIVE

present indicative of haber	add past participle
he **caído**	hemos **caído**
has **caído**	habéis **caído**
ha **caído**	han **caído**

PERFECT SUBJUNCTIVE

present subjunctive of haber	add past participle
haya **caído**	hayamos **caído**
hayas **caído**	hayáis **caído**
haya **caído**	hayan **caído**

PLUPERFECT INDICATIVE

imperfect indicative of haber	add past participle
había **caído**	habíamos **caído**
habías **caído**	habíais **caído**
había **caído**	habían **caído**

PAST PARTICIPLE

caído

PLUPERFECT SUBJUNCTIVE

imperfect subjunctive of haber	add past participle
hubiera **caído**	hubiéramos **caído**
hubieras **caído**	hubierais **caído**
hubiera **caído**	hubieran **caído**

FUTURE PERFECT

future of haber	add past participle
habré **caído**	habremos **caído**
habrás **caído**	habréis **caído**
habrá **caído**	habrán **caído**

CONDITIONAL PERFECT

conditional of haber	add past participle
habría **caído**	habríamos **caído**
habrías **caído**	habríais **caído**
habría **caído**	habrían **caído**

◥◤ Usage examples

Han caído en la trampa. *They have fallen into the trap.*

"El hombre que se levanta es aún más grande que el que no ha caído." *"The man who gets up is even greater than the one who has not fallen at all."*

La torre se está cayendo. *The tower is falling down.*

Una lluvia fuerte caerá en el sur de Francia. *Heavy rain will fall on the south of France.*

La nieve estaba cayendo cuando llegamos. *The snow was falling when we arrived.*

¿Por qué las hojas caen en otoño? *Why do leaves fall in autumn?*

El soldado cayó en las manos del enemigo. *The soldier fell into the enemy's hands.*

La temperatura había caído bajo cero. *The temperature had fallen below zero.*

Mi cumpleaños cae en domingo. *My birthday falls on a Sunday.*

Mi abuela cayó enferma en diciembre. *My grandmother fell ill in December.*

¿Cómo pudiste caer tan bajo? *How could you stoop so low?*

Me cae muy bien tu hermano. *I really like your brother.*

Me cae mal el médico. *I dislike the doctor.*

caerse *to fall; to drop*

Claudia se cayó y se rompió el brazo. *Claudia fell and broke her arm.*

Tenía miedo de que el niño se cayera. *I was afraid that the child would fall.*

Se me cayó el vaso. *I dropped the glass.*

la caída *fall*

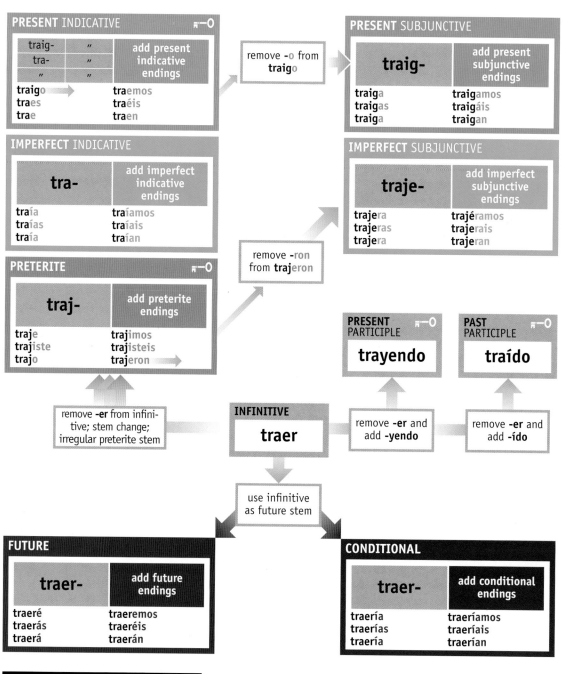

🔑—O Key points

➜ stem changes to **traig-** in 1st person singular of present indicative
➜ irregular stem in preterite: **traj-**

➜ add the ending **-yendo** for present participle
➜ add the ending **-ído** for past participle

PRESENT INDICATIVE   🔑—O

traig-	"	add present indicative endings
tra-	"	
"	"	

traigo	traemos
traes	traéis
trae	traen

remove -o from **traigo**

PRESENT SUBJUNCTIVE

| **traig-** | add present subjunctive endings |

traiga	traigamos
traigas	traigáis
traiga	traigan

IMPERFECT INDICATIVE

| **tra-** | add imperfect indicative endings |

traía	traíamos
traías	traíais
traía	traían

IMPERFECT SUBJUNCTIVE

| **traje-** | add imperfect subjunctive endings |

trajera	trajéramos
trajeras	trajerais
trajera	trajeran

remove -ron from **trajeron**

PRETERITE   🔑—O

| **traj-** | add preterite endings |

traje	trajimos
trajiste	trajisteis
trajo	trajeron

remove -er from infinitive; stem change; irregular preterite stem

PRESENT PARTICIPLE   🔑—O

trayendo

PAST PARTICIPLE   🔑—O

traído

INFINITIVE

traer

remove -er and add -yendo

remove -er and add -ído

use infinitive as future stem

FUTURE

| **traer-** | add future endings |

traeré	traeremos
traerás	traeréis
traerá	traerán

CONDITIONAL

| **traer-** | add conditional endings |

traería	traeríamos
traerías	traeríais
traería	traerían

🧩 Following the same pattern

atraer *to attract*	**extraer** *to extract*
contraer *to contract*	**retraer** *to retract*
distraer *to entertain; to distract*	**sustraer** *to remove; to subtract*

---

haber (in the correct simple tense) + past participle

PERFECT INDICATIVE

present indicative of haber	add past participle
he **traído**	hemos **traído**
has **traído**	habéis **traído**
ha **traído**	han **traído**

PERFECT SUBJUNCTIVE

present subjunctive of haber	add past participle
haya **traído**	hayamos **traído**
hayas **traído**	hayáis **traído**
haya **traído**	hayan **traído**

PLUPERFECT INDICATIVE

imperfect indicative of haber	add past participle
había **traído**	habíamos **traído**
habías **traído**	habíais **traído**
había **traído**	habían **traído**

PAST PARTICIPLE

traído

PLUPERFECT SUBJUNCTIVE

imperfect subjunctive of haber	add past participle
hubiera **traído**	hubiéramos **traído**
hubieras **traído**	hubierais **traído**
hubiera **traído**	hubieran **traído**

FUTURE PERFECT

future of haber	add past participle
habré **traído**	habremos **traído**
habrás **traído**	habréis **traído**
habrá **traído**	habrán **traído**

CONDITIONAL PERFECT

conditional of haber	add past participle
habría **traído**	habríamos **traído**
habrías **traído**	habríais **traído**
habría **traído**	habrían **traído**

◥◣ Usage examples

¿Me puedes traer una servilleta? *Can you bring me a napkin?*

¿Podría traerme la carta, por favor? *Could you bring me the menu, please?*

¿Nos trae la cuenta, por favor? *Can we have the bill, please?*

No hace falta traer nada. *We don't need to bring anything.*

Antonio trae mi entrada. *Antonio is bringing my ticket.*

Trajo un pastel. *She brought a cake.*

¿Has traído tu pasaporte? *Have you brought your passport?*

El alumno dijo que traería el libro a clase. *The student said that he would bring the book to class.*

Traeré mi cámara. *I will bring my camera.*

Que traiga el dinero. *Have him bring the money.*

Esperamos que traigan a sus amigos. *We hope that you will bring your friends.*

Ojalá que lo hubieran traído. *I wish that they had brought it.*

Si hubiera sabido que iba a llover, habría traído un paraguas. *If I had known that it was going to rain, I would have brought an umbrella.*

Me trae buenos recuerdos. *It brings me happy memories.*

Esto traerá problemas. *This will cause problems.*

No trajo más que problemas. *It brought nothing but trouble.*

Traía un vestido. *She was wearing a dress.*

el traje *suit; dress; costume*

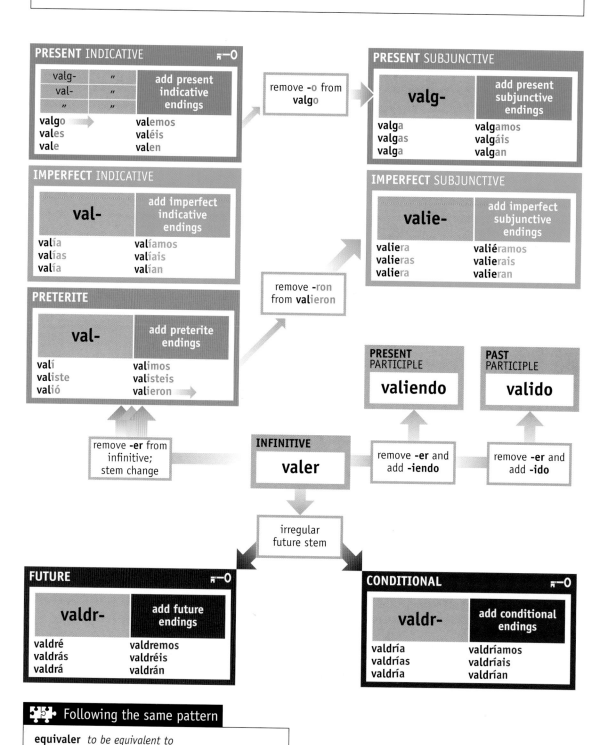

valer to cost; to be worth

Key points

➡ stem changes to **valg-** in 1st person singular of present indicative

➡ irregular future stem: **valdr-**

PRESENT INDICATIVE

valg-	"	add present indicative endings
val-	"	
"	"	

valgo → valemos
vales — valéis
vale — valen

remove -o from **valgo**

PRESENT SUBJUNCTIVE

| **valg-** | add present subjunctive endings |

valga — valgamos
valgas — valgáis
valga — valgan

IMPERFECT INDICATIVE

| **val-** | add imperfect indicative endings |

valía — valíamos
valías — valíais
valía — valían

IMPERFECT SUBJUNCTIVE

| **valie-** | add imperfect subjunctive endings |

valiera — valiéramos
valieras — valierais
valiera — valieran

remove -ron from **valieron**

PRETERITE

| **val-** | add preterite endings |

valí — valimos
valiste — valisteis
valió — valieron

PRESENT PARTICIPLE

valiendo

PAST PARTICIPLE

valido

remove -er from infinitive; stem change

INFINITIVE

valer

remove -er and add -iendo

remove -er and add -ido

irregular future stem

FUTURE

| **valdr-** | add future endings |

valdré — valdremos
valdrás — valdréis
valdrá — valdrán

CONDITIONAL

| **valdr-** | add conditional endings |

valdría — valdríamos
valdrías — valdríais
valdría — valdrían

Following the same pattern

equivaler *to be equivalent to*

> ## **haber** (in the correct simple tense) **+ past participle**

PERFECT INDICATIVE

present indicative of haber	add past participle
he **valido**	hemos **valido**
has **valido**	habéis **valido**
ha **valido**	han **valido**

PERFECT SUBJUNCTIVE

present subjunctive of haber	add past participle
haya **valido**	hayamos **valido**
hayas **valido**	hayáis **valido**
haya **valido**	hayan **valido**

PLUPERFECT INDICATIVE

imperfect indicative of haber	add past participle
había **valido**	habíamos **valido**
habías **valido**	habíais **valido**
había **valido**	habían **valido**

PAST PARTICIPLE
valido

PLUPERFECT SUBJUNCTIVE

imperfect subjunctive of haber	add past participle
hubiera **valido**	hubiéramos **valido**
hubieras **valido**	hubierais **valido**
hubiera **valido**	hubieran **valido**

FUTURE PERFECT

future of haber	add past participle
habré valido	habremos valido
habrás valido	habréis valido
habrá valido	habrán valido

CONDITIONAL PERFECT

conditional of haber	add past participle
habría valido	habríamos valido
habrías valido	habríais valido
habría valido	habrían valido

◥◣ Usage examples

¿Cuánto vale? *How much is it?*

La radio vale cinco euros. *The radio costs five euros.*

No creo que la casa valga cien mil libras. *I don't think the house is worth one hundred thousand pounds.*

Esas joyas no valen nada. *Those jewels are not worth anything.*

Valdrá mucho dinero en el futuro. *It will be worth a lot of money in the future.*

Vale un ojo de la cara. *It's worth a fortune.*

No valdría para ese trabajo. *I would be no good at that job.*

¿Vale la pena? *Is it worth it?*

Vale la pena intentarlo. *It's worth a try.*

Vale la pena visitar Barcelona. *Barcelona is worth a visit.*

No valía la pena. *It wasn't worth it.*

Más vale que estudiemos. *We had better study.*

¡Eso no vale! *That doesn't count!*

Su conducta le valió una reprimenda. *His conduct earned him a reprimand.*

Más vale pájaro en mano que ciento volando. *A bird in the hand is worth two in the bush.*

Más vale prevenir que curar. *An ounce of prevention is worth a pound of cure.*

Más vale tarde que nunca. *Better late than never.*

Como futbolista no vale mucho. *He's not much of a footballer.*

¿Vale? *O.K.?*

el valor *value*

la valía *worth*

⚷─O Key points

➡ stem changes to **pong-** in 1st person singular of present indicative
➡ irregular stem in preterite: **pus-**
➡ irregular past participle: **puesto**
➡ irregular future stem: **pondr-**

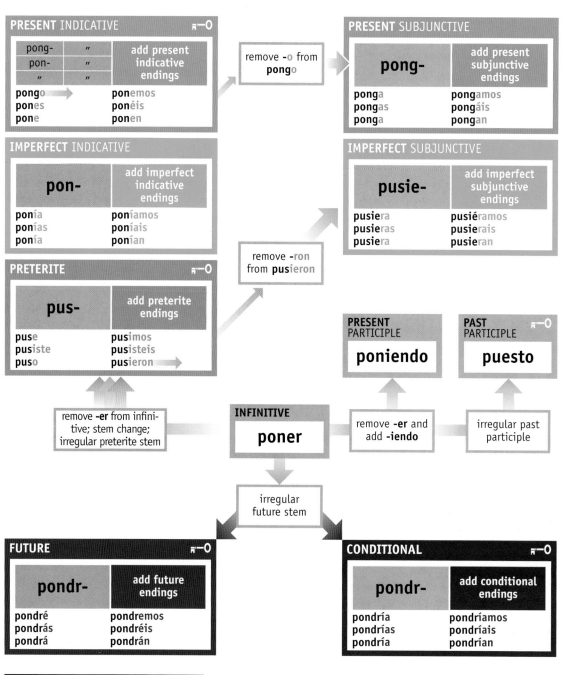

PRESENT INDICATIVE   ⚷─O

pong-	"	add present indicative endings
pon-	"	
"	"	

pongo	ponemos
pones	ponéis
pone	ponen

remove **-o** from **pong**o

PRESENT SUBJUNCTIVE

| pong- | add present subjunctive endings |

ponga	pongamos
pongas	pongáis
ponga	pongan

IMPERFECT INDICATIVE

| pon- | add imperfect indicative endings |

ponía	poníamos
ponías	poníais
ponía	ponían

IMPERFECT SUBJUNCTIVE

| pusie- | add imperfect subjunctive endings |

pusiera	pusiéramos
pusieras	pusierais
pusiera	pusieran

remove **-ron** from **pus**ie**ron**

PRETERITE   ⚷─O

| pus- | add preterite endings |

puse	pusimos
pusiste	pusisteis
puso	pusieron

remove **-er** from infinitive; stem change; irregular preterite stem

INFINITIVE

poner

remove **-er** and add **-iendo**

PRESENT PARTICIPLE

poniendo

PAST PARTICIPLE   ⚷─O

puesto

irregular past participle

irregular future stem

FUTURE   ⚷─O

| pondr- | add future endings |

pondré	pondremos
pondrás	pondréis
pondrá	pondrán

CONDITIONAL   ⚷─O

| pondr- | add conditional endings |

pondría	pondríamos
pondrías	pondríais
pondría	pondrían

🧩 Following the same pattern

componer to make up; to compose, write
contraponer to compare
disponer to arrange; to have at one's disposal; to make use of
disponerse a to get ready
exponer to expose
imponer to impose
indisponer to make ill; to upset

> ## haber (in the correct simple tense) + past participle

PERFECT INDICATIVE

present indicative of haber	add past participle
he **puesto**	hemos **puesto**
has **puesto**	habéis **puesto**
ha **puesto**	han **puesto**

PERFECT SUBJUNCTIVE

present subjunctive of haber	add past participle
haya **puesto**	hayamos **puesto**
hayas **puesto**	hayáis **puesto**
haya **puesto**	hayan **puesto**

PLUPERFECT INDICATIVE

imperfect indicative of haber	add past participle
había **puesto**	habíamos **puesto**
habías **puesto**	habíais **puesto**
había **puesto**	habían **puesto**

PAST PARTICIPLE

puesto

PLUPERFECT SUBJUNCTIVE

imperfect subjunctive of haber	add past participle
hubiera **puesto**	hubiéramos **puesto**
hubieras **puesto**	hubierais **puesto**
hubiera **puesto**	hubieran **puesto**

FUTURE PERFECT

future of haber	add past participle
habré **puesto**	habremos **puesto**
habrás **puesto**	habréis **puesto**
habrá **puesto**	habrán **puesto**

CONDITIONAL PERFECT

conditional of haber	add past participle
habría **puesto**	habríamos **puesto**
habrías **puesto**	habríais **puesto**
habría **puesto**	habrían **puesto**

Usage examples

Pongo las llaves en la mesa. *I am putting the keys on the table.*

Puso la ropa en el armario. *She put the clothes in the wardrobe.*

Pondré mis libros en el estante. *I will put my books on the shelf.*

Sergio, ¿podrías poner el equipaje en la habitación? *Sergio, would you put the luggage in the bedroom?*

¿Dónde he puesto mis cosas? *Where did I put my things?*

No lo has puesto nada de azúcar. *You haven't put any sugar in it.*

Pondré la mesa yo mismo. *I will set the table myself.*

Esperaba que los niños pusieran la mesa. *I was hoping that the children would set the table.*

La pusieron a trabajar en el extranjero. *They sent her to work abroad.*

La gallina puso cinco huevos. *The hen laid five eggs.*

Pusieron una bomba en la estación. *They planted a bomb in the station.*

¿Qué te pongo? *What can I get you?*

Si lo hubiera puesto en el cajón, no lo habría perdido. *If I had put it in the drawer, I would not have lost it.*

Quiero que pongas la música. *I want you to put the music on.*

¿Qué ponen en la televisión esta noche? *What's on the television tonight?*

¿Qué quieres que ponga en el formulario? *What do you want me to put on the form?*

🔑—O **Key points**

➡ three stems in present indicative: **teng-**, **tien-** & **ten-**
➡ irregular stem in preterite: **tuv-**
➡ irregular future stem: **tendr-**

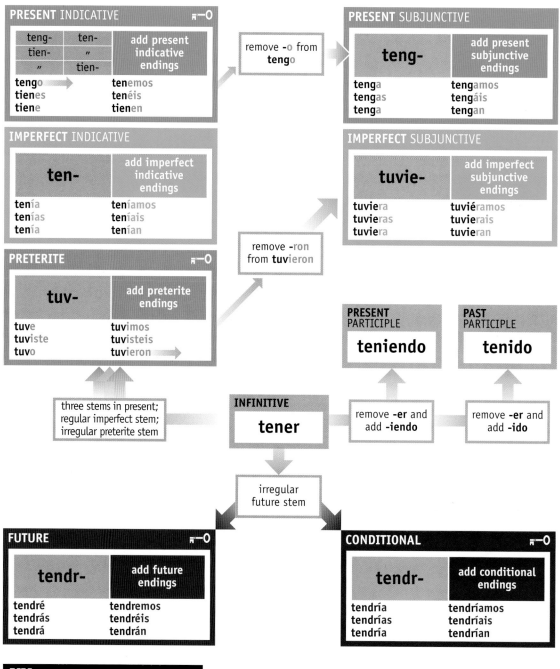

PRESENT INDICATIVE

teng-	ten-	add present indicative endings
tien-	"	
"	tien-	

tengo → tenemos
tienes tenéis
tiene tienen

PRESENT SUBJUNCTIVE

teng-	add present subjunctive endings

tenga tengamos
tengas tengáis
tenga tengan

remove **-o** from **teng**o

IMPERFECT INDICATIVE

ten-	add imperfect indicative endings

tenía teníamos
tenías teníais
tenía tenían

IMPERFECT SUBJUNCTIVE

tuvie-	add imperfect subjunctive endings

tuviera tuviéramos
tuvieras tuvierais
tuviera tuvieran

remove **-ron** from **tuv**ieron

PRETERITE

tuv-	add preterite endings

tuve tuvimos
tuviste tuvisteis
tuvo tuvieron →

PRESENT PARTICIPLE

teniendo

PAST PARTICIPLE

tenido

three stems in present; regular imperfect stem; irregular preterite stem

INFINITIVE

tener

remove **-er** and add **-iendo**

remove **-er** and add **-ido**

irregular future stem

FUTURE

tendr-	add future endings

tendré tendremos
tendrás tendréis
tendrá tendrán

CONDITIONAL

tendr-	add conditional endings

tendría tendríamos
tendrías tendríais
tendría tendrían

🧩 Following the same pattern

abstenerse *to abstain*
contener *to contain*
detener *to detain, stop*
entretener *to entertain*
mantener *to maintain, support*
obtener *to obtain, get*
retener *to retain*
sostener *to support*

---

haber (in the correct simple tense) + past participle

PERFECT INDICATIVE

present indicative of haber	add past participle
he **tenido**	hemos **tenido**
has **tenido**	habéis **tenido**
ha **tenido**	han **tenido**

PERFECT SUBJUNCTIVE

present subjunctive of haber	add past participle
haya **tenido**	hayamos **tenido**
hayas **tenido**	hayáis **tenido**
haya **tenido**	hayan **tenido**

PLUPERFECT INDICATIVE

imperfect indicative of haber	add past participle
había **tenido**	habíamos **tenido**
habías **tenido**	habíais **tenido**
había **tenido**	habían **tenido**

PAST PARTICIPLE
tenido

PLUPERFECT SUBJUNCTIVE

imperfect subjunctive of haber	add past participle
hubiera **tenido**	hubiéramos **tenido**
hubieras **tenido**	hubierais **tenido**
hubiera **tenido**	hubieran **tenido**

FUTURE PERFECT

future of haber	add past participle
habré **tenido**	habremos **tenido**
habrás **tenido**	habréis **tenido**
habrá **tenido**	habrán **tenido**

CONDITIONAL PERFECT

conditional of haber	add past participle
habría **tenido**	habríamos **tenido**
habrías **tenido**	habríais **tenido**
habría **tenido**	habrían **tenido**

◥◢ Usage examples

Tengo tres perros. *I have three dogs.*
Ellos tienen mucho dinero. *They have a lot of money.*
Tuvo dolor de cabeza durante tres días. *He had a headache for three days.*
Si tuviera tiempo, aprendería otro idioma. *If I had the time, I would learn another language.*
¿Cuántos años tienes? *How old are you?*
Tiene quince años. *She is fifteen years old.*
¿Tienes frío ahora? *Are you cold in here?*
Tengo calor. *I am hot.*
Tendrás sed. *You will be thirsty.*
Tenemos mucha hambre. *We are very hungry.*
Ellos tenían razón. *They were right.*
No creo que ella vaya a tener éxito. *I do not think she will succeed.*

Mi hermana tiene miedo de las alturas. *My sister is afraid of heights.*
Tienen celos de nuestro éxito. *They are jealous of our success.*
Tengo prisa. *I'm in a hurry.*
Tenéis que llevar uniforme. *You all have to wear a uniform.*
Tuvimos que esperar mucho rato. *We had to wait for a long time.*
Tuve una pesadilla anoche. *I had a nightmare last night.*
Está teniendo problemas con su nuevo coche. *He's having problems with his new car.*
Tendrá lugar la semana que viene. *It will take place next week.*

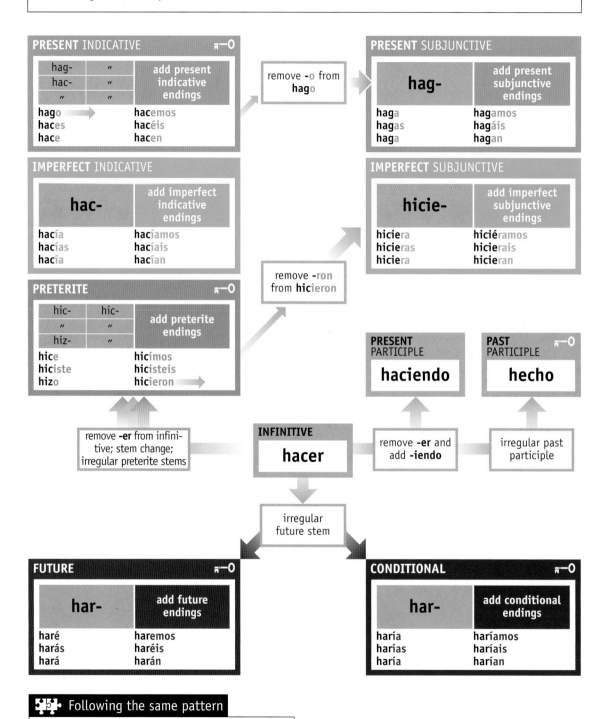

➡ stem changes to **hag-** in 1st person singular of present indicative
➡ two irregular stems in preterite: **hic-** & **hiz-**
➡ irregular past participle: **hecho**
➡ irregular future stem: **har-**

PRESENT INDICATIVE ⚷—O

hag-	"	add present indicative endings
hac-	"	
"	"	

hago	hacemos
haces	hacéis
hace	hacen

remove **-o** from **hag**o

PRESENT SUBJUNCTIVE

hag-	add present subjunctive endings

haga	hagamos
hagas	hagáis
haga	hagan

IMPERFECT INDICATIVE

hac-	add imperfect indicative endings

hacía	hacíamos
hacías	hacíais
hacía	hacían

IMPERFECT SUBJUNCTIVE

hicie-	add imperfect subjunctive endings

hiciera	hiciéramos
hicieras	hicierais
hiciera	hicieran

PRETERITE ⚷—O

hic-	hic-	add preterite endings
"	"	
hiz-	"	

hice	hicimos
hiciste	hicisteis
hizo	hicieron

remove **-ron** from **hic**ieron

PRESENT PARTICIPLE

haciendo

PAST PARTICIPLE ⚷—O

hecho

remove **-er** from infinitive; stem change; irregular preterite stems

INFINITIVE

hacer

remove **-er** and add **-iendo**

irregular past participle

irregular future stem

FUTURE ⚷—O

har-	add future endings

haré	haremos
harás	haréis
hará	harán

CONDITIONAL ⚷—O

har-	add conditional endings

haría	haríamos
harías	haríais
haría	harían

⟐ Following the same pattern

deshacer *to undo*

---

haber (in the correct simple tense) + past participle

PERFECT INDICATIVE

present indicative of haber	add past participle
he **hecho**	hemos **hecho**
has **hecho**	habéis **hecho**
ha **hecho**	han **hecho**

PERFECT SUBJUNCTIVE

present subjunctive of haber	add past participle
haya **hecho**	hayamos **hecho**
hayas **hecho**	hayáis **hecho**
haya **hecho**	hayan **hecho**

PLUPERFECT INDICATIVE

imperfect indicative of haber	add past participle
había **hecho**	habíamos **hecho**
habías **hecho**	habíais **hecho**
había **hecho**	habían **hecho**

PAST PARTICIPLE

hecho

PLUPERFECT SUBJUNCTIVE

imperfect subjunctive of haber	add past participle
hubiera **hecho**	hubiéramos **hecho**
hubieras **hecho**	hubierais **hecho**
hubiera **hecho**	hubieran **hecho**

FUTURE PERFECT

future of haber	add past participle
habré **hecho**	habremos **hecho**
habrás **hecho**	habréis **hecho**
habrá **hecho**	habrán **hecho**

CONDITIONAL PERFECT

conditional of haber	add past participle
habría **hecho**	habríamos **hecho**
habrías **hecho**	habríais **hecho**
habría **hecho**	habrían **hecho**

Usage examples

¿Qué haces? *What are you doing?*

¿Qué hace tu padre? *What does your father do?*

No hizo nada. *He didn't do anything.*

¡Concentrarte en lo que haces! *Concentrate on what you are doing!*

Tengo mucho que hacer. *I have a lot to do.*

Quiero que tú lo hagas. *I want you to do it.*

Habría hecho lo mismo. *I would have done the same.*

¿Qué hace esto en la mesa? *What is this doing on the table?*

Trabajo en este proyecto desde hace dos años. *I have been working on this project for two years.*

Estudian francés desde hace cinco meses. *They have been studying French for five months.*

Hace buen tiempo. *The weather is good.*

¿Qué tiempo hace hoy? *What is the weather like today?*

Ayer hizo mucho frío. *It was very cold yesterday.*

Preferiría que hiciera calor y sol. *I'd rather it were hot and sunny.*

Lo sabrías si hubieras hecho los deberes. *You would know it if you had done the homework.*

La hiciste llorar. *You made her cry.*

Hice la reserva de las entradas. *I had tickets reserved.*

Dos y dos hacen cuatro. *Two and two make four.*

La práctica hace al maestro. *Practice makes perfect.*

Dicho y hecho. *No sooner said than done.*

hacerse *to become; to get*

Se está haciendo tarde. *It's getting late.*

Se hizo médico. *He became a doctor.*

Key points

→ very irregular in present indicative
→ irregular stem in preterite: **hub-**

→ irregular stem in present subjunctive: **hay-**
→ irregular future stem: **habr-**

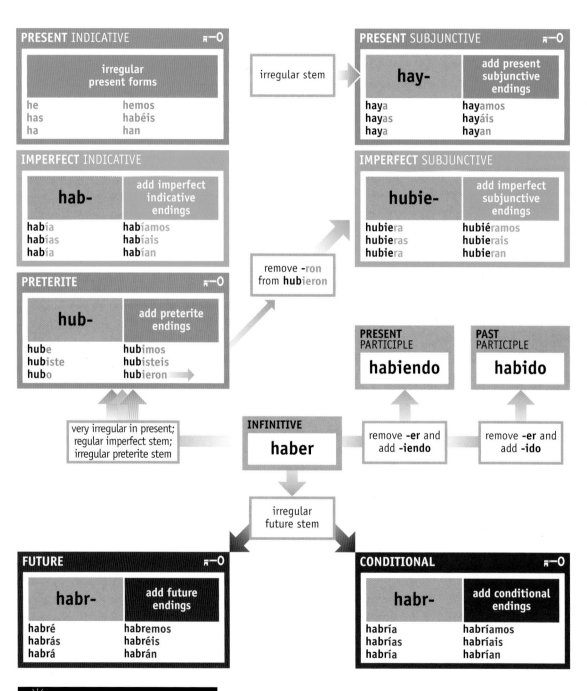

PRESENT INDICATIVE

irregular present forms	
he	hemos
has	habéis
ha	han

irregular stem →

PRESENT SUBJUNCTIVE

hay-	add present subjunctive endings
haya	hayamos
hayas	hayáis
haya	hayan

IMPERFECT INDICATIVE

hab-	add imperfect indicative endings
había	habíamos
habías	habíais
había	habían

IMPERFECT SUBJUNCTIVE

hubie-	add imperfect subjunctive endings
hubiera	hubiéramos
hubieras	hubierais
hubiera	hubieran

remove **-ron** from **hub**ieron

PRETERITE

hub-	add preterite endings
hube	hubimos
hubiste	hubisteis
hubo	hubieron

PRESENT PARTICIPLE

habiendo

PAST PARTICIPLE

habido

very irregular in present; regular imperfect stem; irregular preterite stem

INFINITIVE

haber

remove **-er** and add **-iendo**

remove **-er** and add **-ido**

irregular future stem

FUTURE

habr-	add future endings
habré	habremos
habrás	habréis
habrá	habrán

CONDITIONAL

habr-	add conditional endings
habría	habríamos
habrías	habríais
habría	habrían

Useful tips

The verb **haber** is used almost exclusively as an auxiliary verb to form the compound tenses. Where "to have" means "to possess", Spanish uses **tener** and it would be a mistake to use **haber** instead.

haber (in the correct simple tense) + past participle

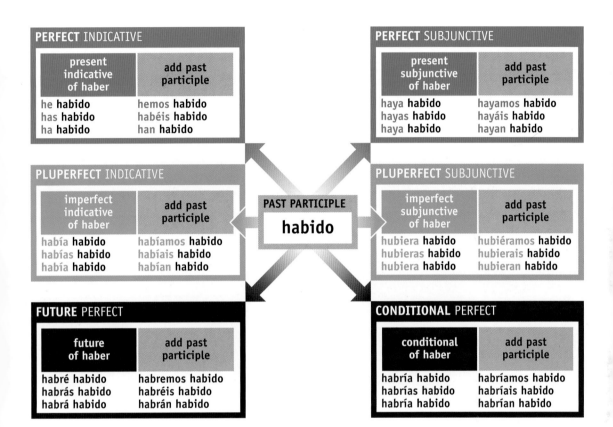

PERFECT INDICATIVE	
present indicative of haber	add past participle
he **habido**	hemos **habido**
has **habido**	habéis **habido**
ha **habido**	han **habido**

PERFECT SUBJUNCTIVE	
present subjunctive of haber	add past participle
haya **habido**	hayamos **habido**
hayas **habido**	hayáis **habido**
haya **habido**	hayan **habido**

PLUPERFECT INDICATIVE	
imperfect indicative of haber	add past participle
había **habido**	habíamos **habido**
habías **habido**	habíais **habido**
había **habido**	habían **habido**

PAST PARTICIPLE

habido

PLUPERFECT SUBJUNCTIVE	
imperfect subjunctive of haber	add past participle
hubiera **habido**	hubiéramos **habido**
hubieras **habido**	hubierais **habido**
hubiera **habido**	hubieran **habido**

FUTURE PERFECT	
future of haber	add past participle
habré **habido**	habremos **habido**
habrás **habido**	habréis **habido**
habrá **habido**	habrán **habido**

CONDITIONAL PERFECT	
conditional of haber	add past participle
habría **habido**	habríamos **habido**
habrías **habido**	habríais **habido**
habría **habido**	habrían **habido**

◥◤ Usage examples

He escrito el informe. *I have written the report.*
¿Qué has hecho hoy? *What have you done today?*
No ha limpiado su habitación. *She hasn't cleaned her room.*
Habéis trabajado todo el día. *You have worked all day.*
Los niños han abierto los regalos. *The children have opened the presents.*
Ya habían comido. *They had already eaten.*
Había visitado el museo antes. *I had visited the museum before.*
Habré cocinado la paella antes de que lleguen los invitados. *I will have cooked the paella before the guests arrive.*
Habrán vuelto de Italia para el doce de febrero. *They will have returned from Italy by the twelfth of February.*

Habrá salido. *He will have left.*
Si hubiera hecho buen tiempo, habríamos ido a la playa. *If the weather had been good, we would have gone to the beach.*
Habrá sido las dos cuando llegué a su casa. *It must have been two o'clock when I got to his house.*
Estoy tan contenta de que hayas venido a verme. *I'm so glad you came to see me.*
Es bueno que haya aprobado el examen. *It's good that he passed the test.*
Si Olivia hubiera estudiado más, habría aprobado el examen. *If Olivia had studied harder, she would have passed the exam.*
Si lo hubiera sabido, no habría ido. *If I had known, I would not have gone.*

→ very irregular in present indicative
→ irregular stem in imperfect indicative: **er-**
→ irregular stem in preterite: **fu-**
→ irregular stem in present subjunctive: **se-**

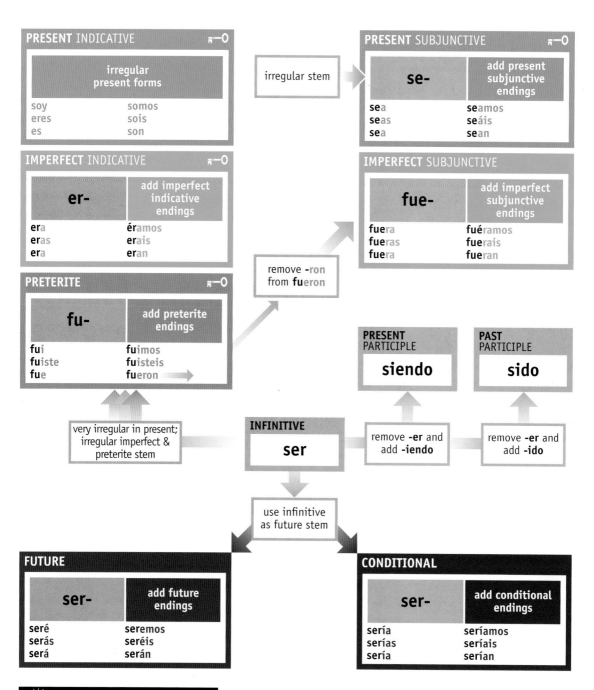

PRESENT INDICATIVE ⚷–O

irregular present forms	
soy	somos
eres	sois
es	son

PRESENT SUBJUNCTIVE ⚷–O

irregular stem →

se-	add present subjunctive endings
sea	seamos
seas	seáis
sea	sean

IMPERFECT INDICATIVE ⚷–O

er-	add imperfect indicative endings
era	éramos
eras	erais
era	eran

IMPERFECT SUBJUNCTIVE

fue-	add imperfect subjunctive endings
fuera	fuéramos
fueras	fuerais
fuera	fueran

PRETERITE ⚷–O

fu-	add preterite endings
fui	fuimos
fuiste	fuisteis
fue	fueron

remove **-ron** from **fu**eron

PRESENT PARTICIPLE

siendo

PAST PARTICIPLE

sido

very irregular in present; irregular imperfect & preterite stem

INFINITIVE

ser

remove **-er** and add **-iendo**

remove **-er** and add **-ido**

use infinitive as future stem

FUTURE

ser-	add future endings
seré	seremos
serás	seréis
será	serán

CONDITIONAL

ser-	add conditional endings
sería	seríamos
serías	seríais
sería	serían

💡 Useful tips

Ser and **estar** both mean "to be", but they are used in different ways. **Ser** is used for statements expressing the fundamental nature of an entity, i.e. "what something or someone is": **Es médico** (He's a doctor); **Es importante** (It is important); **Soy terco** (I'm stubborn). See page 82 to learn about **estar**.

haber (in the correct simple tense) **+ past participle**

PERFECT INDICATIVE

present indicative of haber	add past participle
he **sido**	hemos **sido**
has **sido**	habéis **sido**
ha **sido**	han **sido**

PERFECT SUBJUNCTIVE

present subjunctive of haber	add past participle
haya **sido**	hayamos **sido**
hayas **sido**	hayáis **sido**
haya **sido**	hayan **sido**

PLUPERFECT INDICATIVE

imperfect indicative of haber	add past participle
había **sido**	habíamos **sido**
habías **sido**	habíais **sido**
había **sido**	habían **sido**

PAST PARTICIPLE

sido

PLUPERFECT SUBJUNCTIVE

imperfect subjunctive of haber	add past participle
hubiera **sido**	hubiéramos **sido**
hubieras **sido**	hubierais **sido**
hubiera **sido**	hubieran **sido**

FUTURE PERFECT

future of haber	add past participle
habré sido	habremos sido
habrás sido	habréis sido
habrá sido	habrán sido

CONDITIONAL PERFECT

conditional of haber	add past participle
habría sido	habríamos sido
habrías sido	habríais sido
habría sido	habrían sido

◥◣ Usage examples

¿De dónde eres? *Where are you from?*

Somos de Madrid. *We are from Madrid.*

Soy cartero. *I am a postman.*

Son estudiantes. *They are students.*

Mi hermana es muy inteligente. *My sister is very intelligent.*

Las casas son caras en ese vecindario. *The houses are expensive in that neighbourhood.*

Era muy travieso cuando era niño. *He was very naughty when he was a child.*

La fiesta será en mi casa. *The party will be at my house.*

Seremos famosos. *We will be famous.*

Si fuera rico, viajaría por todo el mundo. *If I were rich, I would travel all over the world.*

El reloj es de Juan. *The watch is Juan's.*

Dos por dos son ocho. *Two times two is four.*

Habría sido un desastre si hubiera llegado tarde. *It would have been a disaster if I had arrived late.*

¿Qué fecha es hoy? *What is the date today?*

Es el dos de junio. *It is the second of June.*

¿Qué hora es? *What time is it?*

Es la una y media. *It is half past one.*

Son las nueve menos cuarto. *It is a quarter to nine.*

El libro será publicado en septiembre. *The book will be published in September.*

El castillo fue construido en el siglo XVI. *The castle was built in the sixteenth century.*

Es natural que estés molesto. *It is natural for you to be upset.*

Puede ser que sea verdad. *It may be true.*

⛏—O Key points

➡ irregular stem in imperfect indicative: **ve-**   ➡ irregular past participle: **visto**

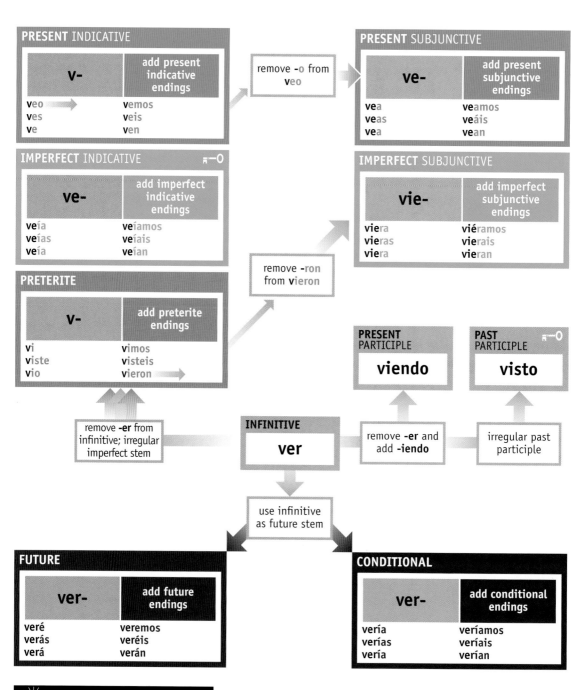

PRESENT INDICATIVE

v-	add present indicative endings
veo	vemos
ves	veis
ve	ven

remove **-o** from **v**eo

PRESENT SUBJUNCTIVE

ve-	add present subjunctive endings
vea	veamos
veas	veáis
vea	vean

IMPERFECT INDICATIVE   ⛏—O

ve-	add imperfect indicative endings
veía	veíamos
veías	veíais
veía	veían

IMPERFECT SUBJUNCTIVE

vie-	add imperfect subjunctive endings
viera	viéramos
vieras	vierais
viera	vieran

remove **-ron** from **v**ieron

PRETERITE

v-	add preterite endings
vi	vimos
viste	visteis
vio	vieron

PRESENT PARTICIPLE

viendo

PAST PARTICIPLE   ⛏—O

visto

remove **-er** from infinitive; irregular imperfect stem

INFINITIVE

ver

remove **-er** and add **-iendo**

irregular past participle

use infinitive as future stem

FUTURE

ver-	add future endings
veré	veremos
verás	veréis
verá	verán

CONDITIONAL

ver-	add conditional endings
vería	veríamos
verías	veríais
vería	verían

🔆 Useful tips

As mentioned on page 13 of the Introduction, there are only three verbs that are irregular in the imperfect indicative tense: **ir** (see page 184), **ser** (see page 128) and **ver** (above). **Ver** is irregular because you cannot form its imperfect indicative stem (**ve-**) by removing -er from the infinitive.

haber (in the correct simple tense) **+ past participle**

PERFECT INDICATIVE

present indicative of haber	add past participle
he **visto**	hemos **visto**
has **visto**	habéis **visto**
ha **visto**	han **visto**

PERFECT SUBJUNCTIVE

present subjunctive of haber	add past participle
haya **visto**	hayamos **visto**
hayas **visto**	hayáis **visto**
haya **visto**	hayan **visto**

PLUPERFECT INDICATIVE

imperfect indicative of haber	add past participle
había **visto**	habíamos **visto**
habías **visto**	habíais **visto**
había **visto**	habían **visto**

PAST PARTICIPLE
visto

PLUPERFECT SUBJUNCTIVE

imperfect subjunctive of haber	add past participle
hubiera **visto**	hubiéramos **visto**
hubieras **visto**	hubierais **visto**
hubiera **visto**	hubieran **visto**

FUTURE PERFECT

future of haber	add past participle
habré **visto**	habremos **visto**
habrás **visto**	habréis **visto**
habrá **visto**	habrán **visto**

CONDITIONAL PERFECT

conditional of haber	add past participle
habría **visto**	habríamos **visto**
habrías **visto**	habríais **visto**
habría **visto**	habrían **visto**

◥◣ Usage examples

¡No veo nada! *I can't see a thing!*
Está viendo la televisión. *He is watching television.*
¡Lo vi con mis propios ojos! *I saw it with my own eyes!*
Te vimos entrar. *We saw you come in.*
No la he visto hoy. *I haven't seen her today.*
Ya había visto la película. *She had already seen the film.*
¿Ves lo que quiero decir? *Do you see what I mean?*
¡Si hubieras visto lo que pasó! *If only you had seen what happened!*
Debes ver a un médico. *You must see a doctor.*
Ha sonado el timbre; ve a ver quién es. *The doorbell rang; go and see who it is.*
¿Podría ver la carta? *May I see the menu?*

¿Viste el partido de fútbol anoche? *Did you see the football match last night?*
Vimos el eclipse. *We saw the eclipse.*
No veo la diferencia. *I can't see the difference.*
Eso está por ver. *It remains to be seen.*
Ver es creer. *Seeing is believing.*
Como vimos en la clase de ayer. *As we saw in yesterday's lesson.*
la vista *sight, vision; view; eyes*
¡Hasta la vista! *See you later!*
la visión *vision*
un vistazo *look, glance*
visto, vista *obvious, clear; seen around*
el visto bueno *approval*
visible *visible*

🔑 Key points

➔ **e** of stem changes to **ie** for stressed syllables in present indicative
➔ irregular stem in preterite: **quis-**

➔ **ie** of stem reverts to **e** for unstressed syllables in present subjunctive
➔ irregular future stem: **querr-**

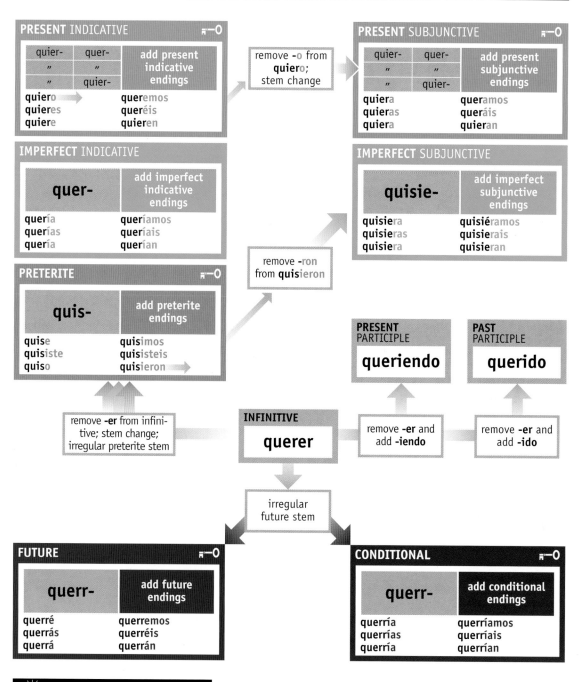

PRESENT INDICATIVE 🔑

quier-	quier-	add present indicative endings
"	"	
"	quer-	

quiero → queremos
quieres   queréis
quiere   quieren

remove **-o** from **quiero**; stem change

PRESENT SUBJUNCTIVE 🔑

quier-	quier-	add present subjunctive endings
"	"	
"	quer-	

quiera   queramos
quieras   queráis
quiera   quieran

IMPERFECT INDICATIVE

| **quer-** | add imperfect indicative endings |

quería   queríamos
querías   queríais
quería   querían

IMPERFECT SUBJUNCTIVE

| **quisie-** | add imperfect subjunctive endings |

quisiera   quisiéramos
quisieras   quisierais
quisiera   quisieran

remove **-ron** from **quisieron**

PRETERITE 🔑

| **quis-** | add preterite endings |

quise   quisimos
quisiste   quisisteis
quiso   quisieron

PRESENT PARTICIPLE
queriendo

PAST PARTICIPLE
querido

remove **-er** from infinitive; stem change; irregular preterite stem

INFINITIVE
querer

remove **-er** and add **-iendo**

remove **-er** and add **-ido**

irregular future stem

FUTURE 🔑

| **querr-** | add future endings |

querré   querremos
querrás   querréis
querrá   querrán

CONDITIONAL 🔑

| **querr-** | add conditional endings |

querría   querríamos
querrías   querríais
querría   querrían

💡 Useful tips

Querer in the preterite tense can express the idea that someone not only wanted to do something but actually attempted to do it. As such, **querer** in the preterite is sometimes translated by the word "tried".

---

haber (in the correct simple tense) **+ past participle**

PERFECT INDICATIVE

present indicative of haber	add past participle
he **querido**	hemos **querido**
has **querido**	habéis **querido**
ha **querido**	han **querido**

PERFECT SUBJUNCTIVE

present subjunctive of haber	add past participle
haya **querido**	hayamos **querido**
hayas **querido**	hayáis **querido**
haya **querido**	hayan **querido**

PLUPERFECT INDICATIVE

imperfect indicative of haber	add past participle
había **querido**	habíamos **querido**
habías **querido**	habíais **querido**
había **querido**	habían **querido**

PAST PARTICIPLE
querido

PLUPERFECT SUBJUNCTIVE

imperfect subjunctive of haber	add past participle
hubiera **querido**	hubieramos **querido**
hubieras **querido**	hubierais **querido**
hubiera **querido**	hubieran **querido**

FUTURE PERFECT

future of haber	add past participle
habré **querido**	habremos **querido**
habrás **querido**	habréis **querido**
habrá **querido**	habrán **querido**

CONDITIONAL PERFECT

conditional of haber	add past participle
habría **querido**	habríamos **querido**
habrías **querido**	habríais **querido**
habría **querido**	habrían **querido**

Usage examples

Queremos una casa a la orilla del mar. *We want a house by the sea.*
Mi hijo quiere un perro. *My son wants a dog.*
Quiero adelgazar. *I want to lose weight.*
Quieren ir de compras. *They want to go shopping.*
Antonio no quería jugar tenis. *Antonio did not want to play tennis.*
Dudo que quiera salir. *I doubt she wants to leave.*
Si hubiera querido quedarme, no habría salido. *If I had wanted to stay, I would not have left.*
Mis padres quieren que aprenda francés. *My parents want me to learn French.*
¿Quieres algo de comer? *Do you want something to eat?*
¿Qué quieres beber? *What would you like to drink?*

¿Quieres pasarme la sal? *Could you pass me the salt?*
Quise llamar un taxi. *I tried to call a taxi.*
El niño no quiso acostarse. *The child refused to go to bed.*
Quisiera decir algo. *I would like to say something.*
Quisiera un kilo de tomates. *I would like a kilo of tomatoes.*
Lo hizo sin querer. *He didn't mean to do it.*
Te quiero. *I love you.*
Quiero mucho a mis padres. *I love my parents very much.*
¿Qué quiere decir esa palabra? *What does that word mean?*
¿Qué quieres decir con eso? *What do you mean by that?*

Key points

➔ **o** of stem changes to **ue** for stressed syllables in present indicative

➔ irregular stem in preterite: **pud-**

➔ **ue** of stem reverts to **o** for unstressed syllables in present subjunctive

➔ irregular present participle: **pudiendo**

➔ irregular future stem: **podr-**

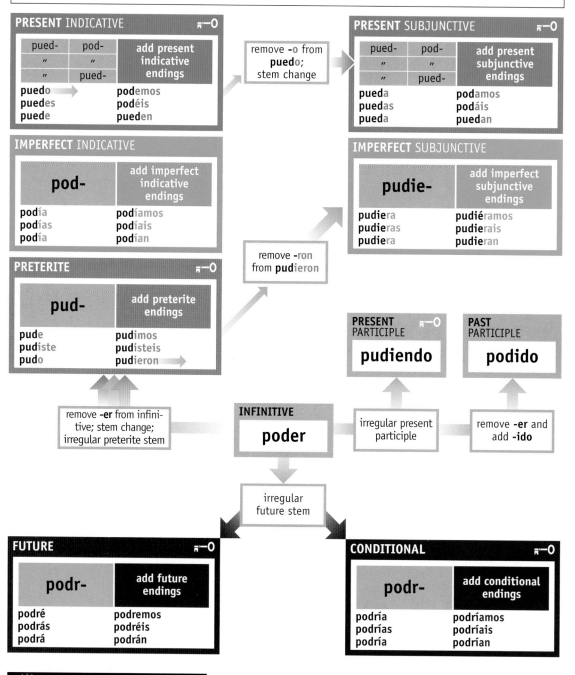

Useful tips

Use **saber** to express the idea of knowing how to do something and use **poder** to convey the idea of being able to do something because circumstances allow: **Sé nadar, pero no puedo nadar en este momento porque me he roto el brazo** (I know how to swim, but I can't swim at the moment because I have broken my arm).

---

haber (in the correct simple tense) **+ past participle**

PERFECT INDICATIVE

present indicative of haber	add past participle
he **podido**	hemos **podido**
has **podido**	habéis **podido**
ha **podido**	han **podido**

PERFECT SUBJUNCTIVE

present subjunctive of haber	add past participle
haya **podido**	hayamos **podido**
hayas **podido**	hayáis **podido**
haya **podido**	hayan **podido**

PLUPERFECT INDICATIVE

imperfect indicative of haber	add past participle
había **podido**	habíamos **podido**
habías **podido**	habíais **podido**
había **podido**	habían **podido**

PAST PARTICIPLE

podido

PLUPERFECT SUBJUNCTIVE

imperfect subjunctive of haber	add past participle
hubiera **podido**	hubiéramos **podido**
hubieras **podido**	hubierais **podido**
hubiera **podido**	hubieran **podido**

FUTURE PERFECT

future of haber	add past participle
habré **podido**	habremos **podido**
habrás **podido**	habréis **podido**
habrá **podido**	habrán **podido**

CONDITIONAL PERFECT

conditional of haber	add past participle
habría **podido**	habríamos **podido**
habrías **podido**	habríais **podido**
habría **podido**	habrían **podido**

❧ Usage examples

Puedo hablar japonés. *I can speak Japanese.*
No puedo creer que Rafael no venga. *I cannot believe that Rafael is not coming.*
¡No puedo evitarlo! *I can't help it!*
Los avestruces no pueden volar. *Ostriches cannot fly.*
No puedes aparcar aquí. *You can't park here.*
Vuelve a casa en cuanto puedas. *Come home as soon as you can.*
No pude terminar los deberes. *I wasn't able to finish the homework.*
No pudimos ir a la fiesta. *We couldn't go to the party.*
No pudieron venir. *They could not come.*
Habría podido ir a la universidad. *I could have gone to university.*

Podríamos ir al cine. *We could go to the cinema.*
No creo que pueda cambiar. *I don't believe I can change.*
¡No puede más! *She can't take any more!*
¿Puedo entrar? *May I come in?*
¿Puede ayudarme, por favor? *Can you help me, please?*
¿Podrías pasarme la sal? *Would you pass me the salt?*
Puedes salir. *You may leave.*
Puede que llueva. *It might rain.*
Puede ser que tengas razón. *You may be right.*
Querer es poder. *Where there's a will, there's a way.*
Saber es poder. *Knowledge is power.*
el poder *power, authority*
poderoso, poderosa *powerful*
el poderío *power, might*

Key points

→ very irregular in 1st person singular of present indicative
→ irregular stem in preterite: **sup-**
→ irregular stem in present subjunctive: **sep-**
→ irregular future stem: **sabr-**

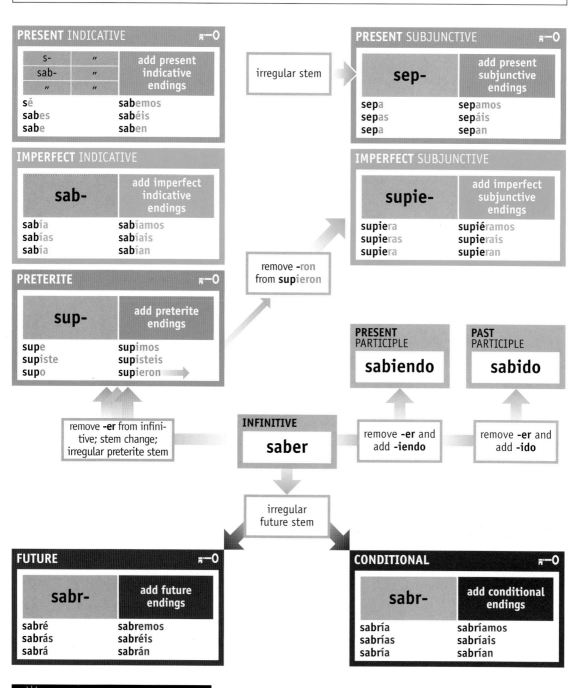

PRESENT INDICATIVE

s-	"	add present
sab-	"	indicative
"	"	endings

sé	sabemos
sabes	sabéis
sabe	saben

irregular stem →

PRESENT SUBJUNCTIVE

sep- add present subjunctive endings

sepa	sepamos
sepas	sepáis
sepa	sepan

IMPERFECT INDICATIVE

sab- add imperfect indicative endings

sabía	sabíamos
sabías	sabíais
sabía	sabían

IMPERFECT SUBJUNCTIVE

supie- add imperfect subjunctive endings

supiera	supiéramos
supieras	supierais
supiera	supieran

remove **-ron** from **sup**ieron

PRETERITE

sup- add preterite endings

supe	supimos
supiste	supisteis
supo	supieron

PRESENT PARTICIPLE
sabiendo

PAST PARTICIPLE
sabido

remove **-er** from infinitive; stem change; irregular preterite stem

INFINITIVE
saber

remove **-er** and add **-iendo**

remove **-er** and add **-ido**

irregular future stem

FUTURE

sabr- add future endings

sabré	sabremos
sabrás	sabréis
sabrá	sabrán

CONDITIONAL

sabr- add conditional endings

sabría	sabríamos
sabrías	sabríais
sabría	sabrían

Useful tips

Saber and **conocer** both mean "to know", but they are used in different contexts. **Saber** is used to express knowledge of a fact or information about something; **conocer** means "to know" in the sense of "to be familiar with".

---

haber (in the correct simple tense) + **past participle**

PERFECT INDICATIVE

present indicative of haber	add past participle
he sabido	hemos sabido
has sabido	habéis sabido
ha sabido	han sabido

PERFECT SUBJUNCTIVE

present subjunctive of haber	add past participle
haya sabido	hayamos sabido
hayas sabido	hayáis sabido
haya sabido	hayan sabido

PLUPERFECT INDICATIVE

imperfect indicative of haber	add past participle
había sabido	habíamos sabido
habías sabido	habíais sabido
había sabido	habían sabido

PAST PARTICIPLE

sabido

PLUPERFECT SUBJUNCTIVE

imperfect subjunctive of haber	add past participle
hubiera sabido	hubiéramos sabido
hubieras sabido	hubierais sabido
hubiera sabido	hubieran sabido

FUTURE PERFECT

future of haber	add past participle
habré sabido	habremos sabido
habrás sabido	habréis sabido
habrá sabido	habrán sabido

CONDITIONAL PERFECT

conditional of haber	add past participle
habría sabido	habríamos sabido
habrías sabido	habríais sabido
habría sabido	habrían sabido

⌇⌇ Usage examples

Lo sé. *I know.*
Saben tu nombre. *They know your name.*
Sabe mucho de historia. *He knows a lot about history.*
Sé tocar el piano. *I know how to play the piano.*
Sabemos conducir. *We know how to drive.*
Mi hermano no sabe nadar. *My brother can't swim.*
No supo qué decir. *She didn't know what to say.*
No sabía que tenía un gato. *I didn't know he had a cat.*
¿Sabías que está embarazada? *Did you know that she was pregnant?*
Sabía que nos perderíamos el juego. *I knew that we would lose the game.*
Sabrás los verbos irregulares de memoria. *You will know the irregular verbs off by heart.*

No sé qué quieres decir. *I don't know what you mean.*
Que yo sepa, habla alemán. *As far as I know, she speaks German.*
Me puse furioso cuando lo supe. *I was furious when I found out.*
¿Cómo lo sabes? *How do you know?*
"Yo sé por qué canta el pájaro enjaulado" (la autobiografía de Maya Angelou) *"I Know Why the Caged Bird Sings" (the autobiography of Maya Angelou)*
saber a algo *to taste of something*
Esta sopa sabe a ajo. *This soup tastes of garlic.*
sabio, sabia *wise, learned*
sabido, sabida *well-known, familiar*
el saber *knowledge*
la sabiduría *wisdom*

Key points

➡ stem changes to **quep-** in 1st person singular of present indicative

➡ irregular stem in preterite: **cup-**
➡ irregular future stem: **cabr-**

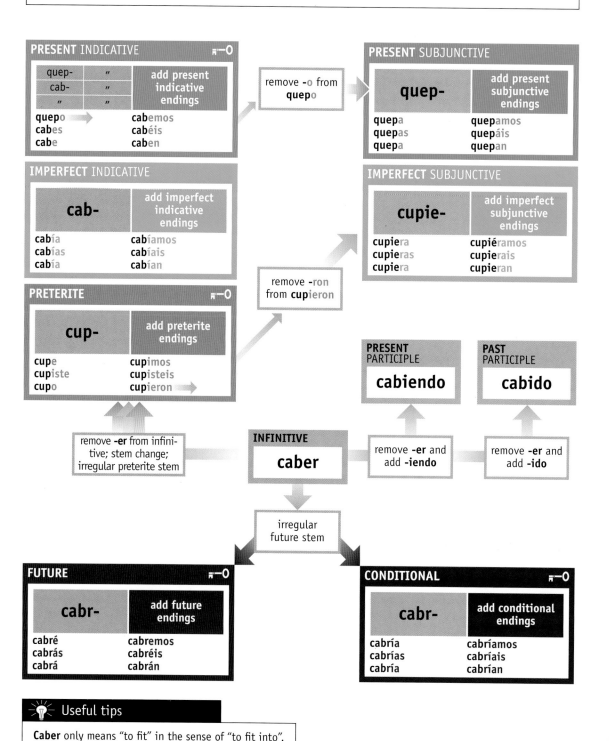

PRESENT INDICATIVE

quep-	"	add present indicative endings
cab-	"	
"	"	

quepo	cabemos
cabes	cabéis
cabe	caben

remove **-o** from **quep**o

PRESENT SUBJUNCTIVE

quep-	add present subjunctive endings

quepa	quepamos
quepas	quepáis
quepa	quepan

IMPERFECT INDICATIVE

cab-	add imperfect indicative endings

cabía	cabíamos
cabías	cabíais
cabía	cabían

IMPERFECT SUBJUNCTIVE

cupie-	add imperfect subjunctive endings

cupiera	cupiéramos
cupieras	cupierais
cupiera	cupieran

remove **-ron** from **cup**ieron

PRETERITE

cup-	add preterite endings

cupe	cupimos
cupiste	cupisteis
cupo	cupieron

PRESENT PARTICIPLE

cabiendo

PAST PARTICIPLE

cabido

remove **-er** from infinitive; stem change; irregular preterite stem

INFINITIVE

caber

remove **-er** and add **-iendo**

remove **-er** and add **-ido**

irregular future stem

FUTURE

cabr-	add future endings

cabré	cabremos
cabrás	cabréis
cabrá	cabrán

CONDITIONAL

cabr-	add conditional endings

cabría	cabríamos
cabrías	cabríais
cabría	cabrían

Useful tips

Caber only means "to fit" in the sense of "to fit into". It cannot be used to refer to the fitting of articles of clothing.

haber (in the correct simple tense) + past participle

PERFECT INDICATIVE

present indicative of haber	add past participle
he **cabido**	hemos **cabido**
has **cabido**	habéis **cabido**
ha **cabido**	han **cabido**

PERFECT SUBJUNCTIVE

present subjunctive of haber	add past participle
haya **cabido**	hayamos **cabido**
hayas **cabido**	hayáis **cabido**
haya **cabido**	hayan **cabido**

PLUPERFECT INDICATIVE

imperfect indicative of haber	add past participle
había **cabido**	habíamos **cabido**
habías **cabido**	habíais **cabido**
había **cabido**	habían **cabido**

PAST PARTICIPLE
cabido

PLUPERFECT SUBJUNCTIVE

imperfect subjunctive of haber	add past participle
hubiera **cabido**	hubiéramos **cabido**
hubieras **cabido**	hubierais **cabido**
hubiera **cabido**	hubieran **cabido**

FUTURE PERFECT

future of haber	add past participle
habré **cabido**	habremos **cabido**
habrás **cabido**	habréis **cabido**
habrá **cabido**	habrán **cabido**

CONDITIONAL PERFECT

conditional of haber	add past participle
habría **cabido**	habríamos **cabido**
habrías **cabido**	habríais **cabido**
habría **cabido**	habrían **cabido**

Usage examples

La cacerola no cabrá en el cajón. *The saucepan won't fit in the draw.*
La maleta habría cabido si tuviéramos un maletero más grande. *The suitcase would have fitted if we had a bigger boot.*
Dudo que el coche quepa en el garaje. *I doubt that the car will fit in the garage.*
El armario no cabe por la puerta. *The wardrobe won't fit through the door.*
¿Quepo yo? *Is there room for me?*
Cabe uno más. *There's room for one more.*
¿Cabe otro en el taxi? *Is there room for one more in the taxi?*
¿Cabremos todos en el coche? *Will we all fit in the car?*

No cabe más. *There's no room for anything else.*
Caben dos litros. *It holds two litres.*
En esta mesa caben cuatro personas. *This table sits four people.*
10 entre 5 cabe a 2. *10 divided by 5 is 2.*
¿Cuántas veces cabe 9 en 81? *How many times does 9 go into 81?*
No cabe duda. *There's no doubt.*
No me cabe en la cabeza. *I don't get it.*
No cabía en sí de gozo. *She was beside herself with joy.*
Cabréis en el ascensor. *You will fit in the lift.*
Las cosas han ido bien, dentro de lo que cabe. *All in all, things have gone well.*
la cabida *capacity; room*

⚷—O Key points

→ **ol** of stem changes to **huel** for stressed syllables in present indicative

→ **huel** of stem reverts to **ol** for unstressed syllables in present subjunctive

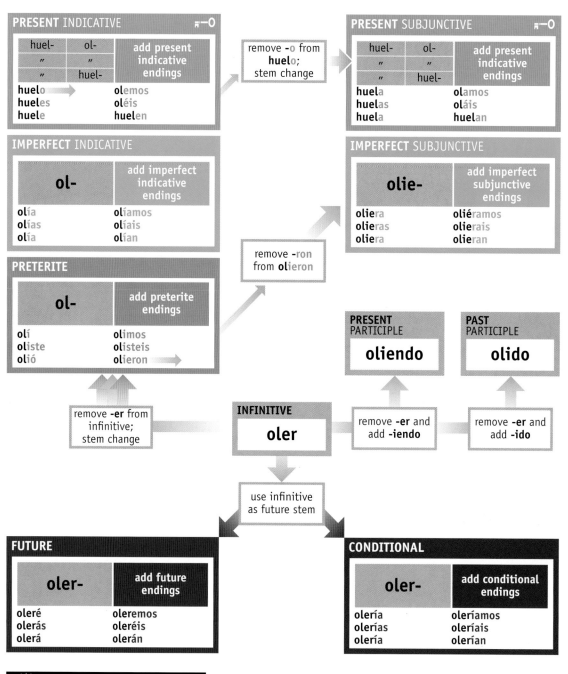

PRESENT INDICATIVE ⚷—O

huel-	ol-	add present indicative endings
"	"	
"	huel-	

huelo	**ol**emos
hueles	**ol**éis
huele	**huel**en

remove **-o** from **huel**o; stem change

PRESENT SUBJUNCTIVE ⚷—O

huel-	ol-	add present indicative endings
"	"	
"	huel-	

huela	**ol**amos
huelas	**ol**áis
huela	**huel**an

IMPERFECT INDICATIVE

ol-	add imperfect indicative endings

olía	**ol**íamos
olías	**ol**íais
olía	**ol**ían

IMPERFECT SUBJUNCTIVE

olie-	add imperfect subjunctive endings

oliera	**olie**ramos
olieras	**olie**rais
oliera	**olie**ran

PRETERITE

ol-	add preterite endings

olí	**ol**imos
oliste	**ol**isteis
olió	**ol**ieron

remove **-ron** from **ol**ieron

PRESENT PARTICIPLE

oliendo

PAST PARTICIPLE

olido

remove **-er** from infinitive; stem change

INFINITIVE

oler

remove **-er** and add **-iendo**

remove **-er** and add **-ido**

use infinitive as future stem

FUTURE

oler-	add future endings

oleré	**oler**emos
olerás	**oler**éis
olerá	**oler**án

CONDITIONAL

oler-	add conditional endings

olería	**oler**íamos
olerías	**oler**íais
olería	**oler**ían

☼ Useful tips

You may expect **oler** to be followed by **de** to mean "to smell of", but this is not the case. **Oler a** is in fact the correct way to say "to smell of".

> ## haber (in the correct simple tense) + past participle

PERFECT INDICATIVE

present indicative of haber	add past participle
he **olido**	hemos **olido**
has **olido**	habéis **olido**
ha **olido**	han **olido**

PERFECT SUBJUNCTIVE

present subjunctive of haber	add past participle
haya **olido**	hayamos **olido**
hayas **olido**	hayáis **olido**
haya **olido**	hayan **olido**

PLUPERFECT INDICATIVE

imperfect indicative of haber	add past participle
había **olido**	habíamos **olido**
habías **olido**	habíais **olido**
había **olido**	habían **olido**

PAST PARTICIPLE

olido

PLUPERFECT SUBJUNCTIVE

imperfect subjunctive of haber	add past participle
hubiera **olido**	hubiéramos **olido**
hubieras **olido**	hubierais **olido**
hubiera **olido**	hubieran **olido**

FUTURE PERFECT

future of haber	add past participle
habré olido	habremos olido
habrás olido	habréis olido
habrá olido	habrán olido

CONDITIONAL PERFECT

conditional of haber	add past participle
habría olido	habríamos olido
habrías olido	habríais olido
habría olido	habrían olido

◤▼ Usage examples

Me gusta oler las flores. *I like to smell the flowers.*
Está oliendo las rosas. *She is smelling the roses.*
Este es el perfume más rico que jamás haya olido. *This is the nicest perfume that I have ever smelled.*
Hemos olido el aire de mar. *We smelled the sea air.*
¡Qué bien huele! *That smells good!*
¡Qué mal huele ese pescado! *That fish smells awful!*
¿A qué huele? *What does it smell like?*
No huele a nada. *It has no smell.*
¿Huele? *Does he smell?*
Oleremos a ajo. *We will smell of garlic.*
¿No hueles a gas? *Can't you smell gas?*
¿Puedes olerlo? *Can you smell it?*
Le olíamos alcohol en el aliento. *We could smell alcohol on his breath.*

El perro olió la maleta. *The dog smelled the suitcase.*
El coche olía a gasolina. *The car smelled of petrol.*
La salsa huele que alimenta. *The sauce smells lovely.*
olerse *to suspect*
No me había olido nada. *I hadn't suspected anything.*
Me huelo algo. *I smell a rat.*
El policía se olió el pastel. *The policeman could smell a rat.*
Me huele que miente. *I suspect he's lying.*
Los animales pueden oler el miedo. *Animals can smell fear.*
(sentido del) olfato *(sense of) smell*
olor *smell*
olor a quemado *smell of burning*
oloroso, olorosa *scented, fragrant*

⚷—O Key points

➜ irregular past participle: **roto**

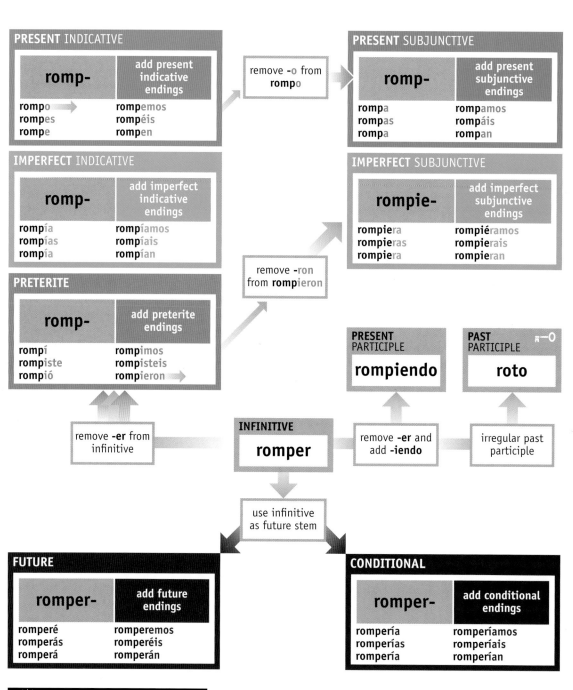

PRESENT INDICATIVE

romp-	add present indicative endings
rompo	rompemos
rompes	rompéis
rompe	rompen

remove **-o** from **romp**o

PRESENT SUBJUNCTIVE

romp-	add present subjunctive endings
rompa	rompamos
rompas	rompáis
rompa	rompan

IMPERFECT INDICATIVE

romp-	add imperfect indicative endings
rompía	rompíamos
rompías	rompíais
rompía	rompían

IMPERFECT SUBJUNCTIVE

rompie-	add imperfect subjunctive endings
rompiera	rompiéramos
rompieras	rompierais
rompiera	rompieran

remove **-ron** from **rompi**eron

PRETERITE

romp-	add preterite endings
rompí	rompimos
rompiste	rompisteis
rompió	rompieron

PRESENT PARTICIPLE

rompiendo

PAST PARTICIPLE   ⚷—O

roto

remove **-er** from infinitive

INFINITIVE

romper

remove **-er** and add **-iendo**

irregular past participle

use infinitive as future stem

FUTURE

romper-	add future endings
romperé	romperemos
romperás	romperéis
romperá	romperán

CONDITIONAL

romper-	add conditional endings
rompería	romperíamos
romperías	romperíais
rompería	romperían

🔆 Useful tips

Although it is not a hard and fast rule, it is worth noting that **romper** is normally used to talk about intentionally breaking something, whereas the reflexive form **romperse** usually refers to breaking something accidentally.

> **haber** (in the correct simple tense) **+ past participle**

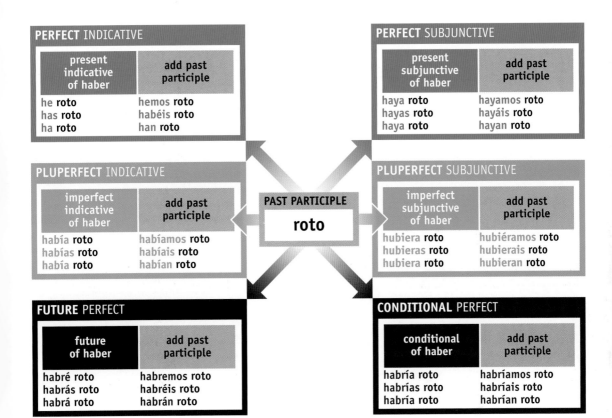

PERFECT INDICATIVE

present indicative of haber	add past participle
he **roto**	hemos **roto**
has **roto**	habéis **roto**
ha **roto**	han **roto**

PERFECT SUBJUNCTIVE

present subjunctive of haber	add past participle
haya **roto**	hayamos **roto**
hayas **roto**	hayáis **roto**
haya **roto**	hayan **roto**

PLUPERFECT INDICATIVE

imperfect indicative of haber	add past participle
había **roto**	habíamos **roto**
habías **roto**	habíais **roto**
había **roto**	habían **roto**

PAST PARTICIPLE
roto

PLUPERFECT SUBJUNCTIVE

imperfect subjunctive of haber	add past participle
hubiera **roto**	hubiéramos **roto**
hubieras **roto**	hubierais **roto**
hubiera **roto**	hubieran **roto**

FUTURE PERFECT

future of haber	add past participle
habré **roto**	habremos **roto**
habrás **roto**	habréis **roto**
habrá **roto**	habrán **roto**

CONDITIONAL PERFECT

conditional of haber	add past participle
habría **roto**	habríamos **roto**
habrías **roto**	habríais **roto**
habría **roto**	habrían **roto**

◥ Usage examples

¿Quién rompió la ventana? *Who broke the window?*
¡Vas a romper la silla! *You're going to break the chair!*
Rompí el florero tirándolo contra la pared. *I broke the vase by throwing it against the wall.*
Ese velocista romperá el record. *That sprinter will break the record.*
Él nunca rompería una promesa. *He would never break a promise.*
No es fácil romper el hielo. *It is not easy to break the ice.*
Quieren que Elena rompa con su novio. *They want Elena to break up with her boyfriend.*
Es hora de que rompamos con una tradición de siglos. *It is time for us to break with a centuries-old tradition.*

Las olas rompen. *The waves are breaking.*
Te veré al romper el alba. *I'll meet you at the crack of dawn.*
Rompimos a reír. *We burst out laughing.*
Rompió a llorar. *She burst into tears.*
romperse *to break, get broken*
¿Cómo se rompió? *How did it break?*
La taza se rompió. *The cup broke.*
Mis gafas se rompieron. *My glasses broke.*
El vaso se rompió. *The glass smashed.*
Me rompí la pierna. *I broke my leg.*
Me he roto el brazo. *I have broken my arm.*
Se rompió el silencio. *The silence was broken.*
roto, rota *broken*
una rotura *breakage*

-ir verbs

➡ -ir verbs are verbs that end in -ir in the infinitive.

⊞—O Key points

➡ this verb follows the regular pattern for **-ir** verbs

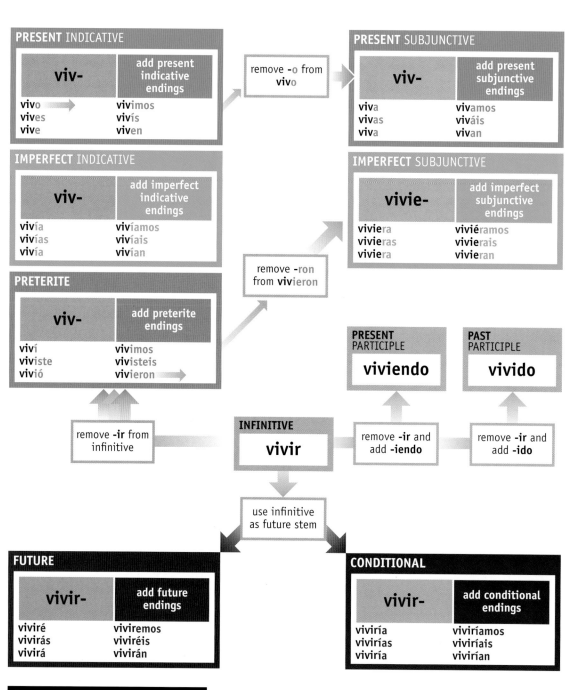

PRESENT INDICATIVE

viv-	add present indicative endings

vivo	vivimos
vives	vivís
vive	viven

remove **-o** from viv**o**

PRESENT SUBJUNCTIVE

viv-	add present subjunctive endings

viva	vivamos
vivas	viváis
viva	vivan

IMPERFECT INDICATIVE

viv-	add imperfect indicative endings

vivía	vivíamos
vivías	vivíais
vivía	vivían

IMPERFECT SUBJUNCTIVE

vivie-	add imperfect subjunctive endings

viviera	viviéramos
vivieras	vivierais
viviera	vivieran

remove **-ron** from viv**ieron**

PRETERITE

viv-	add preterite endings

viví	vivimos
viviste	vivisteis
vivió	vivieron

PRESENT PARTICIPLE
viviendo

PAST PARTICIPLE
vivido

remove **-ir** from infinitive

INFINITIVE
vivir

remove **-ir** and add **-iendo**

remove **-ir** and add **-ido**

use infinitive as future stem

FUTURE

vivir-	add future endings

viviré	viviremos
vivirás	viviréis
vivirá	vivirán

CONDITIONAL

vivir-	add conditional endings

viviría	viviríamos
vivirías	viviríais
viviría	vivirían

🧩 Following the same pattern

añadir *to add*	**interrumpir** *to interrupt*	**recibir** *to receive*
asistir *to attend*	**ocurrir** *to occur*	**subir** *to go up, climb*
discutir *to discuss*	**partir** *to leave*	**sufrir** *to suffer*

haber (in the correct simple tense) + past participle

PERFECT INDICATIVE

present indicative of haber	add past participle
he **vivido**	hemos **vivido**
has **vivido**	habéis **vivido**
ha **vivido**	han **vivido**

PERFECT SUBJUNCTIVE

present subjunctive of haber	add past participle
haya **vivido**	hayamos **vivido**
hayas **vivido**	hayáis **vivido**
haya **vivido**	hayan **vivido**

PLUPERFECT INDICATIVE

imperfect indicative of haber	add past participle
había **vivido**	habíamos **vivido**
habías **vivido**	habíais **vivido**
había **vivido**	habían **vivido**

PAST PARTICIPLE
vivido

PLUPERFECT SUBJUNCTIVE

imperfect subjunctive of haber	add past participle
hubiera **vivido**	hubiéramos **vivido**
hubieras **vivido**	hubierais **vivido**
hubiera **vivido**	hubieran **vivido**

FUTURE PERFECT

future of haber	add past participle
habré vivido	habremos vivido
habrás vivido	habréis vivido
habrá vivido	habrán vivido

CONDITIONAL PERFECT

conditional of haber	add past participle
habría vivido	habríamos vivido
habrías vivido	habríais vivido
habría vivido	habrían vivido

◥◣ Usage examples

¿Dónde vives? *Where do you live?*
Vivimos en los Estados Unidos. *We live in the United States.*
Vivo en un apartamento. *I am living in an apartment.*
Este es un buen sitio para vivir. *This is a nice place to live.*
¿Cuántas personas viven en China? *How many people live in China?*
Mucha gente vive por encima de sus posibilidades. *Many people live beyond their means.*
Viviréis en Roma el año que viene. *You will live in Rome next year.*
Fabio y su mujer Isabel viven en Bilbao. *Fabio and his wife Isabel live in Bilbao.*

Viviríamos en el campo si pudiéramos. *We would live in the countryside if we could.*
Hablaríamos español si viviéramos en España. *We would speak Spanish if we lived in Spain.*
Fernando había vivido feliz hasta que se casó. *Fernando had lived happily until he got married.*
En dos semanas, habré vivido aquí cuatro años. *In two weeks, I will have lived here for four years.*
vivir de algo *to live on something*
Vive de su pensión. *He lives on his pension.*
No daba para vivir. *It was not enough to live on.*
la vida *life*
vivo, viva *alive, living*
en vivo *live (performance)*
"música en vivo" *"live music"*

🔑 Key points

➡ irregular past participle: **escrito**

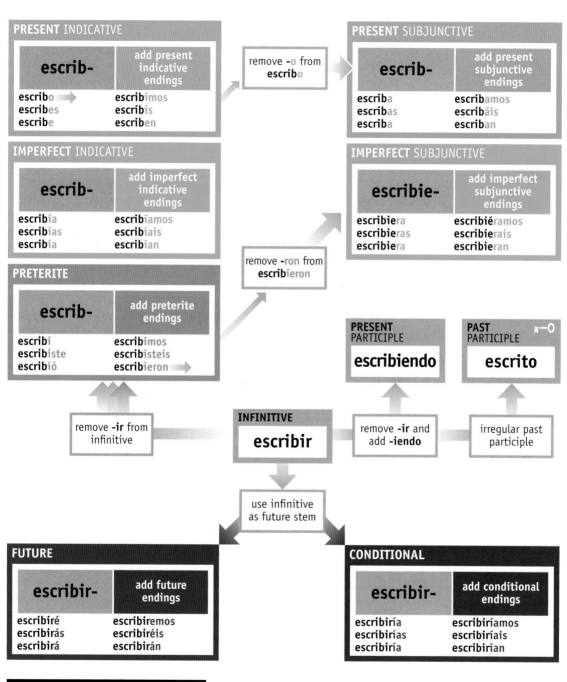

PRESENT INDICATIVE

escrib-	add present indicative endings
escribo	escribimos
escribes	escribís
escribe	escriben

remove -o from **escribo**

PRESENT SUBJUNCTIVE

escrib-	add present subjunctive endings
escriba	escribamos
escribas	escribáis
escriba	escriban

IMPERFECT INDICATIVE

escrib-	add imperfect indicative endings
escribía	escribíamos
escribías	escribíais
escribía	escribían

IMPERFECT SUBJUNCTIVE

escribie-	add imperfect subjunctive endings
escribiera	escribiéramos
escribieras	escribierais
escribiera	escribieran

PRETERITE

escrib-	add preterite endings
escribí	escribimos
escribiste	escribisteis
escribió	escribieron

remove -ron from **escribieron**

PRESENT PARTICIPLE

escribiendo

PAST PARTICIPLE 🔑

escrito

remove -ir from infinitive

INFINITIVE

escribir

remove -ir and add -iendo

irregular past participle

use infinitive as future stem

FUTURE

escribir-	add future endings
escribiré	escribiremos
escribirás	escribiréis
escribirá	escribirán

CONDITIONAL

escribir-	add conditional endings
escribiría	escribiríamos
escribirías	escribiríais
escribiría	escribirían

🧩 Following the same pattern

describir *to describe*
inscribir *to inscribe; to enrol; to register*

suscribir *to sign; to endorse; to subscribe*

-scribir verbs | the compound tenses

> ## haber (in the correct simple tense) + past participle

PERFECT INDICATIVE

present indicative of haber	add past participle
he **escrito**	hemos **escrito**
has **escrito**	habéis **escrito**
ha **escrito**	han **escrito**

PERFECT SUBJUNCTIVE

present subjunctive of haber	add past participle
haya **escrito**	hayamos **escrito**
hayas **escrito**	hayáis **escrito**
haya **escrito**	hayan **escrito**

PLUPERFECT INDICATIVE

imperfect indicative of haber	add past participle
había **escrito**	habíamos **escrito**
habías **escrito**	habíais **escrito**
había **escrito**	habían **escrito**

PAST PARTICIPLE
escrito

PLUPERFECT SUBJUNCTIVE

imperfect subjunctive of haber	add past participle
hubiera **escrito**	hubiéramos **escrito**
hubieras **escrito**	hubierais **escrito**
hubiera **escrito**	hubieran **escrito**

FUTURE PERFECT

future of haber	add past participle
habré **escrito**	habremos **escrito**
habrás **escrito**	habréis **escrito**
habrá **escrito**	habrán **escrito**

CONDITIONAL PERFECT

conditional of haber	add past participle
habría **escrito**	habríamos **escrito**
habrías **escrito**	habríais **escrito**
habría **escrito**	habrían **escrito**

Usage examples

Escribe ella misma sus canciones. *She writes her own songs.*
No había escrito la redacción. *He had not written the essay.*
Mi padre escribe literatura no novelesca. *My father writes non-fiction.*
¿Escribís muchas cartas? *Do you write many letters?*
Estaba escribiendo una carta. *I was writing a letter.*
Escribía poesía en su juventud. *He used to write poetry in his youth.*
Los alumnos tenemos que escribir una redacción por semana. *The pupils have to write one essay a week.*
Habría escrito más si hubiera tenido más tiempo. *I would have written more if I had had more time.*
La novela está bien escrita. *The novel is well written.*

J. R. R. Tolkien escribió "El señor de los anillos". *J. R. R. Tolkien wrote "The Lord of the Rings".*
Fue escrita por Bob Dylan. *It was written by Bob Dylan.*
¿Me escribirás? *Will you write to me?*
Me alegro de que me hayas escrito. *I am glad that you wrote to me.*
escribirse *to write to each other; to be written*
¿Cómo se escribe esa palabra? *How do you spell that word?*
¿Cómo se escribe tu apellido? *How do you spell your surname?*
Los nombres propios se escriben con mayúscula inicial. *Proper nouns are written with a capital letter.*
la escritura *writing; handwriting*
un escritor, una escritora *writer*

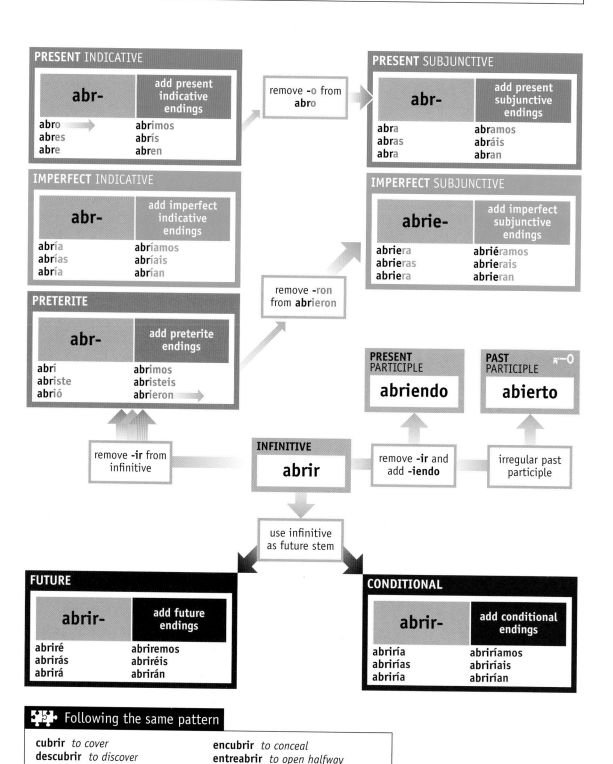 Key points

➡ irregular past participle: **abierto**

PRESENT INDICATIVE

abr-	add present indicative endings
abro	abrimos
abres	abrís
abre	abren

remove **-o** from **abro**

PRESENT SUBJUNCTIVE

abr-	add present subjunctive endings
abra	abramos
abras	abráis
abra	abran

IMPERFECT INDICATIVE

abr-	add imperfect indicative endings
abría	abríamos
abrías	abríais
abría	abrían

IMPERFECT SUBJUNCTIVE

abrie-	add imperfect subjunctive endings
abriera	abriéramos
abrieras	abrierais
abriera	abrieran

remove **-ron** from **abrieron**

PRETERITE

abr-	add preterite endings
abrí	abrimos
abriste	abristeis
abrió	abrieron

PRESENT PARTICIPLE

abriendo

PAST PARTICIPLE

abierto

remove **-ir** from infinitive

INFINITIVE

abrir

remove **-ir** and add **-iendo**

irregular past participle

use infinitive as future stem

FUTURE

abrir-	add future endings
abriré	abriremos
abrirás	abriréis
abrirá	abrirán

CONDITIONAL

abrir-	add conditional endings
abriría	abriríamos
abrirías	abriríais
abriría	abrirían

Following the same pattern

cubrir *to cover*
descubrir *to discover*

encubrir *to conceal*
entreabrir *to open halfway*

---

haber (in the correct simple tense) **+ past participle**

PERFECT INDICATIVE

present indicative of haber	add past participle
he **abierto**	hemos **abierto**
has **abierto**	habéis **abierto**
ha **abierto**	han **abierto**

PERFECT SUBJUNCTIVE

present subjunctive of haber	add past participle
haya **abierto**	hayamos **abierto**
hayas **abierto**	hayáis **abierto**
haya **abierto**	hayan **abierto**

PLUPERFECT INDICATIVE

imperfect indicative of haber	add past participle
había **abierto**	habíamos **abierto**
habías **abierto**	habíais **abierto**
había **abierto**	habían **abierto**

PAST PARTICIPLE

abierto

PLUPERFECT SUBJUNCTIVE

imperfect subjunctive of haber	add past participle
hubiera **abierto**	hubiéramos **abierto**
hubieras **abierto**	hubierais **abierto**
hubiera **abierto**	hubieran **abierto**

FUTURE PERFECT

future of haber	add past participle
habré abierto	habremos abierto
habrás abierto	habréis abierto
habrá abierto	habrán abierto

CONDITIONAL PERFECT

conditional of haber	add past participle
habría abierto	habríamos abierto
habrías abierto	habríais abierto
habría abierto	habrían abierto

◥ Usage examples

¿Quién abrió la puerta? *Who opened the door?*
Esa llave abre el armario. *That key opens the cupboard.*
Quise abrir la ventana. *I tried to open the window.*
Los niños habían abierto todos los regalos para cuando llegamos. *The children had opened all the presents by the time we arrived.*
Los regalos serán abiertos el día de Navidad. *The presents will be opened on Christmas Day.*
Han abierto un nuevo supermercado. *They have opened a new supermarket.*
¿A qué hora abren la farmacia? *What time does the pharmacy open?*
Las tiendas abren a las nueve de la mañana. *The shops open at nine in the morning.*

¿Hay alguna tienda que abra hoy? *Is there any shop that's open today?*
Acabo de abrir una cuenta en el banco. *I have just opened a bank account.*
Dudo que abran un restaurante aquí. *I doubt they will open a restaurant here.*
¿Has abierto el grifo? *Have you turned on the tap?*
abrirse *to open (up)*
De repente, se abrió la puerta. *Suddenly, the door opened.*
abierto, abierta *open*
una mente abierta *an open mind*
abiertamente *openly*
las horas de abrir *opening hours*
apertura *opening*

⌐−O Key points

➡ spelling rule: **g** becomes **j** before **o**

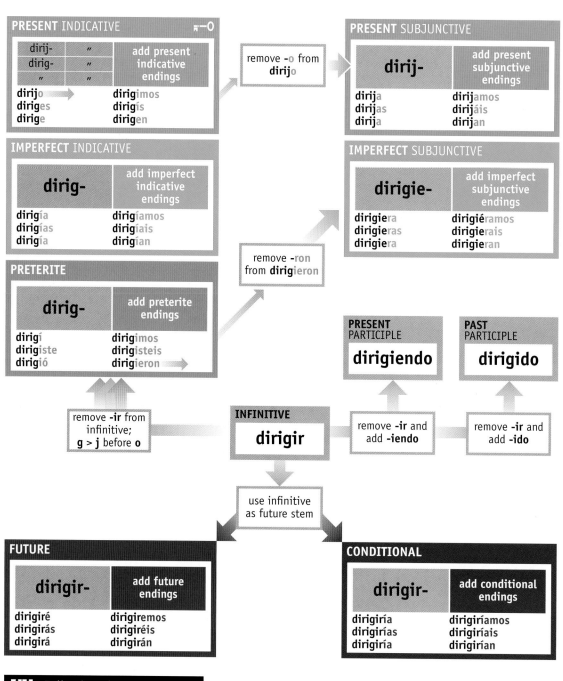

PRESENT INDICATIVE ⌐−O

dirij-	"	add present indicative endings
dirig-	"	
"	"	

dirijo	dirigimos
diriges	dirigís
dirige	dirigen

remove **-o** from **dirij**o

PRESENT SUBJUNCTIVE

| **dirij-** | add present subjunctive endings |

dirija	dirijamos
dirijas	dirijáis
dirija	dirijan

IMPERFECT INDICATIVE

| **dirig-** | add imperfect indicative endings |

dirigía	dirigíamos
dirigías	dirigíais
dirigía	dirigían

IMPERFECT SUBJUNCTIVE

| **dirigie-** | add imperfect subjunctive endings |

dirigiera	dirigiéramos
dirigieras	dirigierais
dirigiera	dirigieran

PRETERITE

| **dirig-** | add preterite endings |

dirigí	dirigimos
dirigiste	dirigisteis
dirigió	dirigieron

remove **-ron** from **dirig**ieron

PRESENT PARTICIPLE

dirigiendo

PAST PARTICIPLE

dirigido

remove **-ir** from infinitive; **g > j** before **o**

INFINITIVE

dirigir

remove **-ir** and add **-iendo**

remove **-ir** and add **-ido**

use infinitive as future stem

FUTURE

| **dirigir-** | add future endings |

dirigiré	dirigiremos
dirigirás	dirigiréis
dirigirá	dirigirán

CONDITIONAL

| **dirigir-** | add conditional endings |

dirigiría	dirigiríamos
dirigirías	dirigiríais
dirigiría	dirigirían

▚▞ Following the same pattern

erigir to build, erect	**restringir** to restrict
exigir to demand	**resurgir** to reappear, revive
fingir to feign, pretend	**surgir** to emerge

---

haber (in the correct simple tense) + **past participle**

PERFECT INDICATIVE

present indicative of haber	add past participle
he dirigido	hemos dirigido
has dirigido	habéis dirigido
ha dirigido	han dirigido

PERFECT SUBJUNCTIVE

present subjunctive of haber	add past participle
haya dirigido	hayamos dirigido
hayas dirigido	hayáis dirigido
haya dirigido	hayan dirigido

PLUPERFECT INDICATIVE

imperfect indicative of haber	add past participle
había dirigido	habíamos dirigido
habías dirigido	habíais dirigido
había dirigido	habían dirigido

PAST PARTICIPLE

dirigido

PLUPERFECT SUBJUNCTIVE

imperfect subjunctive of haber	add past participle
hubiera dirigido	hubiéramos dirigido
hubieras dirigido	hubierais dirigido
hubiera dirigido	hubieran dirigido

FUTURE PERFECT

future of haber	add past participle
habré dirigido	habremos dirigido
habrás dirigido	habréis dirigido
habrá dirigido	habrán dirigido

CONDITIONAL PERFECT

conditional of haber	add past participle
habría dirigido	habríamos dirigido
habrías dirigido	habríais dirigido
habría dirigido	habrían dirigido

Usage examples

Dirige la empresa muy bien. *He manages the business very well.*

Dirijo el departamento de inglés. *I run the English department.*

¿Quién dirige éste negocio? *Who is running this business?*

David dirigirá el proyecto. *David will direct the project.*

Le dirigí la mirada. *I looked at him.*

La carta estaba dirigida a ti. *The letter was addressed to you.*

Nos dirigimos a ustedes para invitarles a nuestra conferencia anual. *We are writing to invite you to our annual conference.*

Dirigieron las fuerzas móviles al lugar exacto. *They guided the emergency services to the right location.*

La película fue escrita y dirigida por Woody Allen. *The film was written and directed by Woody Allen.*

dirigirse *to go to; to speak to*

¿A dónde te diriges? *Where are you going?*

Me dirigía a casa cuando le vi. *I was on my way home when I saw him.*

El camping al que se dirigieron estaba muy lejos. *The campsite that they went to was really far away.*

¿Se dirige usted a mí? *Are you addressing me?*

Se dirigieron a mí. *They addressed me.*

No se ha dirigido a mí en toda la mañana. *He hasn't said a word to me all morning.*

el/la dirigente *leader*

dirigente *leading*

las clases dirigentes *ruling classes*

Key points

→ spelling rule: **gu** becomes **g** before **o**

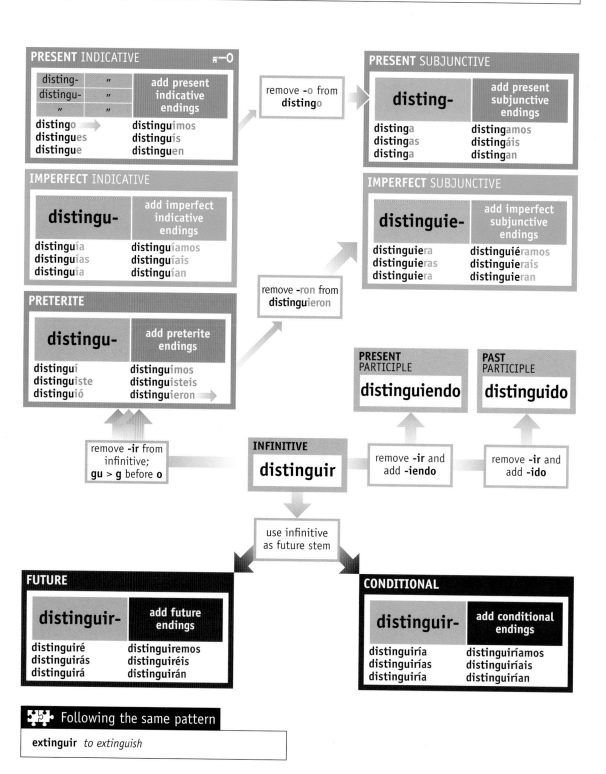

PRESENT INDICATIVE

disting-	"	add present indicative endings
distingu-	"	
"	"	

distingo → distinguimos
distingues   distinguís
distingue   distinguen

remove **-o** from
distingo

PRESENT SUBJUNCTIVE

| **disting-** | add present subjunctive endings |

distinga   distingamos
distingas   distingáis
distinga   distingan

IMPERFECT INDICATIVE

| **distingu-** | add imperfect indicative endings |

distinguía   distinguíamos
distinguías   distinguíais
distinguía   distinguían

IMPERFECT SUBJUNCTIVE

| **distinguie-** | add imperfect subjunctive endings |

distinguiera   distinguiéramos
distinguieras   distinguierais
distinguiera   distinguieran

remove **-ron** from
distinguieron

PRETERITE

| **distingu-** | add preterite endings |

distinguí   distinguimos
distinguiste   distinguisteis
distinguió → distinguieron

PRESENT PARTICIPLE

distinguiendo

PAST PARTICIPLE

distinguido

remove **-ir** from
infinitive;
gu > g before **o**

INFINITIVE

distinguir

remove **-ir** and
add **-iendo**

remove **-ir** and
add **-ido**

use infinitive
as future stem

FUTURE

| **distinguir-** | add future endings |

distinguiré   distinguiremos
distinguirás   distinguiréis
distinguirá   distinguirán

CONDITIONAL

| **distinguir-** | add conditional endings |

distinguiría   distinguiríamos
distinguirías   distinguiríais
distinguiría   distinguirían

Following the same pattern

extinguir to extinguish

> **haber** (in the correct simple tense) **+ past participle**

PERFECT INDICATIVE

present indicative of haber	add past participle
he **distinguido**	hemos **distinguido**
has **distinguido**	habéis **distinguido**
ha **distinguido**	han **distinguido**

PERFECT SUBJUNCTIVE

present subjunctive of haber	add past participle
haya **distinguido**	hayamos **distinguido**
hayas **distinguido**	hayáis **distinguido**
haya **distinguido**	hayan **distinguido**

PLUPERFECT INDICATIVE

imperfect indicative of haber	add past participle
había **distinguido**	habíamos **distinguido**
habías **distinguido**	habíais **distinguido**
había **distinguido**	habían **distinguido**

PAST PARTICIPLE
distinguido

PLUPERFECT SUBJUNCTIVE

imperfect subjunctive of haber	add past participle
hubiera **distinguido**	hubiéramos **distinguido**
hubieras **distinguido**	hubierais **distinguido**
hubiera **distinguido**	hubieran **distinguido**

FUTURE PERFECT

future of haber	add past participle
habré **distinguido**	habremos **distinguido**
habrás **distinguido**	habréis **distinguido**
habrá **distinguido**	habrán **distinguido**

CONDITIONAL PERFECT

conditional of haber	add past participle
habría **distinguido**	habríamos **distinguido**
habrías **distinguido**	habríais **distinguido**
habría **distinguido**	habrían **distinguido**

Usage examples

La ley distingue entre parejas casadas y las que no lo están. *The law distinguishes between married and unmarried couples.*

Los gemelos son tan parecidos que es difícil distinguir a uno del otro. *The twins are so alike that it is difficult to tell one from the other.*

No pude distinguir cuál era el original. *I couldn't tell which was the original.*

Apenas puedo distinguir el perfil de la ciudad por la niebla. *I can hardly make out the city's profile in the fog.*

Los consumidores no distinguirán entre los dos productos. *The consumers will not distinguish between the two products.*

No distingue entre el verde y el rojo. *He cannot distinguish between green and red.*

Los daltónicos no distinguen bien los colores. *The colour-blind cannot correctly distinguish between colours.*

A lo lejos se distingue el castillo. *The castle can be made out in the distance.*

¿Cómo distinguir entre el bien y el mal? *How can one distinguish between good and evil?*

Su humildad le distingue de los demás políticos. *His humility sets him apart from other politicians.*

distinguirse *to distinguish oneself*
distinguido, distinguida *distinguished*
la distinción *distinction*
distintivo, distintiva *distinctive*
Distinguí a mi padre en todas las fotos. *I picked out my father in all of the photos.*

⚷—O Key points

➔ spelling rule: add **y** to stem before **o** or **e**   ➔ add the ending **-yendo** for present participle

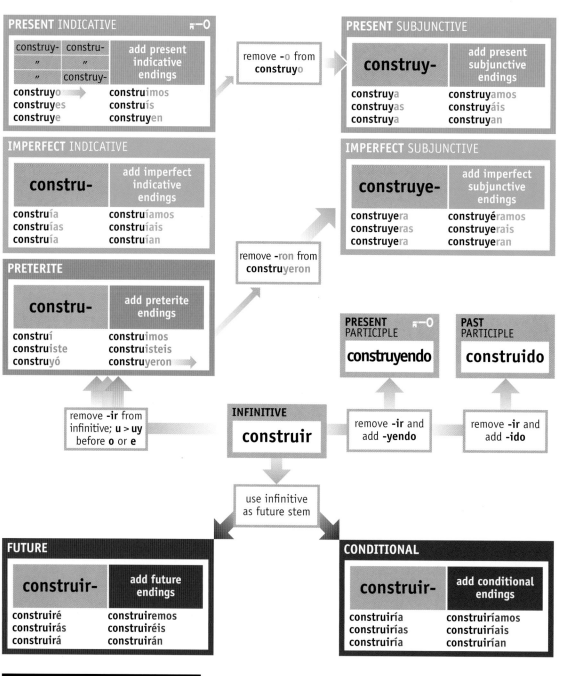

PRESENT INDICATIVE   ⚷—O

construy-	constru-	add present indicative endings
"	"	
"	construy-	

construyo	construimos
construyes	construís
construye	construyen

remove **-o** from **construyo**

PRESENT SUBJUNCTIVE

construy-	add present subjunctive endings

construya	construyamos
construyas	construyáis
construya	construyan

IMPERFECT INDICATIVE

constru-	add imperfect indicative endings

construía	construíamos
construías	construíais
construía	construían

IMPERFECT SUBJUNCTIVE

construye-	add imperfect subjunctive endings

construyera	construyéramos
construyeras	construyerais
construyera	construyeran

remove **-ron** from **construyeron**

PRETERITE

constru-	add preterite endings

construí	construimos
construiste	construisteis
construyó	construyeron

PRESENT PARTICIPLE   ⚷—O

construyendo

PAST PARTICIPLE

construido

remove **-ir** from infinitive; **u > uy** before **o** or **e**

INFINITIVE

construir

remove **-ir** and add **-yendo**

remove **-ir** and add **-ido**

use infinitive as future stem

FUTURE

construir-	add future endings

construiré	construiremos
construirás	construiréis
construirá	construirán

CONDITIONAL

construir-	add conditional endings

construiría	construiríamos
construirías	construiríais
construiría	construirían

🧩 Following the same pattern

concluir to conclude	**destruir** to destroy	**incluir** to include
constituir to constitute	**disminuir** to decrease; to reduce	**influir** to influence
contribuir to contribute	**huir** to run away; to avoid	**sustituir** to replace, substitute

---

haber (in the correct simple tense) **+ past participle**

PERFECT INDICATIVE

present indicative of haber	add past participle
he **construido**	hemos **construido**
has **construido**	habéis **construido**
ha **construido**	han **construido**

PERFECT SUBJUNCTIVE

present subjunctive of haber	add past participle
haya **construido**	hayamos **construido**
hayas **construido**	hayáis **construido**
haya **construido**	hayan **construido**

PLUPERFECT INDICATIVE

imperfect indicative of haber	add past participle
había **construido**	habíamos **construido**
habías **construido**	habíais **construido**
había **construido**	habían **construido**

PAST PARTICIPLE
construido

PLUPERFECT SUBJUNCTIVE

imperfect subjunctive of haber	add past participle
hubiera **construido**	hubiéramos **construido**
hubieras **construido**	hubierais **construido**
hubiera **construido**	hubieran **construido**

FUTURE PERFECT

future of haber	add past participle
habré **construido**	habremos **construido**
habrás **construido**	habréis **construido**
habrá **construido**	habrán **construido**

CONDITIONAL PERFECT

conditional of haber	add past participle
habría **construido**	habríamos **construido**
habrías **construido**	habríais **construido**
habría **construido**	habrían **construido**

◥◣ Usage examples

Noé construyó un arca. *Noah built an ark.*

Quiero construir una casa de muñecas. *I want to build a doll's house.*

Están construyendo un rascacielos. *They are building a skyscraper.*

¿Cuánto tiempo habían estado construyendo la casa? *How long had they been building the house?*

Llevan dos años construyendo el puente. *They have been building the bridge for two years.*

Van a construir un centro comercial en la ciudad. *They are going to build a shopping centre in the city.*

Estoy construyendo un sitio web. *I am building a website.*

Hizo construir un palacio en Estambul. *He had a palace built in Istanbul.*

Estaba construyendo un cobertizo cuando empezó a llover. *I was building a shed when it started to rain.*

Cuando ella volvió a casa, ya había construido el muro. *When she returned home, he'd already built the wall.*

Lo habría construido sin planos. *I would have built it without any plans.*

Construiría la frase de otra forma. *I would construct this sentence in another way.*

la construcción *construction, building*

la construcción naval *shipbuilding*

en construcción *under construction*

un constructor, una constructora *builder*

constructivo, constructiva *constructive*

un constructo *construct*

Key points

→ spelling rule: **c** becomes **zc** before **o**

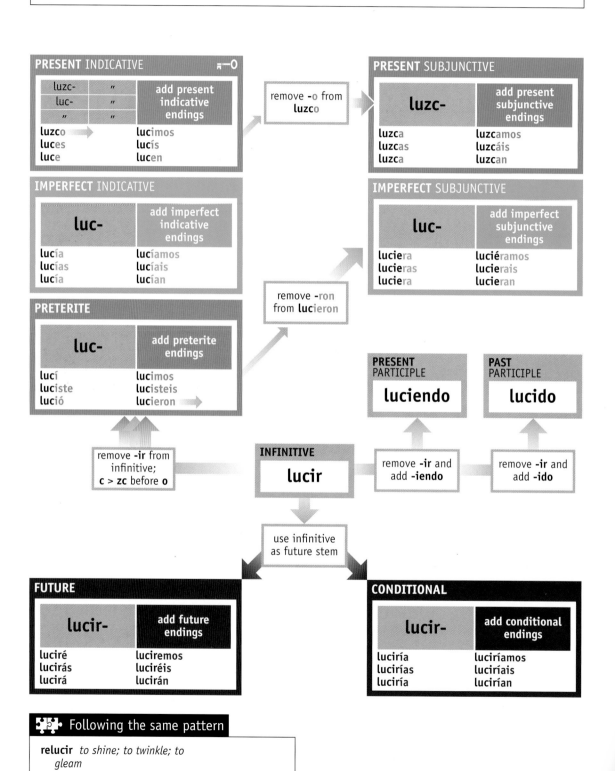

PRESENT INDICATIVE

luzc-	"	add present indicative endings
luc-	"	
"	"	

luzco	lucimos
luces	lucís
luce	lucen

remove **-o** from **luzco**

PRESENT SUBJUNCTIVE

| **luzc-** | add present subjunctive endings |

luzca	luzcamos
luzcas	luzcáis
luzca	luzcan

IMPERFECT INDICATIVE

| **luc-** | add imperfect indicative endings |

lucía	lucíamos
lucías	lucíais
lucía	lucían

IMPERFECT SUBJUNCTIVE

| **luc-** | add imperfect subjunctive endings |

luciera	luciéramos
lucieras	lucierais
luciera	lucieran

remove **-ron** from **lucieron**

PRETERITE

| **luc-** | add preterite endings |

lucí	lucimos
luciste	lucisteis
lució	lucieron

PRESENT PARTICIPLE

luciendo

PAST PARTICIPLE

lucido

remove **-ir** from infinitive; **c > zc** before **o**

INFINITIVE

lucir

remove **-ir** and add **-iendo**

remove **-ir** and add **-ido**

use infinitive as future stem

FUTURE

| **lucir-** | add future endings |

luciré	luciremos
lucirás	luciréis
lucirá	lucirán

CONDITIONAL

| **lucir-** | add conditional endings |

luciría	luciríamos
lucirías	luciríais
luciría	lucirían

Following the same pattern

relucir to shine; to twinkle; to gleam

haber (in the correct simple tense) + **past participle**

PERFECT INDICATIVE

present indicative of haber	add past participle
he **lucido**	hemos **lucido**
has **lucido**	habéis **lucido**
ha **lucido**	han **lucido**

PERFECT SUBJUNCTIVE

present subjunctive of haber	add past participle
haya **lucido**	hayamos **lucido**
hayas **lucido**	hayáis **lucido**
haya **lucido**	hayan **lucido**

PLUPERFECT INDICATIVE

imperfect indicative of haber	add past participle
había **lucido**	habíamos **lucido**
habías **lucido**	habíais **lucido**
había **lucido**	habían **lucido**

PAST PARTICIPLE

lucido

PLUPERFECT SUBJUNCTIVE

imperfect subjunctive of haber	add past participle
hubiera **lucido**	hubiéramos **lucido**
hubieras **lucido**	hubierais **lucido**
hubiera **lucido**	hubieran **lucido**

FUTURE PERFECT

future of haber	add past participle
habré **lucido**	habremos **lucido**
habrás **lucido**	habréis **lucido**
habrá **lucido**	habrán **lucido**

CONDITIONAL PERFECT

conditional of haber	add past participle
habría **lucido**	habríamos **lucido**
habrías **lucido**	habríais **lucido**
habría **lucido**	habrían **lucido**

◥▶ Usage examples

Era una noche hermosa y las estrellas lucían. *It was a beautiful night and the stars were shining.*

Las flores lucirían mucho más en la sala de estar. *The flowers would look much better in the living room.*

La corbata luce más con esta camisa. *The tie looks better with this shirt.*

No luce nada. *It doesn't look very good.*

La novia lucirá un vestido blanco. *The bride will wear a white dress.*

Lucía una chaqueta azul. *He was sporting a blue jacket.*

Quiero lucir mi nuevo vestido. *I want to show off my new dress.*

Es una lástima que no haya lucido en los estudios. *It is a pity he did not excel as a student.*

En circunstancias diferentes habría lucido en las elecciones. *In different circumstances, I would have excelled in the elections.*

Podrás lucir el cuerpo que siempre has soñado. *You will be able to show off the body that you have always dreamed of.*

lucirse *to excel oneself*

Se lució en el examen. *He excelled himself in the exam.*

¡Te has lucido! *You've really outdone yourself!*

lucido, lucida *magnificent, splendid*

lúcido, lúcida *lucid*

luciente *bright, shining*

una luz *light; electricity*

el lucimiento *brilliance, sparkle*

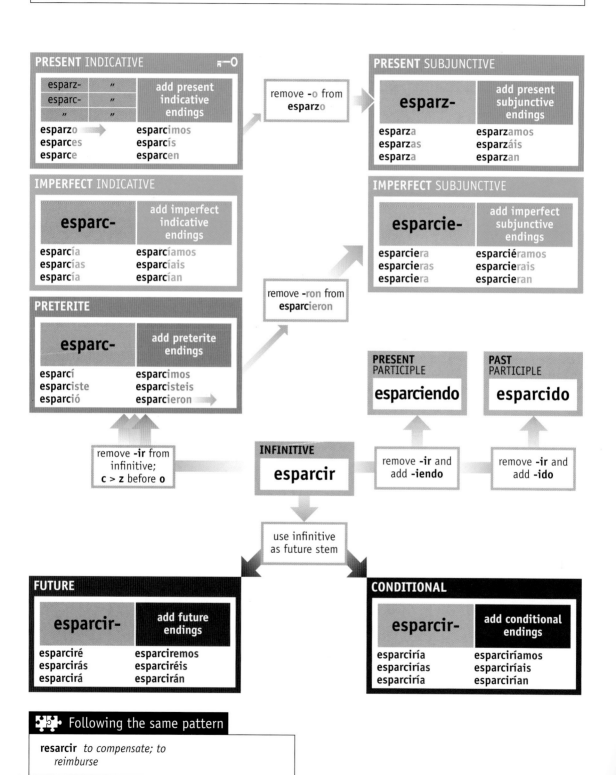

⚷—O Key points

➡ spelling rule: **c** becomes **z** before **o**

PRESENT INDICATIVE   ⚷—O

esparz-	"	add present
esparc-	"	indicative
"	"	endings

esparzo →	esparcimos
esparces	esparcís
esparce	esparcen

remove **-o** from **esparzo**

PRESENT SUBJUNCTIVE

| **esparz-** | add present subjunctive endings |

esparza	esparzamos
esparzas	esparzáis
esparza	esparzan

IMPERFECT INDICATIVE

| **esparc-** | add imperfect indicative endings |

esparcía	esparcíamos
esparcías	esparcíais
esparcía	esparcían

IMPERFECT SUBJUNCTIVE

| **esparcie-** | add imperfect subjunctive endings |

esparciera	esparciéramos
esparcieras	esparcierais
esparciera	esparcieran

remove **-ron** from **esparcieron**

PRETERITE

| **esparc-** | add preterite endings |

esparcí	esparcimos
esparciste	esparcisteis
esparció	esparcieron →

remove **-ir** from infinitive; **c > z** before **o**

INFINITIVE

esparcir

PRESENT PARTICIPLE

esparciendo

remove **-ir** and add **-iendo**

PAST PARTICIPLE

esparcido

remove **-ir** and add **-ido**

use infinitive as future stem

FUTURE

| **esparcir-** | add future endings |

esparciré	esparciremos
esparcirás	esparciréis
esparcirá	esparcirán

CONDITIONAL

| **esparcir-** | add conditional endings |

esparciría	esparciríamos
esparcirías	esparciríais
esparciría	esparcirían

🧩 Following the same pattern

resarcir to compensate; to reimburse

---

haber (in the correct simple tense) + past participle

PERFECT INDICATIVE

present indicative of haber	add past participle
he **esparcido**	hemos **esparcido**
has **esparcido**	habéis **esparcido**
ha **esparcido**	han **esparcido**

PERFECT SUBJUNCTIVE

present subjunctive of haber	add past participle
haya **esparcido**	hayamos **esparcido**
hayas **esparcido**	hayáis **esparcido**
haya **esparcido**	hayan **esparcido**

PLUPERFECT INDICATIVE

imperfect indicative of haber	add past participle
había **esparcido**	habíamos **esparcido**
habías **esparcido**	habíais **esparcido**
había **esparcido**	habían **esparcido**

PAST PARTICIPLE
esparcido

PLUPERFECT SUBJUNCTIVE

imperfect subjunctive of haber	add past participle
hubiera **esparcido**	hubiéramos **esparcido**
hubieras **esparcido**	hubierais **esparcido**
hubiera **esparcido**	hubieran **esparcido**

FUTURE PERFECT

future of haber	add past participle
habré **esparcido**	habremos **esparcido**
habrás **esparcido**	habréis **esparcido**
habrá **esparcido**	habrán **esparcido**

CONDITIONAL PERFECT

conditional of haber	add past participle
habría **esparcido**	habríamos **esparcido**
habrías **esparcido**	habríais **esparcido**
habría **esparcido**	habrían **esparcido**

◥ Usage examples

Esparcí las semillas en el jardín. *I scattered the seeds in the garden.*

El agricultor esparcía las semillas en el campo. *The farmer was sowing the seeds in the field.*

El viento ha esparcido los pétalos. *The wind has scattered the petals.*

Esparciría arena por el suelo. *I would scatter sand on the floor.*

Dedicó su vida a esparcir la palabra de Dios. *She devoted her life to spreading the word of God.*

Esparcimos sus cenizas en el parque. *We scattered her ashes in the park.*

Las cenizas del dramaturgo se esparcirán en la Bahía de Cádiz. *The playwright's ashes will be scattered in the Bay of Cádiz.*

esparcirse *to be scattered, be spread; to relax, enjoy oneself*

El cólera se esparció por todo el barrio bajo. *Cholera spread throughout the slum.*

Los rumores se esparcieron por toda la aldea. *The rumours spread throughout the village.*

Ojalá que no esparcieras rumores. *I wish you would not spread rumours.*

La noticia se esparció como un reguero de pólvora. *The news spread like wildfire.*

Los periódicos se encargan de esparcir la noticia. *The newspapers are responsible for spreading the news.*

La marea negra se está esparciendo rápidamente. *The oil slick is spreading rapidly.*

el esparcimiento *spreading; relaxation, recreation*

⌐—O Key points

→ spelling rule: **c** becomes **zc** before **o**

→ irregular stem in preterite: **conduj-**

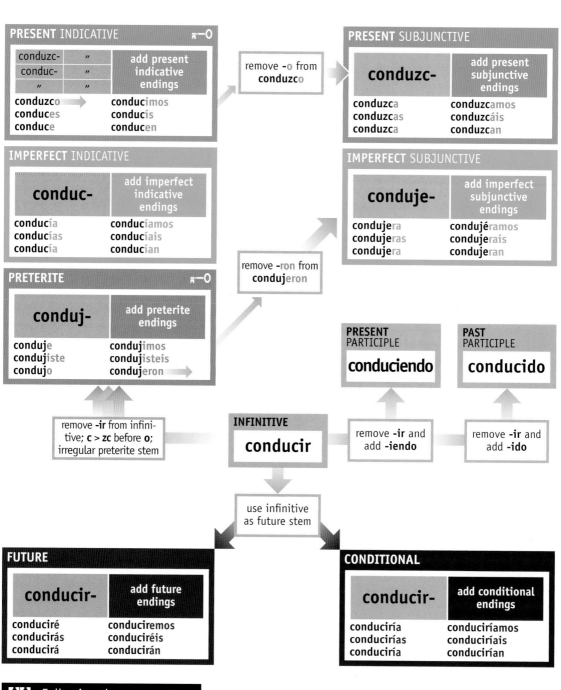

PRESENT INDICATIVE   ⌐—O

conduzc-	"	add present indicative endings
conduc-	"	
"	"	

conduzco →	conducimos
conduces	conducís
conduce	conducen

remove **-o** from **conduzco**

PRESENT SUBJUNCTIVE

| conduzc- | add present subjunctive endings |

conduzca	conduzcamos
conduzcas	conduzcáis
conduzca	conduzcan

IMPERFECT INDICATIVE

| conduc- | add imperfect indicative endings |

conducía	conducíamos
conducías	conducíais
conducía	conducían

IMPERFECT SUBJUNCTIVE

| conduje- | add imperfect subjunctive endings |

condujera	condujéramos
condujeras	condujerais
condujera	condujeran

remove **-ron** from **condujeron**

PRETERITE   ⌐—O

| conduj- | add preterite endings |

conduje	condujimos
condujiste	condujisteis
condujo	condujeron →

PRESENT PARTICIPLE

conduciendo

PAST PARTICIPLE

conducido

remove **-ir** from infinitive; **c > zc** before **o**; irregular preterite stem

INFINITIVE

conducir

remove **-ir** and add **-iendo**

remove **-ir** and add **-ido**

use infinitive as future stem

FUTURE

| conducir- | add future endings |

conduciré	conduciremos
conducirás	conduciréis
conducirá	conducirán

CONDITIONAL

| conducir- | add conditional endings |

conduciría	conduciríamos
conducirías	conduciríais
conduciría	conducirían

⁙ Following the same pattern

deducir to deduce	**producir** to produce	**reproducir** to reproduce
inducir to induce	**reconducir** to bring back	**seducir** to seduce
introducir to introduce	**reducir** to reduce	**traducir** to translate

> # haber (in the correct simple tense) + past participle

PERFECT INDICATIVE

present indicative of haber	add past participle
he **conducido**	hemos **conducido**
has **conducido**	habéis **conducido**
ha **conducido**	han **conducido**

PERFECT SUBJUNCTIVE

present subjunctive of haber	add past participle
haya **conducido**	hayamos **conducido**
hayas **conducido**	hayáis **conducido**
haya **conducido**	hayan **conducido**

PLUPERFECT INDICATIVE

imperfect indicative of haber	add past participle
había **conducido**	habíamos **conducido**
habías **conducido**	habíais **conducido**
había **conducido**	habían **conducido**

PAST PARTICIPLE
conducido

PLUPERFECT SUBJUNCTIVE

imperfect subjunctive of haber	add past participle
hubiera **conducido**	hubiéramos **conducido**
hubieras **conducido**	hubierais **conducido**
hubiera **conducido**	hubieran **conducido**

FUTURE PERFECT

future of haber	add past participle
habré **conducido**	habremos **conducido**
habrás **conducido**	habréis **conducido**
habrá **conducido**	habrán **conducido**

CONDITIONAL PERFECT

conditional of haber	add past participle
habría **conducido**	habríamos **conducido**
habrías **conducido**	habríais **conducido**
habría **conducido**	habrían **conducido**

Usage examples

Conduce muy bien. *She drives very well.*

Juan conduce rápido. *Juan drives fast.*

No sé conducir. *I can't drive.*

Suelo conducir al trabajo. *I usually drive to work.*

Conducirá el camión hasta Londres. *He will drive the lorry to London.*

Si hubiera hecho calor, habríamos conducido a la playa. *If the weather had been hot, we would have driven to the beach.*

A las seis, habrán conducido cuatro horas sin parar. *By six o'clock, they will have driven for four hours straight.*

Iba conduciendo un coche deportivo cuando lo vi. *He was driving a sports car when I saw him.*

Conduciremos con cuidado. *We will drive carefully.*

Le pedimos que no condujera tan rápido. *We asked him not to drive so fast.*

Esta calle conduce al cementerio. *This road leads to the cemetery.*

Condujo el partido a la victoria en las elecciones. *He led the party to victory in the elections.*

El cobre conduce la electricidad. *Copper conducts electricity.*

un conductor, una conductora *driver; host, presenter*

la conducción *driving*

la conducta *behaviour, conduct*

conductual *behavioural*

un conducto *duct, tube; pipe, conduit*

un permiso de conducir *driving licence*

un examen de conducir *driving test*

⌐−O Key points

→ **i** of stem changes to **ie** for stressed syllables in present indicative

→ **ie** of stem reverts to **i** for unstressed syllables in present subjunctive

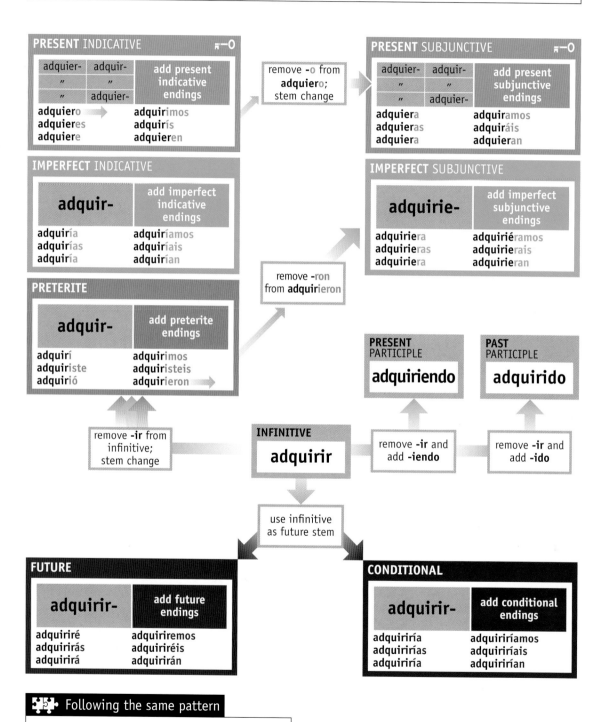

PRESENT INDICATIVE ⌐−O

adquier-	adquir-	add present indicative endings
"	"	
"	adquier-	

adquiero → adquirimos
adquieres adquirís
adquiere adquieren

PRESENT SUBJUNCTIVE ⌐−O

remove **-o** from **adquiero**; stem change

adquier-	adquir-	add present subjunctive endings
"	"	
"	adquier-	

adquiera adquiramos
adquieras adquiráis
adquiera adquieran

IMPERFECT INDICATIVE

adquir-	add imperfect indicative endings

adquiría adquiríamos
adquirías adquiríais
adquiría adquirían

IMPERFECT SUBJUNCTIVE

adquirie-	add imperfect subjunctive endings

adquiriera adquiriéramos
adquirieras adquirierais
adquiriera adquirieran

remove **-ron** from **adquirieron**

PRETERITE

adquir-	add preterite endings

adquirí adquirimos
adquiriste adquiristeis
adquirió adquirieron →

PRESENT PARTICIPLE

adquiriendo

PAST PARTICIPLE

adquirido

remove **-ir** from infinitive; stem change

INFINITIVE

adquirir

remove **-ir** and add **-iendo**

remove **-ir** and add **-ido**

use infinitive as future stem

FUTURE

adquirir-	add future endings

adquiriré adquiriremos
adquirirás adquiriréis
adquirirá adquirirán

CONDITIONAL

adquirir-	add conditional endings

adquiriría adquiriríamos
adquirirías adquiriríais
adquiriría adquirirían

🧩 Following the same pattern

inquirir to investigate, look into; to inquire

---

haber (in the correct simple tense) **+ past participle**

PERFECT INDICATIVE

present indicative of haber	add past participle
he adquirido	hemos adquirido
has adquirido	habéis adquirido
ha adquirido	han adquirido

PERFECT SUBJUNCTIVE

present subjunctive of haber	add past participle
haya adquirido	hayamos adquirido
hayas adquirido	hayáis adquirido
haya adquirido	hayan adquirido

PLUPERFECT INDICATIVE

imperfect indicative of haber	add past participle
había adquirido	habíamos adquirido
habías adquirido	habíais adquirido
había adquirido	habían adquirido

PAST PARTICIPLE

adquirido

PLUPERFECT SUBJUNCTIVE

imperfect subjunctive of haber	add past participle
hubiera adquirido	hubiéramos adquirido
hubieras adquirido	hubierais adquirido
hubiera adquirido	hubieran adquirido

FUTURE PERFECT

future of haber	add past participle
habré adquirido	habremos adquirido
habrás adquirido	habréis adquirido
habrá adquirido	habrán adquirido

CONDITIONAL PERFECT

conditional of haber	add past participle
habría adquirido	habríamos adquirido
habrías adquirido	habríais adquirido
habría adquirido	habrían adquirido

Usage examples

Adquirió una propiedad en Francia. *He purchased a property in France.*

Lo adquiriría por ese precio. *I would buy it for that price.*

La corporación adquirió una participación del 30% en una compañía naviera. *The corporation acquired a 30% stake in a shipping company.*

Poco a poco la alumna adquiría confianza. *The student was gradually gaining confidence.*

Si adquiero más experiencia, podré conseguir un empleo mejor. *If I gain more experience, I will be able to get a better job.*

Adquirirá mucha experiencia durante la formación. *She will acquire a lot of experience during the training.*

Es importante que los estudiantes adquieran nuevas habilidades. *It is important that the students acquire new skills.*

El futbolista ha adquirido renombre en los últimos años. *The footballer has attained international renown in recent years.*

El sector público ha adquirido gran importancia en la economía nacional. *The public sector has taken on great importance in the national economy.*

el adquisidor, la adquisidora *buyer, purchaser*

la adquisición *acquisition, purchase*

la adquisición de la lengua *language acquisition*

adquisidor, adquisidora *acquisitive*

No estamos en condiciones de adquirir la franquicia. *We are not in a position to buy the franchise.*

🔑─O Key points

➜ **e** of stem changes to **i** for stressed syllables in present indicative

➜ stem changes to **pid-** in 3rd person of preterite
➜ irregular present participle: **pidiendo**

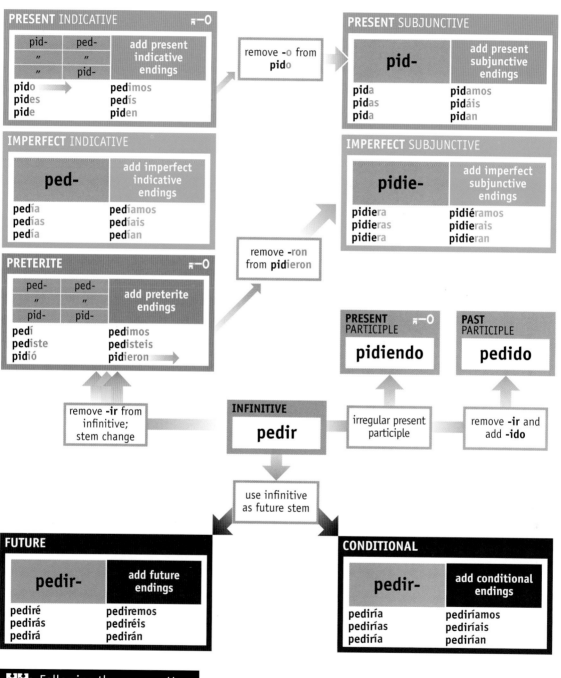

PRESENT INDICATIVE 🔑─O

pid-	ped-	add present indicative endings
"	"	
"	pid-	

pido	pedimos
pides	pedís
pide	piden

PRESENT SUBJUNCTIVE

remove **-o** from **pid**o

pid-	add present subjunctive endings

pida	pidamos
pidas	pidáis
pida	pidan

IMPERFECT INDICATIVE

ped-	add imperfect indicative endings

pedía	pedíamos
pedías	pedíais
pedía	pedían

IMPERFECT SUBJUNCTIVE

pidie-	add imperfect subjunctive endings

pidiera	pidiéramos
pidieras	pidierais
pidiera	pidieran

remove **-ron** from **pid**ieron

PRETERITE 🔑─O

ped-	ped-	add preterite endings
"	"	
pid-	pid-	

pedí	pedimos
pediste	pedisteis
pidió	pidieron

PRESENT PARTICIPLE 🔑─O

pidiendo

PAST PARTICIPLE

pedido

remove **-ir** from infinitive; stem change

INFINITIVE

pedir

irregular present participle

remove **-ir** and add **-ido**

use infinitive as future stem

FUTURE

pedir-	add future endings

pediré	pediremos
pedirás	pediréis
pedirá	pedirán

CONDITIONAL

pedir-	add conditional endings

pediría	pediríamos
pedirías	pediríais
pediría	pedirían

🧩 Following the same pattern

competir *to compete*	**expedir** *to issue*	**repetir** *to repeat*
concebir *to conceive*	**impedir** *to prevent*	**servir** *to serve*
despedir *to say goodbye to, dismiss*	**medir** *to measure*	**vestir** *to dress*

haber (in the correct simple tense) **+ past participle**

PERFECT INDICATIVE

present indicative of haber	add past participle
he **pedido**	hemos **pedido**
has **pedido**	habéis **pedido**
ha **pedido**	han **pedido**

PERFECT SUBJUNCTIVE

present subjunctive of haber	add past participle
haya **pedido**	hayamos **pedido**
hayas **pedido**	hayáis **pedido**
haya **pedido**	hayan **pedido**

PLUPERFECT INDICATIVE

imperfect indicative of haber	add past participle
había **pedido**	habíamos **pedido**
habías **pedido**	habíais **pedido**
había **pedido**	habían **pedido**

PAST PARTICIPLE
pedido

PLUPERFECT SUBJUNCTIVE

imperfect subjunctive of haber	add past participle
hubiera **pedido**	hubiéramos **pedido**
hubieras **pedido**	hubierais **pedido**
hubiera **pedido**	hubieran **pedido**

FUTURE PERFECT

future of haber	add past participle
habré **pedido**	habremos **pedido**
habrás **pedido**	habréis **pedido**
habrá **pedido**	habrán **pedido**

CONDITIONAL PERFECT

conditional of haber	add past participle
habría **pedido**	habríamos **pedido**
habrías **pedido**	habríais **pedido**
habría **pedido**	habrían **pedido**

Usage examples

La estudiante pide un bolígrafo. *The student is asking for a pen.*

¿Qué pides? *What are you asking for?*

Siempre te doy lo que me pides. *I always give you what you ask for.*

¿Cuánto pides por este coche? *How much do you want for this car?*

Te pido que me des más información. *I request that you give me more information.*

No te estoy pidiendo cuentas. *I am not asking you for an explanation.*

Le he pedido a mi amigo que me ayude. *I have asked my friend to help me.*

Pedí un incremento salarial al jefe. *I asked the boss for a pay rise.*

Pidió hablar con el médico. *He asked to speak to the doctor.*

Voy a pedir una hamburguesa. *I am going to order a hamburger.*

Hemos pedido dos cafés. *We have ordered two coffees.*

Pediré un favor a mi padre. *I will ask my father for a favour.*

pedir prestado *to ask to borrow*

Pidieron dinero prestado. *They asked to borrow some money.*

pedir socorro *to ask for help*

un pedido *order; request*

hacer un pedido *to place an order*

un pedimento *petition*

una pedida *marriage proposal*

🔑—O Key points

➡ **e** of stem changes to **i** for stressed syllables in present indicative

➡ **e** of stem changes to **i** for 3rd person in preterite
➡ irregular present participle: **riñendo**

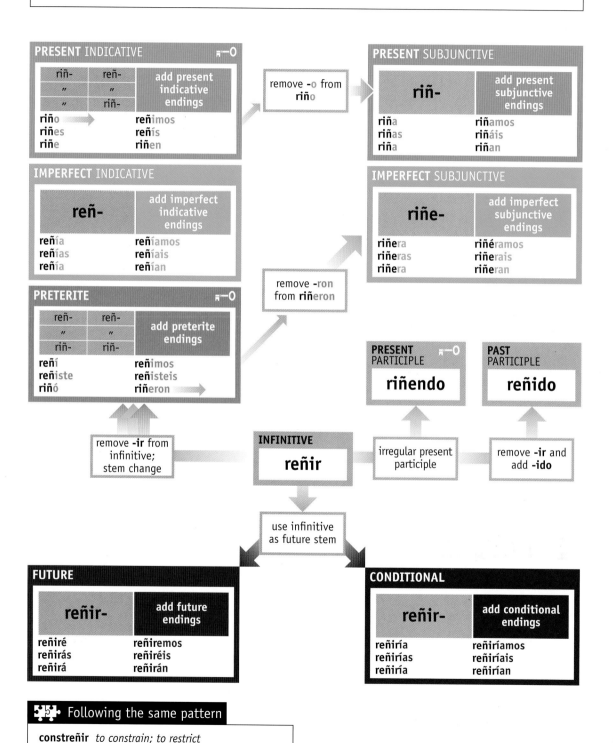

PRESENT INDICATIVE 🔑—O

riñ-	reñ-	add present indicative endings
"	"	
"	riñ-	

riño	reñimos
riñes	reñís
riñe	riñen

remove **-o** from **riño**

PRESENT SUBJUNCTIVE

| riñ- | add present subjunctive endings |

riña	riñamos
riñas	riñáis
riña	riñan

IMPERFECT INDICATIVE

| reñ- | add imperfect indicative endings |

reñía	reñíamos
reñías	reñíais
reñía	reñían

IMPERFECT SUBJUNCTIVE

| riñe- | add imperfect subjunctive endings |

riñera	riñéramos
riñeras	riñerais
riñera	riñeran

remove **-ron** from **riñeron**

PRETERITE 🔑—O

reñ-	reñ-	add preterite endings
"	"	
riñ-	riñ-	

reñí	reñimos
reñiste	reñisteis
riñó	riñeron

PRESENT PARTICIPLE 🔑—O

riñendo

PAST PARTICIPLE

reñido

remove **-ir** from infinitive; stem change

INFINITIVE

reñir

irregular present participle

remove **-ir** and add **-ido**

use infinitive as future stem

FUTURE

| reñir- | add future endings |

reñiré	reñiremos
reñirás	reñiréis
reñirá	reñirán

CONDITIONAL

| reñir- | add conditional endings |

reñiría	reñiríamos
reñirías	reñiríais
reñiría	reñirían

🧩 Following the same pattern

constreñir *to constrain; to restrict*
teñir *to dye; to stain*

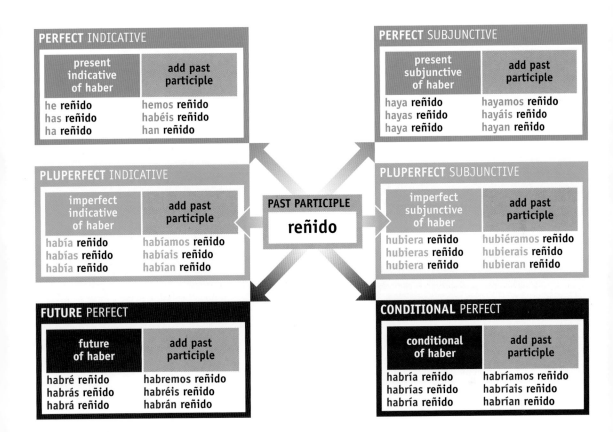

haber (in the correct simple tense) + past participle

PERFECT INDICATIVE

present indicative of haber	add past participle
he reñido	hemos reñido
has reñido	habéis reñido
ha reñido	han reñido

PERFECT SUBJUNCTIVE

present subjunctive of haber	add past participle
haya reñido	hayamos reñido
hayas reñido	hayáis reñido
haya reñido	hayan reñido

PLUPERFECT INDICATIVE

imperfect indicative of haber	add past participle
había reñido	habíamos reñido
habías reñido	habíais reñido
había reñido	habían reñido

PAST PARTICIPLE
reñido

PLUPERFECT SUBJUNCTIVE

imperfect subjunctive of haber	add past participle
hubiera reñido	hubiéramos reñido
hubieras reñido	hubierais reñido
hubiera reñido	hubieran reñido

FUTURE PERFECT

future of haber	add past participle
habré reñido	habremos reñido
habrás reñido	habréis reñido
habrá reñido	habrán reñido

CONDITIONAL PERFECT

conditional of haber	add past participle
habría reñido	habríamos reñido
habrías reñido	habríais reñido
habría reñido	habrían reñido

Usage examples

Los niños se han pasado todo el día riñendo. *The children have spent the whole day bickering.*

Los dos hermanos reñían mucho. *The two brothers used to quarrel a lot.*

Siempre riñe con sus amigos. *She's always arguing with her friends.*

Ha reñido con su hermana. *He's fallen out with his sister.*

Estoy cansado de reñir. *I am tired of arguing.*

Reñimos por asuntos de dinero. *We argued about money.*

Estaban riñendo por el balón de fútbol. *They were squabbling over the football.*

Por cualquier tontería riñen. *They argue over the smallest things.*

Quiero que dejéis de reñir. *I want you to stop bickering.*

Creo que el jefe me va a reñir. *I think that the boss is going to tell me off.*

Siempre me riñe. *He always tells me off.*

Mis padres me riñeron. *My parents told me off.*

No se trata de reñir a nadie. *It is not a question of admonishing anybody.*

Le reñí por no hacer los deberes. *I scolded him for not having done the homework.*

Nos riñó por romper el florero. *She told us off for breaking the vase.*

la riña *quarrel; fight, brawl*

una riña callejera *street fight*

reñido, reñida *hard-fought*

Key points

→ three stems in present indicative: **sig-**, **sigu-** & **segu-**

→ stem changes to **sigu-** in 3rd person of preterite
→ irregular present participle: **siguiendo**

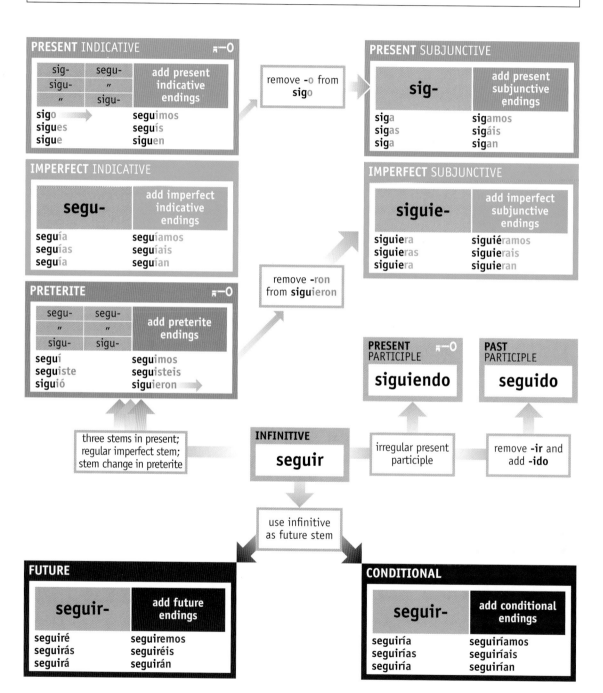

PRESENT INDICATIVE

sig-	segu-	add present indicative endings
sigu-	"	
"	sigu-	

sigo	seguimos
sigues	seguís
sigue	siguen

remove -o from **sigo**

PRESENT SUBJUNCTIVE

sig-	add present subjunctive endings

siga	sigamos
sigas	sigáis
siga	sigan

IMPERFECT INDICATIVE

segu-	add imperfect indicative endings

seguía	seguíamos
seguías	seguíais
seguía	seguían

IMPERFECT SUBJUNCTIVE

siguie-	add imperfect subjunctive endings

siguiera	siguiéramos
siguieras	siguierais
siguiera	siguieran

PRETERITE

segu-	segu-	add preterite endings
"	"	
sigu-	sigu-	

seguí	seguimos
seguiste	seguisteis
siguió	siguieron

remove -ron from **siguieron**

PRESENT PARTICIPLE

siguiendo

PAST PARTICIPLE

seguido

three stems in present; regular imperfect stem; stem change in preterite

INFINITIVE

seguir

irregular present participle

remove -ir and add -ido

use infinitive as future stem

FUTURE

seguir-	add future endings

seguiré	seguiremos
seguirás	seguiréis
seguirá	seguirán

CONDITIONAL

seguir-	add conditional endings

seguiría	seguiríamos
seguirías	seguiríais
seguiría	seguirían

Following the same pattern

conseguir *to get, obtain*
perseguir *to pursue, chase*
proseguir *to continue, carry on*

---

haber (in the correct simple tense) **+ past participle**

PERFECT INDICATIVE

present indicative of haber	add past participle
he **seguido**	hemos **seguido**
has **seguido**	habéis **seguido**
ha **seguido**	han **seguido**

PERFECT SUBJUNCTIVE

present subjunctive of haber	add past participle
haya **seguido**	hayamos **seguido**
hayas **seguido**	hayáis **seguido**
haya **seguido**	hayan **seguido**

PLUPERFECT INDICATIVE

imperfect indicative of haber	add past participle
había **seguido**	habíamos **seguido**
habías **seguido**	habíais **seguido**
había **seguido**	habían **seguido**

PAST PARTICIPLE

seguido

PLUPERFECT SUBJUNCTIVE

imperfect subjunctive of haber	add past participle
hubiera **seguido**	hubiéramos **seguido**
hubieras **seguido**	hubierais **seguido**
hubiera **seguido**	hubieran **seguido**

FUTURE PERFECT

future of haber	add past participle
habré seguido	habremos seguido
habrás seguido	habréis seguido
habrá seguido	habrán seguido

CONDITIONAL PERFECT

conditional of haber	add past participle
habría seguido	habríamos seguido
habrías seguido	habríais seguido
habría seguido	habrían seguido

◣◥ Usage examples

La primavera sigue al invierno. *Spring follows winter.*
Yo te sigo a la fiesta. *I will follow you to the party.*
Creo que alguien nos sigue. *I think that someone is following us.*
El sendero sigue el río. *The path follows the river.*
Es importante que sigáis las instrucciones. *It is important that you follow the instructions.*
Seguiré los consejos de mi madre. *I will follow my mother's advice.*
Seguía un curso de inglés. *She was doing an English language course.*
¡Sigue lloviendo! *It's still raining!*
Siguieron viendo la televisión. *They continued watching the television.*
José sigue enfadado. *José is still angry.*

La ciudad entera sigue sin electricidad. *The entire city is still without electricity.*
Si la situación sigue así, tendremos que cancelar el evento. *If this carries on, we are going to have to cancel the event.*
El presidente entró, seguido del embajador. *The president entered, followed by the ambassador.*
un seguidor, una seguidora *follower*
siguiente *following, next*
al día siguiente *the following day*
en seguida *immediately*
seguido *straight on, straight ahead*
seguido, seguida *consecutive; continuous*
según *according to*
sigue (al dorso) *continued (overleaf)*

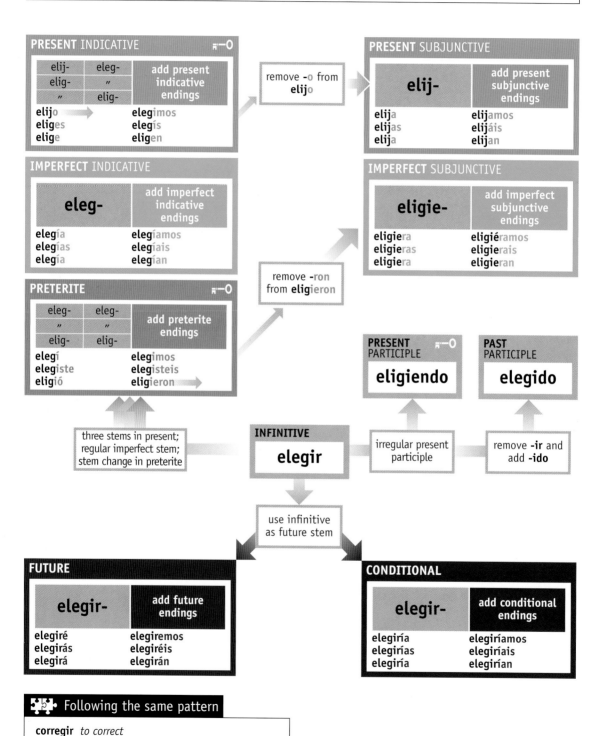

→ three stems in present indicative: **elij-**, **elig-** & **eleg-**

→ stem changes to **elig-** in 3rd person of preterite
→ irregular present participle: **eligiendo**

PRESENT INDICATIVE 🔑—O

elij-	eleg-	add present indicative endings
elig-	"	
"	elig-	

elijo → elegimos
eliges · elegís
elige · eligen

PRESENT SUBJUNCTIVE

elij-	add present subjunctive endings

elija · elijamos
elijas · elijáis
elija · elijan

remove **-o** from **elij**o

IMPERFECT INDICATIVE

eleg-	add imperfect indicative endings

elegía · elegíamos
elegías · elegíais
elegía · elegían

IMPERFECT SUBJUNCTIVE

eligie-	add imperfect subjunctive endings

eligiera · eligiéramos
eligieras · eligierais
eligiera · eligieran

remove **-ron** from **elig**ieron

PRETERITE 🔑—O

eleg-	eleg-	add preterite endings
"	"	
elig-	elig-	

elegí · elegimos
elegiste · elegisteis
eligió · eligieron

PRESENT 🔑—O PARTICIPLE

eligiendo

PAST PARTICIPLE

elegido

three stems in present; regular imperfect stem; stem change in preterite

INFINITIVE

elegir

irregular present participle

remove **-ir** and add **-ido**

use infinitive as future stem

FUTURE

elegir-	add future endings

elegiré · elegiremos
elegirás · elegiréis
elegirá · elegirán

CONDITIONAL

elegir-	add conditional endings

elegiría · elegiríamos
elegirías · elegiríais
elegiría · elegirían

🧩 Following the same pattern

corregir to correct
reelegir to re-elect
regir to govern; to be valid

---

haber (in the correct simple tense) + past participle

PERFECT INDICATIVE

present indicative of haber	add past participle
he **elegido**	hemos **elegido**
has **elegido**	habéis **elegido**
ha **elegido**	han **elegido**

PERFECT SUBJUNCTIVE

present subjunctive of haber	add past participle
haya **elegido**	hayamos **elegido**
hayas **elegido**	hayáis **elegido**
haya **elegido**	hayan **elegido**

PLUPERFECT INDICATIVE

imperfect indicative of haber	add past participle
había **elegido**	habíamos **elegido**
habías **elegido**	habíais **elegido**
había **elegido**	habían **elegido**

PAST PARTICIPLE
elegido

PLUPERFECT SUBJUNCTIVE

imperfect subjunctive of haber	add past participle
hubiera **elegido**	hubiéramos **elegido**
hubieras **elegido**	hubierais **elegido**
hubiera **elegido**	hubieran **elegido**

FUTURE PERFECT

future of haber	add past participle
habré elegido	habremos elegido
habrás elegido	habréis elegido
habrá elegido	habrán elegido

CONDITIONAL PERFECT

conditional of haber	add past participle
habría elegido	habríamos elegido
habrías elegido	habríais elegido
habría elegido	habrían elegido

Usage examples

Elijo a mis amigos con cuidado. *I choose my friends carefully.*

No sabía qué modelo elegir. *She didn't know which model to choose.*

¿Cuál han elegido? *Which one did they choose?*

No hay mucho donde elegir. *There isn't much to choose from.*

Los estudiantes tienen demasiadas asignaturas para elegir. *The students have too many subjects to choose from.*

Es importante que elijamos bien. *It is important that we choose well.*

Debimos elegir la otra opción. *We should have chosen the other option.*

Elegiría éste. *I would choose this one.*

Habría elegido el azul. *I would have chosen the blue one.*

Nunca habrían elegido una película tan triste. *They never would have chosen such a sad film.*

Eligió renunciar. *He chose to resign.*

Elegimos ir a Italia. *We chose to go to Italy.*

Cada cuatro años, los estadounidenses eligen a un nuevo líder. *Every four years, the Americans elect a new leader.*

Habremos elegido un nuevo parlamento para el doce de junio. *We will have elected a new parliament by the twelfth of June.*

elegible *eligible*

la elección *choice; election*

un elector, una electora *voter*

🔑 Key points

→ **e** of stem changes to **ie** for stressed syllables in present indicative
→ stem changes to **sint-** in 3rd person of preterite
→ **ie** of stem changes to **i** for unstressed syllables in present subjunctive
→ irregular present participle: **sintiendo**

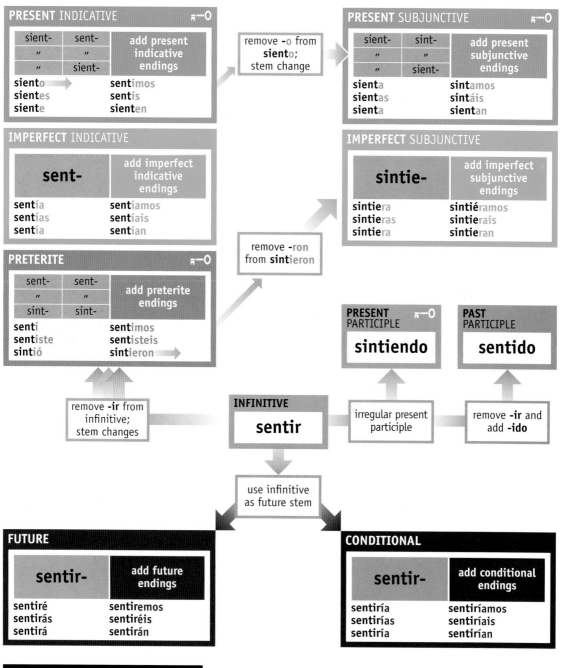

PRESENT INDICATIVE

sient-	sent-	add present indicative endings
"	"	
"	sient-	

siento	sentimos
sientes	sentís
siente	sienten

PRESENT SUBJUNCTIVE

sient-	sint-	add present subjunctive endings
"	"	
"	sient-	

sienta	sintamos
sientas	sintáis
sienta	sientan

remove **-o** from **siento**; stem change

IMPERFECT INDICATIVE

| **sent-** | add imperfect indicative endings |

sentía	sentíamos
sentías	sentíais
sentía	sentían

IMPERFECT SUBJUNCTIVE

| **sintie-** | add imperfect subjunctive endings |

sintiera	sintiéramos
sintieras	sintierais
sintiera	sintieran

remove **-ron** from **sintieron**

PRETERITE

sent-	sent-	add preterite endings
"	"	
sint-	sint-	

sentí	sentimos
sentiste	sentisteis
sintió	sintieron

PRESENT PARTICIPLE
sintiendo

PAST PARTICIPLE
sentido

remove **-ir** from infinitive; stem changes

INFINITIVE
sentir

irregular present participle

remove **-ir** and add **-ido**

use infinitive as future stem

FUTURE

| **sentir-** | add future endings |

sentiré	sentiremos
sentirás	sentiréis
sentirá	sentirán

CONDITIONAL

| **sentir-** | add conditional endings |

sentiría	sentiríamos
sentirías	sentiríais
sentiría	sentirían

🧩 Following the same pattern

advertir to warn; to advise; to notice
convertir to convert

herir to injure, hurt, wound
hervir to boil
invertir to invest; to invert

mentir to lie
preferir to prefer
referir to refer, relate; to recount

haber (in the correct simple tense) + past participle

PERFECT INDICATIVE

present indicative of haber	add past participle
he **sentido**	hemos **sentido**
has **sentido**	habéis **sentido**
ha **sentido**	han **sentido**

PERFECT SUBJUNCTIVE

present subjunctive of haber	add past participle
haya **sentido**	hayamos **sentido**
hayas **sentido**	hayáis **sentido**
haya **sentido**	hayan **sentido**

PLUPERFECT INDICATIVE

imperfect indicative of haber	add past participle
había **sentido**	habíamos **sentido**
habías **sentido**	habíais **sentido**
había **sentido**	habían **sentido**

PAST PARTICIPLE

sentido

PLUPERFECT SUBJUNCTIVE

imperfect subjunctive of haber	add past participle
hubiera **sentido**	hubiéramos **sentido**
hubieras **sentido**	hubierais **sentido**
hubiera **sentido**	hubieran **sentido**

FUTURE PERFECT

future of haber	add past participle
habré **sentido**	habremos **sentido**
habrás **sentido**	habréis **sentido**
habrá **sentido**	habrán **sentido**

CONDITIONAL PERFECT

conditional of haber	add past participle
habría **sentido**	habríamos **sentido**
habrías **sentido**	habríais **sentido**
habría **sentido**	habrían **sentido**

◆ Usage examples

Estoy sintiendo un fuerte dolor en la espalda. *I am feeling a sharp pain in my back.*

Apenas sentí la inyección. *I hardly felt the injection.*

Sientas lo que sientas, no te rindas. *No matter how you feel, don't give up.*

Siento que hacemos progresos. *I feel that we are making progress.*

No quiero que sientas que tú tienes que hacerlo. *I don't want you to feel as though you have to do it.*

Sintió como si fuera a vomitar. *She felt as though she was going to be sick.*

Lo siento mucho. *I'm really sorry.*

Lo siento, pero no puedo asistir a la reunión. *I'm sorry, but I cannot attend the meeting.*

Siento que te vayas. *I'm sorry you're leaving.*

Sentimos que ustedes no puedan venir. *We regret that you cannot come.*

sentirse *to feel*

Se sentirá mucho mejor después de descansar un poco. *She will feel much better after getting some rest.*

Me siento tan solo. *I feel so lonely.*

Se siente mal. *She feels ill.*

¿Cómo te sientes? *How do you feel?*

Si hubiéramos mentido, me habría sentido muy mal. *If we had lied, I would have felt very bad.*

el sentimiento *feeling*

el sentir *feelings; opinion, view*

los (cinco) sentidos *the (five) senses*

sentido, sentida *heartfelt*

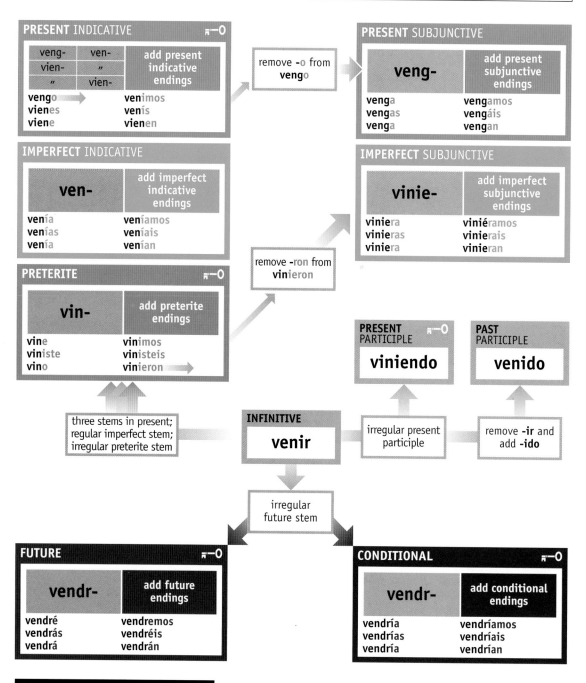

🔑—O Key points

➡ three stems in present indicative: **veng-**, **vien-** & **ven-**
➡ irregular stem in preterite: **vin-**
➡ irregular future stem: **vendr-**
➡ irregular present participle: **viniendo**

PRESENT INDICATIVE 🔑—O

veng-	ven-	add present indicative endings
vien-	"	
"	vien-	

veng**o**	ven**imos**
vien**es**	ven**ís**
vien**e**	vien**en**

remove -o from **veng**o

PRESENT SUBJUNCTIVE

veng-	add present subjunctive endings

veng**a**	veng**amos**
veng**as**	veng**áis**
veng**a**	veng**an**

IMPERFECT INDICATIVE

ven-	add imperfect indicative endings

ven**ía**	ven**íamos**
ven**ías**	ven**íais**
ven**ía**	ven**ían**

IMPERFECT SUBJUNCTIVE

vinie-	add imperfect subjunctive endings

vinie**ra**	vinié**ramos**
vinie**ras**	vinie**rais**
vinie**ra**	vinie**ran**

remove -ron from **vin**ieron

PRETERITE 🔑—O

vin-	add preterite endings

vin**e**	vin**imos**
vin**iste**	vin**isteis**
vin**o**	vin**ieron**

PRESENT PARTICIPLE 🔑—O

viniendo

PAST PARTICIPLE

venido

three stems in present; regular imperfect stem; irregular preterite stem

INFINITIVE

venir

irregular present participle

remove -ir and add -ido

irregular future stem

FUTURE 🔑—O

vendr-	add future endings

vendr**é**	vendr**emos**
vendr**ás**	vendr**éis**
vendr**á**	vendr**án**

CONDITIONAL 🔑—O

vendr-	add conditional endings

vendr**ía**	vendr**íamos**
vendr**ías**	vendr**íais**
vendr**ía**	vendr**ían**

🧩 Following the same pattern

convenir *to be advisable; to suit; to agree*
intervenir *to intervene*

prevenir *to prevent; to warn*
provenir de *to come from*

---

haber (in the correct simple tense) **+ past participle**

PERFECT INDICATIVE

present indicative of haber	add past participle
he **venido**	hemos **venido**
has **venido**	habéis **venido**
ha **venido**	han **venido**

PERFECT SUBJUNCTIVE

present subjunctive of haber	add past participle
haya **venido**	hayamos **venido**
hayas **venido**	hayáis **venido**
haya **venido**	hayan **venido**

PLUPERFECT INDICATIVE

imperfect indicative of haber	add past participle
había **venido**	habíamos **venido**
habías **venido**	habíais **venido**
había **venido**	habían **venido**

PAST PARTICIPLE
venido

PLUPERFECT SUBJUNCTIVE

imperfect subjunctive of haber	add past participle
hubiera **venido**	hubiéramos **venido**
hubieras **venido**	hubierais **venido**
hubiera **venido**	hubieran **venido**

FUTURE PERFECT

future of haber	add past participle
habré **venido**	habremos **venido**
habrás **venido**	habréis **venido**
habrá **venido**	habrán **venido**

CONDITIONAL PERFECT

conditional of haber	add past participle
habría venido	habríamos venido
habrías venido	habríais venido
habría venido	habrían venido

Usage examples

Viene a las seis. *She's coming at six o'clock.*

Vine tarde a la fiesta. *I came late to the party.*

Los invitados vienen a las dos. *The guests are coming at two.*

¿Vendrán? *Will they come?*

¿Puedes venir un momento? *Can you come here a minute?*

Vinimos en tren. *We came by train.*

Hemos venido a verte. *We have come to see you.*

No creo que venga. *I don't think he will come.*

Quizás vengamos con ustedes. *Perhaps we will come with you.*

¿Te gustaría venir conmigo? *Would you like to come with me?*

Me alegro que hayan venido. *I am glad that you came.*

Insistí en que viniera. *I insisted that he come.*

Ojalá hubiera venido. *I wish he had come.*

Mi amigo me dijo que vendría. *My friend told me he would come.*

Isabel habría venido, pero estaba enferma. *Isabel would have come, but she was sick.*

Esta palabra viene del latín. *This word comes from Latin.*

Marzo viene antes de abril. *March comes before April.*

Vienen en distintos tamaños. *They come in different sizes.*

Eso no viene al caso. *That's beside the point.*

la venida *arrival*

la semana que viene *next week*

el mes que viene *next month*

⚷ Key points

➡ three stems in present indicative: **dig-**, **dic-** & **dec-**   ➡ irregular past participle: **dicho**
➡ irregular stem in preterite: **dij-**   ➡ irregular future stem: **dir-**
➡ irregular present participle: **diciendo**

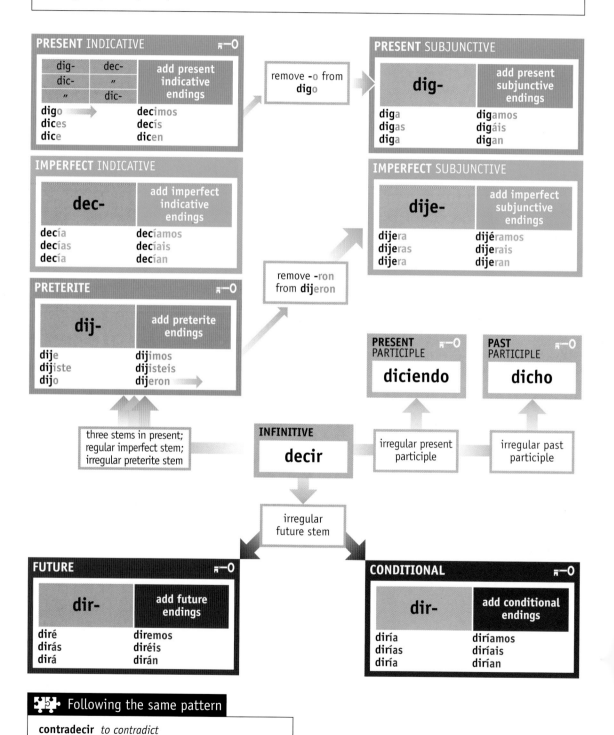

PRESENT INDICATIVE ⚷

dig-	dec-	add present indicative endings
dic-	"	
"	dic-	
digo	decimos
dices	decís
dice	dicen

remove **-o** from **dig**o

PRESENT SUBJUNCTIVE

dig-	add present subjunctive endings
diga	digamos
digas	digáis
diga	digan

IMPERFECT INDICATIVE

dec-	add imperfect indicative endings
decía	decíamos
decías	decíais
decía	decían

IMPERFECT SUBJUNCTIVE

dije-	add imperfect subjunctive endings
dijera	dijéramos
dijeras	dijerais
dijera	dijeran

remove **-ron** from **dije**ron

PRETERITE ⚷

dij-	add preterite endings
dije	dijimos
dijiste	dijisteis
dijo	dijeron

PRESENT PARTICIPLE ⚷
diciendo

PAST PARTICIPLE ⚷
dicho

three stems in present;
regular imperfect stem;
irregular preterite stem

INFINITIVE
decir

irregular present participle

irregular past participle

irregular future stem

FUTURE ⚷

dir-	add future endings
diré	diremos
dirás	diréis
dirá	dirán

CONDITIONAL ⚷

dir-	add conditional endings
diría	diríamos
dirías	diríais
diría	dirían

🧩 Following the same pattern

contradecir *to contradict*

haber (in the correct simple tense) + past participle

PERFECT INDICATIVE

present indicative of haber	add past participle
he **dicho**	hemos **dicho**
has **dicho**	habéis **dicho**
ha **dicho**	han **dicho**

PERFECT SUBJUNCTIVE

present subjunctive of haber	add past participle
haya **dicho**	hayamos **dicho**
hayas **dicho**	hayáis **dicho**
haya **dicho**	hayan **dicho**

PLUPERFECT INDICATIVE

imperfect indicative of haber	add past participle
había **dicho**	habíamos **dicho**
habías **dicho**	habíais **dicho**
había **dicho**	habían **dicho**

PAST PARTICIPLE

dicho

PLUPERFECT SUBJUNCTIVE

imperfect subjunctive of haber	add past participle
hubiera **dicho**	hubiéramos **dicho**
hubieras **dicho**	hubierais **dicho**
hubiera **dicho**	hubieran **dicho**

FUTURE PERFECT

future of haber	add past participle
habré **dicho**	habremos **dicho**
habrás **dicho**	habréis **dicho**
habrá **dicho**	habrán **dicho**

CONDITIONAL PERFECT

conditional of haber	add past participle
habría **dicho**	habríamos **dicho**
habrías **dicho**	habríais **dicho**
habría **dicho**	habrían **dicho**

Usage examples

Ellos nos dicen la verdad. *They are telling us the truth.*
¿Qué dijiste? *What did you say?*
¿Cómo ha dicho usted? *I beg your pardon?*
Dijeron que ganarían. *They said they would win.*
Me dijo que ella llegaría tarde. *She told me that she would be late.*
Le dijiste que la película era buena. *You told her that the film was good.*
Dicen que Barcelona es una ciudad hermosa. *They say that Barcelona is a beautiful city.*
Mi mujer siempre me está diciendo que aprenda otro idioma. *My wife is always telling me to learn another language.*
Diría que éste es un buen consejo. *I would say that this is good advice.*

No estoy diciendo mentiras. *I'm not lying.*
¿Cómo se dice "aparcamiento" en inglés? *How do you say "aparcamiento" in English?*
Me han dicho que te vas a casar. *I've been told that you are getting married.*
¿Hubieras ido a mi fiesta si te lo hubiera dicho? *Would you have gone to my party if I had told you?*
Habría dicho que sí. *I would have said yes.*
querer decir *to mean*
¿Qué quiere decir esta palabra? *What does this word mean?*
¿Qué quieres decir? *What do you mean?*
Se fue sin decir nada. *He left without saying a word.*
es decir *that is to say*
un dicho *saying*

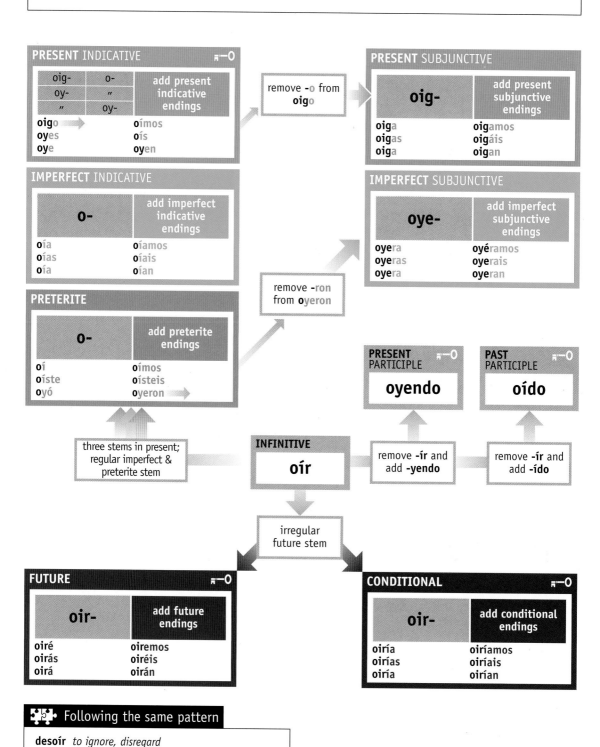

Key points

→ three stems in present indicative: **oig-**, **oy-** & **o-**
→ add the ending **-yendo** for present participle
→ add the ending **-ído** for past participle
→ irregular future stem: **oir-**

PRESENT INDICATIVE

oig-	o-	add present
oy-	"	indicative
"	oy-	endings

oigo → oímos
oyes oís
oye   oyen

remove **-o** from **oig**o

PRESENT SUBJUNCTIVE

| **oig-** | add present subjunctive endings |

oiga   oigamos
oigas oigáis
oiga   oigan

IMPERFECT INDICATIVE

| **o-** | add imperfect indicative endings |

oía   oíamos
oías oíais
oía   oían

IMPERFECT SUBJUNCTIVE

| **oye-** | add imperfect subjunctive endings |

oyera   oyéramos
oyeras oyerais
oyera   oyeran

remove **-ron** from **o**yeron

PRETERITE

| **o-** | add preterite endings |

oí   oímos
oíste oísteis
oyó   oyeron

PRESENT PARTICIPLE

oyendo

PAST PARTICIPLE

oído

three stems in present; regular imperfect & preterite stem

INFINITIVE

oír

remove **-ír** and add **-yendo**

remove **-ír** and add **-ído**

irregular future stem

FUTURE

| **oir-** | add future endings |

oiré   oiremos
oirás oiréis
oirá   oirán

CONDITIONAL

| **oir-** | add conditional endings |

oiría   oiríamos
oirías oiríais
oiría   oirían

Following the same pattern

desoír to ignore, disregard

haber (in the correct simple tense) + past participle

PERFECT INDICATIVE

present indicative of haber	add past participle
he oído	hemos oído
has oído	habéis oído
ha oído	han oído

PERFECT SUBJUNCTIVE

present subjunctive of haber	add past participle
haya oído	hayamos oído
hayas oído	hayáis oído
haya oído	hayan oído

PLUPERFECT INDICATIVE

imperfect indicative of haber	add past participle
había oído	habíamos oído
habías oído	habíais oído
había oído	habían oído

PAST PARTICIPLE

oído

PLUPERFECT SUBJUNCTIVE

imperfect subjunctive of haber	add past participle
hubiera oído	hubiéramos oído
hubieras oído	hubierais oído
hubiera oído	hubieran oído

FUTURE PERFECT

future of haber	add past participle
habré oído	habremos oído
habrás oído	habréis oído
habrá oído	habrán oído

CONDITIONAL PERFECT

conditional of haber	add past participle
habría oído	habríamos oído
habrías oído	habríais oído
habría oído	habrían oído

◥◤ Usage examples

No oigo nada con tanto ruido. *I can't hear a thing with so much noise.*

¿Me oyes? *Can you hear me?*

No te oí. *I didn't hear you.*

No oí todo lo que dijo. *I didn't hear everything she said.*

Nadie nos oirá. *No one will hear us.*

Si hubiera gritado más fuerte, le habría oído. *If he had shouted louder, I would have heard him.*

Puede ser que no nos hayan oído. *They may not have heard us.*

Tenía miedo de que me oyeran. *I was afraid that they would hear me.*

¿Oíste el discurso? *Did you hear the speech?*

¿Has oído ese ruido? *Did you hear that noise?*

Les oímos cantar. *We heard them singing.*

Oía la radio cuando llamó. *I was listening to the radio when he called.*

Lo oí en la radio. *I heard it on the radio.*

Habrá oído lo que pasó. *She must have heard what happened.*

Al oír la noticia, se enfadó. *When he heard the news, he got angry.*

No podía creer lo que estaba oyendo. *He couldn't believe what he was hearing.*

Me sorprende oír eso. *I'm surprised to hear that.*

Hemos oído que te vas. *We have heard that you are leaving.*

Has oído hablar de él. *You've heard of him.*

el oído *ear; hearing*

Key points

→ **e** of stem changes to **i** for stressed syllables in present indicative
→ **i** of stem changes to **i** for unstressed syllables in present subjunctive

→ stem changes to **r-** in 3rd person of preterite
→ irregular present participle: **riendo**
→ add the ending **-ído** for past participle
→ irregular future stem: **reir-**

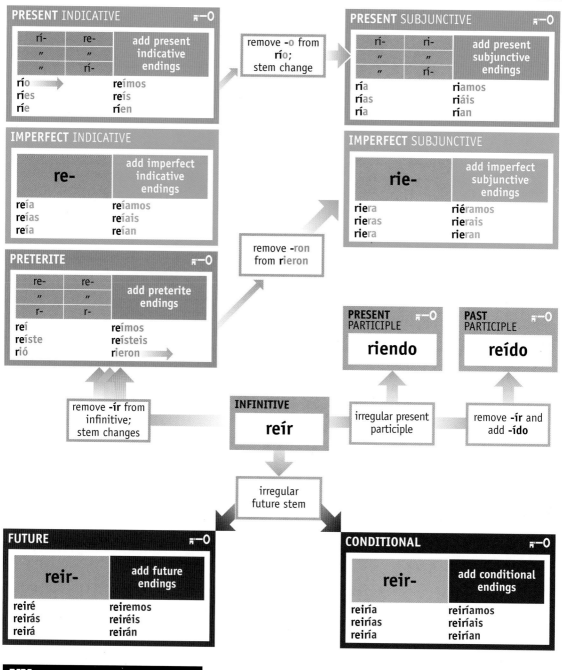

PRESENT INDICATIVE

rí-	re-	add present indicative endings
"	"	
"	rí-	

río	reímos
ríes	reís
ríe	ríen

remove **-o** from **río**; stem change

PRESENT SUBJUNCTIVE

rí-	rí-	add present subjunctive endings
"	"	
"	rí-	

ría	riamos
rías	riáis
ría	rían

IMPERFECT INDICATIVE

| re- | add imperfect indicative endings |

reía	reíamos
reías	reíais
reía	reían

IMPERFECT SUBJUNCTIVE

| rie- | add imperfect subjunctive endings |

riera	riéramos
rieras	rierais
riera	rieran

remove **-ron** from **rieron**

PRETERITE

re-	re-	add preterite endings
"	"	
r-	r-	

reí	reímos
reíste	reísteis
rió	rieron

PRESENT PARTICIPLE
riendo

PAST PARTICIPLE
reído

remove **-ír** from infinitive; stem changes

INFINITIVE
reír

irregular present participle

remove **-ír** and add **-ído**

irregular future stem

FUTURE

| reir- | add future endings |

reiré	reiremos
reirás	reiréis
reirá	reirán

CONDITIONAL

| reir- | add conditional endings |

reiría	reiríamos
reirías	reiríais
reiría	reirían

Following the same pattern

freír *to fry*
sonreír *to smile*

> **haber** (in the correct simple tense) **+ past participle**

PERFECT INDICATIVE

present indicative of haber	add past participle
he **reído**	hemos **reído**
has **reído**	habéis **reído**
ha **reído**	han **reído**

PERFECT SUBJUNCTIVE

present subjunctive of haber	add past participle
haya **reído**	hayamos **reído**
hayas **reído**	hayáis **reído**
haya **reído**	hayan **reído**

PLUPERFECT INDICATIVE

imperfect indicative of haber	add past participle
había **reído**	habíamos **reído**
habías **reído**	habíais **reído**
había **reído**	habían **reído**

PAST PARTICIPLE

reído

PLUPERFECT SUBJUNCTIVE

imperfect subjunctive of haber	add past participle
hubiera **reído**	hubiéramos **reído**
hubieras **reído**	hubierais **reído**
hubiera **reído**	hubieran **reído**

FUTURE PERFECT

future of haber	add past participle
habré **reído**	habremos **reído**
habrás **reído**	habréis **reído**
habrá **reído**	habrán **reído**

CONDITIONAL PERFECT

conditional of haber	add past participle
habría **reído**	habríamos **reído**
habrías **reído**	habríais **reído**
habría **reído**	habrían **reído**

◢◣ Usage examples

Pedro se ríe de todos. *Pedro laughs at everyone.*
Mi hermano ríe todo el tiempo. *My brother laughs all the time.*
No dejó de reír. *She didn't stop laughing.*
No reiría. *He wouldn't laugh.*
Me haces reír. *You make me laugh.*
Los niños ríen mucho. *The children laugh a lot.*
Siempre reían en clase. *They used to always laugh in class.*
Se reirán cuando se enteren. *They will laugh when they find out.*
Se rió cuando oyó la noticia. *He laughed when he heard the news.*
Reía mientras contaba la historia. *She was laughing while I was telling the story.*

Si Tina hubiera estado aquí, se habría reído. *If Tina had been here, she would have laughed.*
Me reí más fuerte de lo que me había reído en años. *I laughed harder than I had laughed in years.*
El que ríe el último, ríe mejor. *He who laughs last, laughs best.*
¿De qué se ríe? *What's he laughing at?*
No creo que se rían de ti. *I don't think they're laughing at you.*
Le pedí que no se riera de mí. *I asked him not to laugh at me.*
la risa *laugh, laughter*
una cosa de risa *a laughing matter*
risueño, risueña *smiling; cheerful*
el hazmerreír *laughing stock*

Key points

➔ very irregular in present indicative
➔ irregular stem in imperfect indicative: **ib-**
➔ irregular stem in preterite: **fu-**

➔ irregular stem in present subjunctive: **vay-**
➔ add the ending **-yendo** for present participle

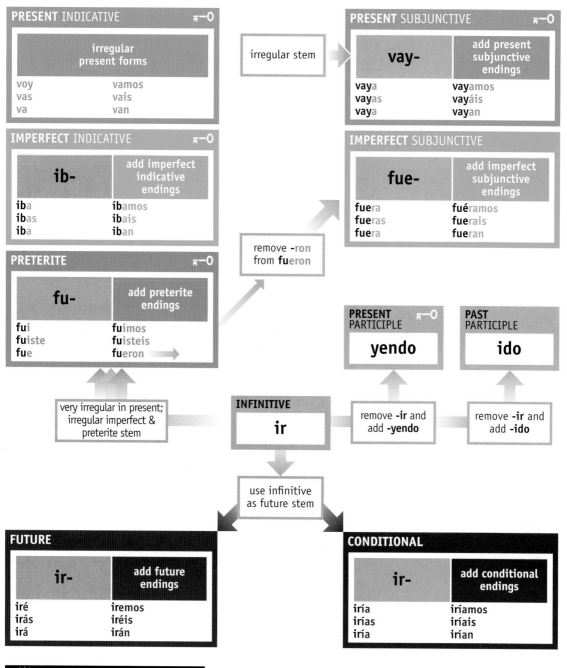

PRESENT INDICATIVE

irregular present forms	
voy	vamos
vas	vais
va	van

irregular stem

PRESENT SUBJUNCTIVE

vay-	add present subjunctive endings
vaya	vayamos
vayas	vayáis
vaya	vayan

IMPERFECT INDICATIVE

ib-	add imperfect indicative endings
iba	íbamos
ibas	ibais
iba	iban

IMPERFECT SUBJUNCTIVE

fue-	add imperfect subjunctive endings
fuera	fuéramos
fueras	fuerais
fuera	fueran

remove **-ron** from **fu**eron

PRETERITE

fu-	add preterite endings
fui	fuimos
fuiste	fuisteis
fue	fueron

PRESENT PARTICIPLE
yendo

PAST PARTICIPLE
ido

very irregular in present; irregular imperfect & preterite stem

INFINITIVE
ir

remove **-ir** and add **-yendo**

remove **-ir** and add **-ido**

use infinitive as future stem

FUTURE

ir-	add future endings
iré	iremos
irás	iréis
irá	irán

CONDITIONAL

ir-	add conditional endings
iría	iríamos
irías	iríais
iría	irían

Useful tips

The verb **ir** is often used to talk about something that is going to happen in the future. The particular construction used for this purpose is the present tense of **ir** followed by the preposition **a** and then an infinitive. Here is an example: **Vamos a cenar** (We are going to have dinner).

> **haber** (in the correct simple tense) **+ past participle**

PERFECT INDICATIVE

present indicative of haber	add past participle
he **ido**	hemos **ido**
has **ido**	habéis **ido**
ha **ido**	han **ido**

PERFECT SUBJUNCTIVE

present subjunctive of haber	add past participle
haya **ido**	hayamos **ido**
hayas **ido**	hayáis **ido**
haya **ido**	hayan **ido**

PLUPERFECT INDICATIVE

imperfect indicative of haber	add past participle
había **ido**	habíamos **ido**
habías **ido**	habíais **ido**
había **ido**	habían **ido**

PAST PARTICIPLE

ido

PLUPERFECT SUBJUNCTIVE

imperfect subjunctive of haber	add past participle
hubiera **ido**	hubiéramos **ido**
hubieras **ido**	hubierais **ido**
hubiera **ido**	hubieran **ido**

FUTURE PERFECT

future of haber	add past participle
habré **ido**	habremos **ido**
habrás **ido**	habréis **ido**
habrá **ido**	habrán **ido**

CONDITIONAL PERFECT

conditional of haber	add past participle
habría **ido**	habríamos **ido**
habrías **ido**	habríais **ido**
habría **ido**	habrían **ido**

Usage examples

Voy a la playa. *I am going to the beach.*

No voy con ellos. *I am not going with them.*

El tren va de Granada a Barcelona. *The train goes from Granada to Barcelona.*

Mañana vamos a Londres. *Tomorrow we are going to London.*

Fuimos en coche. *We went by car.*

¿Qué vas a hacer esta tarde? *What are you going to do this afternoon?*

Van a visitar a sus amigos. *They are going to visit their friends.*

Va a perder el autobús. *She is going to miss the bus.*

¿Cómo te va? *How's it going?*

¿Cómo fue el partido de fútbol? *How did the football match go?*

Los niños iban al parque todos los días. *The children used to go to the park every day.*

El domingo iré de compras. *I will go shopping on Sunday.*

Es probable que vaya al cine. *It's likely that she will go to the cinema.*

Isabel quería que fuera también. *Isabel wanted me to go as well.*

Ella había ido el día anterior. *She had gone the day before.*

Si hubiera ido a la fiesta ayer, la habría visto. *If I had gone to the party yesterday, I would have seen her.*

Me está yendo mal en la universidad. *Things are not going well at university.*

¿Me va bien esto? *Does this suit me?*

Key points

➡ stem changes to **salg-** in 1st person singular of present indicative

➡ irregular future stem: **saldr-**

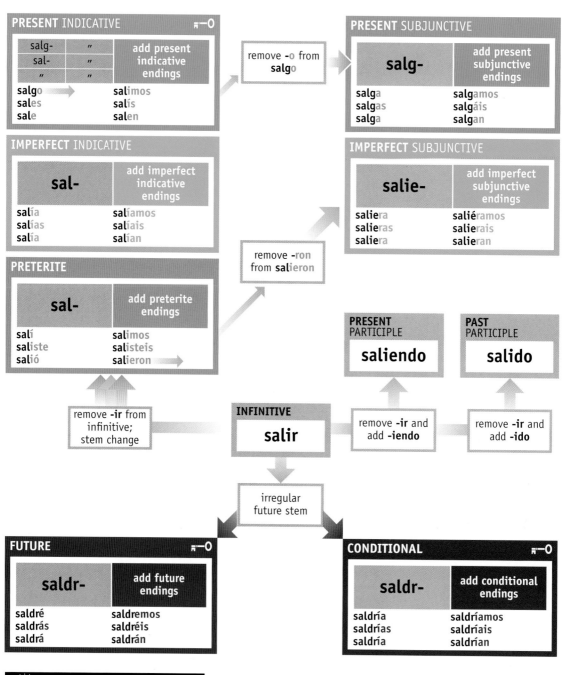

PRESENT INDICATIVE

salg-	"	add present indicative endings
sal-	"	
"	"	

salgo	salimos
sales	salís
sale	salen

remove **-o** from **salg**o

PRESENT SUBJUNCTIVE

| salg- | add present subjunctive endings |

salga	salgamos
salgas	salgáis
salga	salgan

IMPERFECT INDICATIVE

| sal- | add imperfect indicative endings |

salía	salíamos
salías	salíais
salía	salían

IMPERFECT SUBJUNCTIVE

| salie- | add imperfect subjunctive endings |

saliera	saliéramos
salieras	salierais
saliera	salieran

remove **-ron** from **sal**ieron

PRETERITE

| sal- | add preterite endings |

salí	salimos
saliste	salisteis
salió	salieron

PRESENT PARTICIPLE

saliendo

PAST PARTICIPLE

salido

remove **-ir** from infinitive; stem change

INFINITIVE

salir

remove **-ir** and add **-iendo**

remove **-ir** and add **-ido**

irregular future stem

FUTURE

| saldr- | add future endings |

saldré	saldremos
saldrás	saldréis
saldrá	saldrán

CONDITIONAL

| saldr- | add conditional endings |

saldría	saldríamos
saldrías	saldríais
saldría	saldrían

Useful tips

Although **salir** is used to talk about leaving in the sense of "going away", the verb **dejar** is used to talk about leaving an object somewhere.

haber (in the correct simple tense) + past participle

PERFECT INDICATIVE

present indicative of haber	add past participle
he **salido**	hemos **salido**
has **salido**	habéis **salido**
ha **salido**	han **salido**

PERFECT SUBJUNCTIVE

present subjunctive of haber	add past participle
haya **salido**	hayamos **salido**
hayas **salido**	hayáis **salido**
haya **salido**	hayan **salido**

PLUPERFECT INDICATIVE

imperfect indicative of haber	add past participle
había **salido**	habíamos **salido**
habías **salido**	habíais **salido**
había **salido**	habían **salido**

PAST PARTICIPLE

salido

PLUPERFECT SUBJUNCTIVE

imperfect subjunctive of haber	add past participle
hubiera **salido**	hubiéramos **salido**
hubieras **salido**	hubierais **salido**
hubiera **salido**	hubieran **salido**

FUTURE PERFECT

future of haber	add past participle
habré salido	habremos **salido**
habrás salido	habréis **salido**
habrá salido	habrán **salido**

CONDITIONAL PERFECT

conditional of haber	add past participle
habría salido	habríamos salido
habrías salido	habríais salido
habría salido	habrían salido

🕮 Usage examples

¿A qué hora sale el tren? *What time does the train leave?*

Salen de la oficina a las cinco. *They leave the office at five.*

Saldrá temprano del trabajo hoy. *She will leave work early today.*

Salgo el martes para Berlín. *I leave for Berlin on Tuesday.*

Cierra la puerta cuando salgas. *Close the door when you leave.*

Ha salido. *He's gone out.*

¿Por qué ha salido Rafael? *Why has Rafael gone out?*

No creo que hayan salido. *I don't think they went out.*

Cuando llegué, ya había salido. *When I arrived, he had already left.*

Sus padres salieron hace cinco minutos. *His parents left five minutes ago.*

Salgo a jugar al tenis. *I'm going out to play tennis.*

¿Quieres salir a comer? *Do you want to eat out?*

Raquel y yo salimos al cine esta noche. *Raquel and I are going to the cinema tonight.*

Laura está saliendo con Eduardo. *Laura is going out with Eduardo.*

Su nueva novela sale en septiembre. *Her new novel comes out in September.*

Todo salió bien. *Everything turned out well.*

Sale a su padre. *He takes after his father.*

la salida *exit; departure*

la salida de emergencia *emergency exit*

la salida de incendios *fire exit*

→ **o** of stem changes to **ue** for stressed syllables in present indicative

→ **ue** of stem changes to **u** for unstressed syllables in present subjunctive

→ stem changes to **durm-** in 3rd person of preterite

→ irregular present participle: **durmiendo**

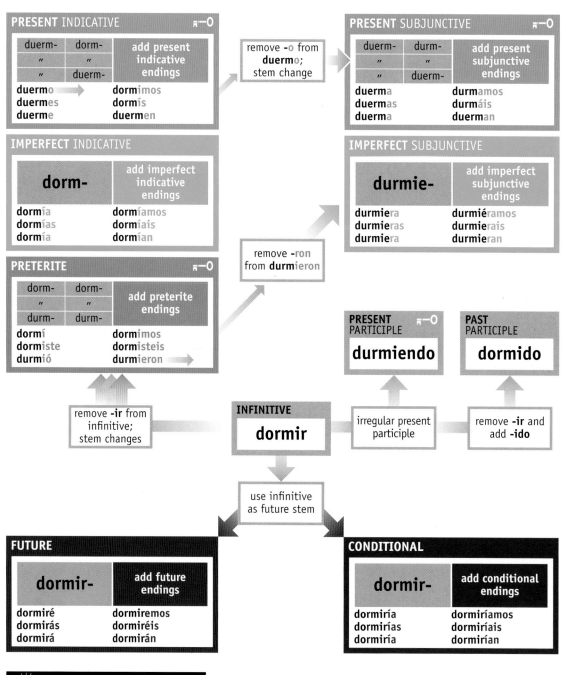

PRESENT INDICATIVE   ⚷—O

duerm-	dorm-	add present indicative endings
"	"	
"	duerm-	

duermo	→	dormimos
duermes		dormís
duerme		duermen

remove **-o** from **duermo**; stem change

PRESENT SUBJUNCTIVE   ⚷—O

duerm-	durm-	add present subjunctive endings
"	"	
"	duerm-	

duerma	durmamos
duermas	durmáis
duerma	duerman

IMPERFECT INDICATIVE

dorm-	add imperfect indicative endings

dormía	dormíamos
dormías	dormíais
dormía	dormían

IMPERFECT SUBJUNCTIVE

durmie-	add imperfect subjunctive endings

durmiera	durmiéramos
durmieras	durmierais
durmiera	durmieran

remove **-ron** from **durmieron**

PRETERITE   ⚷—O

dorm-	dorm-	add preterite endings
"	"	
durm-	durm-	

dormí	dormimos
dormiste	dormisteis
durmió	→ durmieron

PRESENT PARTICIPLE   ⚷—O

durmiendo

PAST PARTICIPLE

dormido

remove **-ir** from infinitive; stem changes

INFINITIVE

dormir

irregular present participle

remove **-ir** and add **-ido**

use infinitive as future stem

FUTURE

dormir-	add future endings

dormiré	dormiremos
dormirás	dormiréis
dormirá	dormirán

CONDITIONAL

dormir-	add conditional endings

dormiría	dormiríamos
dormirías	dormiríais
dormiría	dormirían

💡 Useful tips

Stem-changing -ir verbs have the same vowel in the stem of the present participle as in the third person of the preterite tense.

haber (in the correct simple tense) + past participle

PERFECT INDICATIVE

present indicative of haber	add past participle
he **dormido**	hemos **dormido**
has **dormido**	habéis **dormido**
ha **dormido**	han **dormido**

PERFECT SUBJUNCTIVE

present subjunctive of haber	add past participle
haya **dormido**	hayamos **dormido**
hayas **dormido**	hayáis **dormido**
haya **dormido**	hayan **dormido**

PLUPERFECT INDICATIVE

imperfect indicative of haber	add past participle
había **dormido**	habíamos **dormido**
habías **dormido**	habíais **dormido**
había **dormido**	habían **dormido**

PAST PARTICIPLE
dormido

PLUPERFECT SUBJUNCTIVE

imperfect subjunctive of haber	add past participle
hubiera **dormido**	hubiéramos **dormido**
hubieras **dormido**	hubierais **dormido**
hubiera **dormido**	hubieran **dormido**

FUTURE PERFECT

future of haber	add past participle
habré **dormido**	habremos **dormido**
habrás **dormido**	habréis **dormido**
habrá **dormido**	habrán **dormido**

CONDITIONAL PERFECT

conditional of haber	add past participle
habría **dormido**	habríamos **dormido**
habrías **dormido**	habríais **dormido**
habría **dormido**	habrían **dormido**

◥◢ Usage examples

Traté de dormir. *I tried to sleep.*

Duermo muy bien por la noche. *I sleep very well at night.*

Dormían profundamente. *They were sleeping soundly.*

David dormía cuando sonó la alarma. *David was sleeping when the alarm rang.*

Duerme hasta el mediodía. *She sleeps until midday.*

Los niños están durmiendo. *The children are sleeping.*

El gato duerme debajo de la cama. *The cat sleeps under the bed.*

Dormirás bien esta noche. *You will sleep well tonight.*

No dormiría en esa cama. *I would not sleep in that bed.*

Anoche no dormí más de dos horas. *Last night I only slept for two hours.*

Dormí hasta la tarde. *I slept through till the afternoon.*

Ha dormido toda la mañana. *He has slept the whole morning.*

Es increíble que duermas tanto. *It's incredible that you sleep so much.*

Si no me hubieras llamado esta mañana, habría dormido todo día. *If you hadn't called me this morning, I would have slept all day.*

Esperaba que durmieras más. *I hoped that you would sleep longer.*

Que duermas bien. *Sleep tight.*

La madre durmió al bebé. *The mother got the baby off to sleep.*

Estas clases me duermen. *These lectures send me to sleep.*

🔑 Key points

➡ **o** of stem changes to **ue** for stressed syllables in present indicative

➡ stem changes to **mur-** in 3rd person of preterite

➡ **ue** of stem changes to **u** for unstressed syllables in present subjunctive

➡ irregular present participle: **muriendo**

➡ irregular past participle: **muerto**

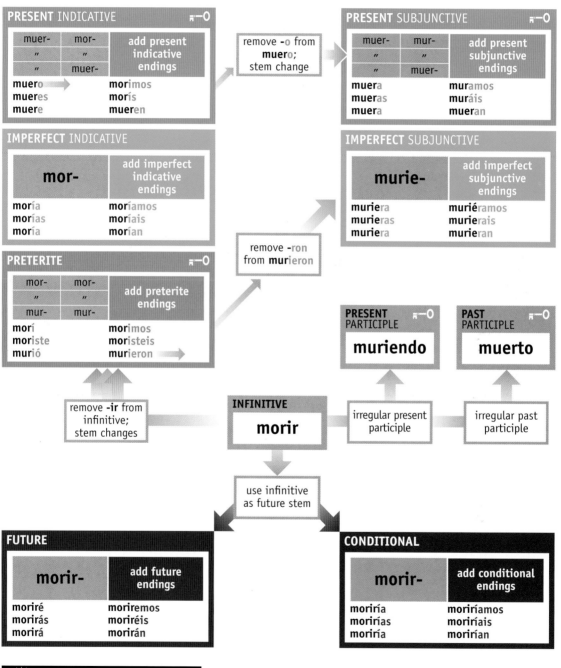

PRESENT INDICATIVE 🔑

muer-	mor-	add present indicative endings
"	"	
"	muer-	

muero	morimos
mueres	morís
muere	mueren

remove **-o** from **muero**; stem change

PRESENT SUBJUNCTIVE 🔑

muer-	mur-	add present subjunctive endings
"	"	
"	muer-	

muera	muramos
mueras	muráis
muera	mueran

IMPERFECT INDICATIVE

mor-	add imperfect indicative endings

moría	moríamos
morías	moríais
moría	morían

IMPERFECT SUBJUNCTIVE

murie-	add imperfect subjunctive endings

muriera	muriéramos
murieras	murierais
muriera	murieran

remove **-ron** from **murieron**

PRETERITE 🔑

mor-	mor-	add preterite endings
"	"	
mur-	mur-	

morí	morimos
moriste	moristeis
murió	murieron

PRESENT PARTICIPLE 🔑

muriendo

PAST PARTICIPLE 🔑

muerto

remove **-ir** from infinitive; stem changes

INFINITIVE

morir

irregular present participle

irregular past participle

use infinitive as future stem

FUTURE

morir-	add future endings

moriré	moriremos
morirás	moriréis
morirá	morirán

CONDITIONAL

morir-	add conditional endings

moriría	moriríamos
morirías	moriríais
moriría	morirían

💡 Useful tips

Morir would follow exactly the same pattern as **dormir** (page 188) were it not for the fact that **morir** has an irregular past participle.

> **haber** (in the correct simple tense) + **past participle**

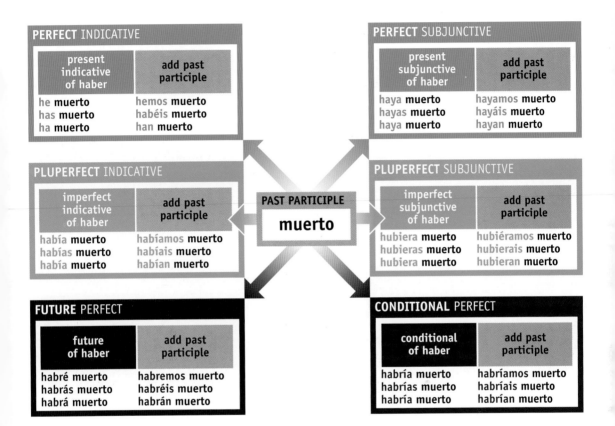

PERFECT INDICATIVE

present indicative of haber	add past participle
he **muerto**	hemos **muerto**
has **muerto**	habéis **muerto**
ha **muerto**	han **muerto**

PERFECT SUBJUNCTIVE

present subjunctive of haber	add past participle
haya **muerto**	hayamos **muerto**
hayas **muerto**	hayáis **muerto**
haya **muerto**	hayan **muerto**

PLUPERFECT INDICATIVE

imperfect indicative of haber	add past participle
había **muerto**	habíamos **muerto**
habías **muerto**	habíais **muerto**
había **muerto**	habían **muerto**

PAST PARTICIPLE
muerto

PLUPERFECT SUBJUNCTIVE

imperfect subjunctive of haber	add past participle
hubiera **muerto**	hubiéramos **muerto**
hubieras **muerto**	hubierais **muerto**
hubiera **muerto**	hubieran **muerto**

FUTURE PERFECT

future of haber	add past participle
habré **muerto**	habremos **muerto**
habrás **muerto**	habréis **muerto**
habrá **muerto**	habrán **muerto**

CONDITIONAL PERFECT

conditional of haber	add past participle
habría **muerto**	habríamos **muerto**
habrías **muerto**	habríais **muerto**
habría **muerto**	habrían **muerto**

Usage examples

El presidente ha muerto de un infarto. *The president has died of a heart attack.*

Mi abuela está muriendo. *My grandmother is dying.*

Se murió el año pasado. *He died last year.*

Murieron en accidente aéreo. *They died in an aeroplane accident.*

Las plantas murieron porque no las regué. *The plants died because I did not water them.*

¿Qué pasará cuando me muera? *What will happen when I die?*

Se le ha muerto el perro. *His dog has died.*

Habrían luchado hasta morir. *They would have fought to the death.*

Tengo miedo a morir. *I am afraid to die.*

Los dodos iban muriendo. *The dodos were dying.*

Tiene miedo de que su madre muera. *He is afraid that his mother will die.*

Mis pensamientos están con las familias de los soldados que han muerto. *My thoughts are with the families of the soldiers who have died.*

Te morirás de frío. *You'll freeze to death.*

Me muero por jugar al tenis. *I am dying to play tennis.*

Se mueren de aburrimiento. *They are bored to death.*

Se moriría de vergüenza. *She would die of shame.*

La esperanza nunca morirá. *Hope will never die.*

muerto, muerta *dead*

la muerte *death*

morir de muerte natural *to die of natural causes*

mortal *mortal, fatal*

la mortalidad *mortality*

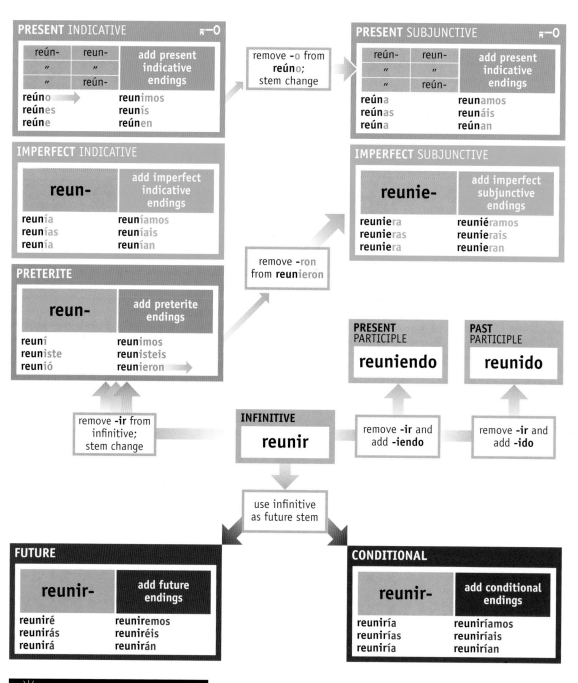

➜ **u** of stem changes to **ú** for stressed syllables in present indicative

➜ **ú** of stem reverts to **u** for unstressed syllables in present subjunctive

PRESENT INDICATIVE 🔑—O

reún-	reun-	add present indicative endings
"	"	
"	reún-	

reúno　　　reunimos
reúnes　　　reunís
reúne　　　reúnen

PRESENT SUBJUNCTIVE 🔑—O

reún-	reun-	add present indicative endings
"	"	
"	reún-	

reúna　　　reunamos
reúnas　　　reunáis
reúna　　　reúnan

remove **-o** from **reúno**; stem change

IMPERFECT INDICATIVE

| reun- | add imperfect indicative endings |

reunía　　　reuníamos
reunías　　　reuníais
reunía　　　reunían

IMPERFECT SUBJUNCTIVE

| reunie- | add imperfect subjunctive endings |

reuniera　　　reuniéramos
reunieras　　　reunierais
reuniera　　　reunieran

remove **-ron** from **reunieron**

PRETERITE

| reun- | add preterite endings |

reuní　　　reunimos
reuniste　　　reunisteis
reunió　　　reunieron

PRESENT PARTICIPLE

reuniendo

PAST PARTICIPLE

reunido

remove **-ir** from infinitive; stem change

INFINITIVE

reunir

remove **-ir** and add **-iendo**

remove **-ir** and add **-ido**

use infinitive as future stem

FUTURE

| reunir- | add future endings |

reuniré　　　reuniremos
reunirás　　　reuniréis
reunirá　　　reunirán

CONDITIONAL

| reunir- | add conditional endings |

reuniría　　　reuniríamos
reunirías　　　reuniríais
reuniría　　　reunirían

---

haber (in the correct simple tense) **+ past participle**

PERFECT INDICATIVE

present indicative of haber	add past participle
he **reunido**	hemos **reunido**
has **reunido**	habéis **reunido**
ha **reunido**	han **reunido**

PERFECT SUBJUNCTIVE

present subjunctive of haber	add past participle
haya **reunido**	hayamos **reunido**
hayas **reunido**	hayáis **reunido**
haya **reunido**	hayan **reunido**

PLUPERFECT INDICATIVE

imperfect indicative of haber	add past participle
había **reunido**	habíamos **reunido**
habías **reunido**	habíais **reunido**
había **reunido**	habían **reunido**

PAST PARTICIPLE

reunido

PLUPERFECT SUBJUNCTIVE

imperfect subjunctive of haber	add past participle
hubiera **reunido**	hubiéramos **reunido**
hubieras **reunido**	hubierais **reunido**
hubiera **reunido**	hubieran **reunido**

FUTURE PERFECT

future of haber	add past participle
habré **reunido**	habremos **reunido**
habrás **reunido**	habréis **reunido**
habrá **reunido**	habrán **reunido**

CONDITIONAL PERFECT

conditional of haber	add past participle
habría **reunido**	habríamos **reunido**
habrías **reunido**	habríais **reunido**
habría **reunido**	habrían **reunido**

Usage examples

Reuniremos todos los datos antes de tomar una decisión. *We will gather all the facts before making a decision.*

El jefe reunió a todos los trabajadores. *The boss gathered all the workers.*

Reunía sellos. *I used to collect stamps.*

Una vez que haya reunido suficiente dinero, compraré un coche. *Once I have raised enough money, I will buy a car.*

Habremos reunido doscientos mil dólares para finales de año. *We will have raised two hundred thousand dollars by the end of the year.*

Deben reunir esfuerzos. *They should join forces.*

El aspirante reunió los requisitos. *The candidate met the requirements.*

El concurso está abierto a cualquier persona que reúna los siguientes requisitos. *The competition is open to any person who meets the following requirements.*

reunirse *to meet; to get together*

Me reúno con Fiona. *I am meeting Fiona.*

¿Cuándo nos reunimos? *When are we meeting?*

Los representantes de los distintos países se reunieron para discutir el tratado. *The representatives of the different countries met to discuss the treaty.*

¿Con que frecuencia te reúnes con tus amigos? *How often do you get together with your friends?*

la reunión *meeting; gathering, get-together*

una reunión de trabajo *business meeting*

una reunión informativa *briefing*

🔑—O Key points

➡ **i** of stem changes to **í** for stressed syllables in present indicative

➡ **í** of stem reverts to **i** for unstressed syllables in present subjunctive

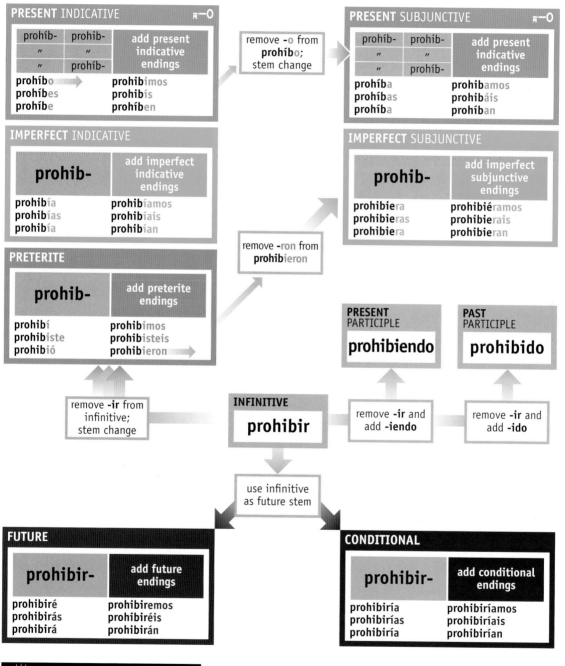

PRESENT INDICATIVE   🔑—O

prohíb-	prohib-	add present indicative endings
"	"	
"	prohib-	
prohíbo		prohibimos
prohíbes		prohibís
prohíbe		prohíben

remove **-o** from **prohíbo**; stem change

PRESENT SUBJUNCTIVE   🔑—O

prohíb-	prohib-	add present indicative endings
"	"	
"	prohib-	
prohíba		prohibamos
prohíbas		prohibáis
prohíba		prohíban

IMPERFECT INDICATIVE

prohib-	add imperfect indicative endings
prohibía	prohibíamos
prohibías	prohibíais
prohibía	prohibían

IMPERFECT SUBJUNCTIVE

prohib-	add imperfect subjunctive endings
prohibiera	prohibiéramos
prohibieras	prohibierais
prohibiera	prohibieran

remove **-ron** from **prohibieron**

PRETERITE

prohib-	add preterite endings
prohibí	prohibimos
prohibiste	prohibisteis
prohibió	prohibieron

PRESENT PARTICIPLE
prohibiendo

PAST PARTICIPLE
prohibido

remove **-ir** from infinitive; stem change

INFINITIVE
prohibir

remove **-ir** and add **-iendo**

remove **-ir** and add **-ido**

use infinitive as future stem

FUTURE

prohibir-	add future endings
prohibiré	prohibiremos
prohibirás	prohibiréis
prohibirá	prohibirán

CONDITIONAL

prohibir-	add conditional endings
prohibiría	prohibiríamos
prohibirías	prohibiríais
prohibiría	prohibirían

💡 Useful tips

Verbs of ordering (such as **prohibir**) are normally followed by an infinitive without an intervening preposition. Other such verbs include **mandar** (to order) and **permitir** (to allow).

haber (in the correct simple tense) + past participle

PERFECT INDICATIVE

present indicative of haber	add past participle
he **prohibido**	hemos **prohibido**
has **prohibido**	habéis **prohibido**
ha **prohibido**	han **prohibido**

PERFECT SUBJUNCTIVE

present subjunctive of haber	add past participle
haya **prohibido**	hayamos **prohibido**
hayas **prohibido**	hayáis **prohibido**
haya **prohibido**	hayan **prohibido**

PLUPERFECT INDICATIVE

imperfect indicative of haber	add past participle
había **prohibido**	habíamos **prohibido**
habías **prohibido**	habíais **prohibido**
había **prohibido**	habían **prohibido**

PAST PARTICIPLE

prohibido

PLUPERFECT SUBJUNCTIVE

imperfect subjunctive of haber	add past participle
hubiera **prohibido**	hubiéramos **prohibido**
hubieras **prohibido**	hubierais **prohibido**
hubiera **prohibido**	hubieran **prohibido**

FUTURE PERFECT

future of haber	add past participle
habré **prohibido**	habremos **prohibido**
habrás **prohibido**	habréis **prohibido**
habrá **prohibido**	habrán **prohibido**

CONDITIONAL PERFECT

conditional of haber	add past participle
habría **prohibido**	habríamos **prohibido**
habrías **prohibido**	habríais **prohibido**
habría **prohibido**	habrían **prohibido**

◥ Usage examples

La ley prohibirá fumar en lugares públicos. *The law will ban smoking in public places.*

Les prohibieron hablar durante el examen. *They were forbidden from talking during the exam.*

Mi madre me ha prohibido jugar con ella. *My mother forbade me from playing with her.*

Nuestro contrato de alquiler prohíbe que tengamos mascotas en el apartamento. *Our tenancy agreement forbids us from keeping pets in the apartment.*

Si dependiera de mí, lo prohibiría. *If it were up to me, I would ban it.*

Si hubiera sido elegido, habría prohibido el uso de armas químicas. *If he had been elected, he would have banned the use of chemical weapons.*

Me alegro de que hayáis prohibido los toros. *I am glad that you have banned bullfighting.*

Lo habrán prohibido para entonces. *They will have banned it by then.*

Insistí en que lo prohibieran. *I insisted that they ban it.*

Han prohibido la poligamia. *They have banned polygamy.*

No pude ir porque mis padres me habían prohibido salir de casa. *I could not go because my parents had forbidden me from going out.*

la prohibición *prohibition, ban; embargo*
prohibitivo, prohibitiva *prohibitive*
prohibido *banned, prohibited, forbidden*
PROHIBIDO FUMAR *NO SMOKING*

Indices

English-Spanish verb index

This index shows possible translations for common English verbs. Each Spanish verb given as a possible translation is followed by the page number of the verbMAP that shows the pattern for that verb. Some English verbs have been given multiple entries in the index as there is very often more than one way to translate a verb from English into Spanish. The preposition "to" in front of the English infinitive has been omitted.

abandon **abandonar**........(56)
able: be able to **poder**...(134)
abolish **abolir**..............(146)
absorb **absorber**............(96)
abuse **abusar**................(56)
accelerate **acelerar**........(56)
accept **aceptar**..............(56)
accommodate (lodge)
    alojar.....................(56)
accommodate (oblige)
    complacer................(98)
accompany **acompañar**....(56)
accomplish **lograr**..........(56)
accumulate **acumular**......(56)
accuse **acusar**................(56)
achieve **lograr**...............(56)
acquire **adquirir**..........(164)
act **actuar**....................(72)
activate **activar**.............(56)
adapt **adaptar**...............(56)
add **añadir**..................(146)
add (up) **sumar**.............(56)
adjust **ajustar**...............(56)
admire **admirar**.............(56)
admit **admitir**..............(146)
adopt **adoptar**...............(56)
adore **adorar**.................(56)
advance **avanzar**...........(60)
advise **aconsejar**............(56)
advocate **abogar por**.......(62)
age **envejecer**...............(98)
aggravate **agravar**..........(56)
agree **estar de acuerdo**...(82)
aim **apuntar**..................(56)
alarm **alarmar**...............(56)
align **alinear**.................(56)
allocate **asignar**.............(56)
allow **permitir**.............(146)

alter **cambiar**................(56)
alternate **alternar**..........(56)
amaze **asombrar**............(56)
amuse **divertir**.............(174)
analyse **analizar**............(60)
anger **enfadar**...............(56)
announce **anunciar**.........(56)
annoy **molestar**.............(56)
answer **contestar**...........(56)
anticipate **prever**..........(130)
apologise **disculparse**.....(56)
appear **aparecer**............(98)
appear (seem) **parecer**....(98)
apply **aplicar**................(58)
appoint **nombrar**............(56)
appreciate (value)
    apreciar.................(56)
appreciate (be grateful for)
    agradecer................(98)
approach **acercarse**.........(58)
approve **aprobar**............(68)
argue **discutir**..............(146)
arrange (in a certain order)
    ordenar..................(56)
arrange (to do something)
    organizar.................(60)
arrest **detener**.............(122)
arrive **llegar**.................(62)
ascend **ascender**..........(104)
ask **preguntar**...............(56)
ask (for) **pedir**.............(166)
aspire **aspirar a**.............(56)
assemble (put together)
    montar....................(56)
assemble (gather)
    reunirse.................(192)
assign **asignar**...............(56)
assist **ayudar**................(56)

associate **asociar**............(56)
assume **suponer**...........(120)
assure **asegurar**.............(56)
attack **atacar**................(58)
attain **alcanzar**..............(60)
attend **asistir (a)**.........(146)
attract **atraer**..............(116)
avoid **evitar**..................(56)
balance **equilibrar**..........(56)
ban **prohibir**...............(194)
bang **golpear**.................(56)
bark **ladrar**...................(56)
base **basar**....................(56)
battle **luchar**.................(56)
be **ser**........................(128)
be **estar**......................(82)
bear **soportar**................(56)
beat **golpear**.................(56)
beat (defeat) **derrotar**.....(56)
become **hacerse**...........(124)
beg **mendigar**................(62)
begin **empezar**...............(74)
behave **portarse**.............(56)
believe **creer**...............(112)
belong to **pertenecer a**...(98)
bend **doblar**..................(56)
bet **apostar**...................(68)
betray **traicionar**............(56)
bite **morder**.................(106)
blame **culpar**.................(56)
bleed **sangrar**................(56)
bless **bendecir**.............(178)
blink **parpadear**.............(56)
block **bloquear**..............(56)
blow **soplar**...................(56)
boast **alardear**...............(56)
boil **hervir**..................(174)
bore **aburrir**................(146)

Spanish verb index

This index contains more than 3,000 Spanish verbs in the infinitive. The number after each verb is the page number of the verbMAP that shows the pattern for that verb.

distribuir to distribute..(156)
disuadir to dissuade .....(146)
divagar to digress...........(62)
divergir to diverge ....(152)
diversificar to diversify...(58)
divertir to amuse,
    entertain ....(174)
divertirse to enjoy
    oneself ....(174)
dividir to divide...........(146)
divisar to make out,
    discern ....(56)
divorciar to divorce........(56)
divorciarse to get
    divorced ....(56)
divulgar to divulge,
    disclose ....(62)
doblar to fold; to turn; to
    dub ....(56)
doctorarse to get a
    doctorate.................(56)
documentar to document.(56)
doler to hurt ....(106)
domar to tame, train ......(56)
domesticar to tame,
    domesticate..............(58)
dominar to dominate......(56)
donar to donate............(56)
dopar to drug, dope........(56)
doparse to take drugs .....(56)
dorar to gild; to brown....(56)
dormir to sleep............(188)
dormirse to fall asleep..(188)
dormitar to doze, snooze.(56)
dosificar to measure out .(58)
dotar to provide with......(56)
dragar to dredge ....(62)
dramatizar to dramatise..(60)
driblar to dribble (sport).(56)
drogar to drug ....(62)
drogarse to take drugs....(62)
ducharse to shower, take a
    shower....................(56)
dudar to doubt ....(56)
dulcificar to mellow ....(58)
duplicar to duplicate; to
    double ....(58)
durar to last................(56)
echar to throw..............(56)
echarse to lie down ....(56)
eclipsar to eclipse..........(56)

economizar to save,
    economise................(60)
edificar to construct; to
    edify ....(58)
editar to publish...........(56)
educar to educate; to bring
    up; to train ....(58)
efectuar to carry out ......(72)
ejecutar to execute, carry
    out, perform ....(56)
ejemplificar to exemplify.(58)
ejercer to practise, exercise;
    to exert...................(100)
ejercitar to exercise; to
    train, drill.................(56)
elaborar to produce,
    manufacture; to
    elaborate ....(56)
electrificar to electrify ...(58)
electrizar to electrify......(60)
electrocutar
    to electrocute............(56)
electrocutarse to get
    electrocuted ....(56)
elegir to choose; to
    elect ....(172)
elevar to raise, elevate....(56)
eliminar to eliminate......(56)
elogiar to praise, eulogise.(56)
elucidar to elucidate ......(56)
eludir to elude, avoid ...(146)
emanar de to emanate
    from........................(56)
emancipar to emancipate.(56)
emanciparse to become
    emancipated..............(56)
emascular to emasculate.(56)
embadurnar to smear,
    daub ....(56)
embalar to pack, wrap up.(56)
embarazar to hamper; to
    make pregnant...........(60)
embarcar to embark, put on
    board......................(58)
embargar to seize, impound;
    to overwhelm.............(62)
embarullar to mess up....(56)
embarullarse to get into a
    muddle, get mixed up .(56)
embelesar to captivate...(56)
embellecer to embellish .(98)

embestir to attack; to
    charge (e.g. bull) .....(166)
emborrachar to make
    drunk ....(56)
emborracharse to get
    drunk ....(56)
emboscar to ambush ......(58)
embotellar to bottle.......(56)
embriagar to intoxicate ..(62)
embriagarse to become
    intoxicated...............(62)
embrollar to confuse; to
    embroil....................(56)
embrutecer to stultify ....(98)
embutir to stuff...........(146)
emerger to emerge.......(102)
emigrar to emigrate ....(56)
emitir to emit ....(146)
emocionar to move, touch;
    to thrill...................(56)
emocionarse to be moved;
    to get excited ....(56)
empañar to steam, mist
    up..........................(56)
empantanar to swamp....(56)
empapar to soak, drench;
    to soak up................(56)
empaparse to get soaked.(56)
empaquetar to pack, wrap
    up..........................(56)
emparejar to match, pair;
    to level, make level....(56)
emparentar to become
    related (through
    marriage) ....(66)
empatar to draw, be equal
    (esp. in sport) ....(56)
empeñar to pawn; to
    pledge ....(56)
empeñarse to get into
    debt ....(56)
empeorar to make worse,
    worsen.....................(56)
empeorarse to get worse,
    worsen.....................(56)
empezar to start, begin ..(74)
emplazar to site, position.(60)
emplear to use; to
    employ ....(56)
empotrar to build in,
    embed ....(56)